Zen and Psychotherapy

Integrating Traditional
and Nontraditional Approaches

Chris Mruk, PhD, was trained in general psychology at Michigan State University in 1971 and in clinical psychology at Duquesne University in 1981. His clinical background includes working in inpatient and outpatient mental health settings, supervising a methadone program in Detroit, Michigan, working in emergency psychiatric services, directing a counseling center at St. Francis College in Pennsylvania, doing some private practice, and serving as a consulting psychologist to Firelands Regional Medical Center in Sandusky, Ohio. He is licensed as a clinical psychologist in Ohio and Pennsylvania.

Chris's academic experience includes some 20 years of teaching psychology and training mental health professionals. He is a professor of psychology at Bowling Green State University, Firelands College, Ohio, where he has won the college's Distinguished Teaching and Distinguished Scholar awards. His publications include a number of academically oriented articles, several chapters, and *Self-Esteem: Research, Theory, and Practice*. This book, which is now in its second edition, is also published by Springer Publishing and published in England. Chris and his wife Marsha, whose career involves directing large-scale mental health programs, live in Sandusky, Ohio.

Joan Hartzell, RN, MA, graduated from the St. Joseph's School of Nursing in Fort Wayne, Indiana, in 1950. After working in medical hospital care positions for some eight years, she found herself so interested in mental health issues that she switched to psychiatric nursing. This work included providing mental health care on inpatient units, doing psychiatric consultations on medical units and at nursing home facilities, and then supervising mental health programs, such as the St. Lawrence Community Mental Health Center in Lansing, Michigan. This work included developing a 24-hour comprehensive psychiatric emergency service that was recognized as an exemplary program by the National Institute of Mental Health in 1974–75.

Shortly afterward, Joan realized that her approach to providing mental health care had much more in common with Zen than with the scientific empiricism of modern psychiatry. After beginning her study of the teachings of the Buddha in the early 1980s, she explored other nontraditional approaches, including Native American healing. Then, Joan completed a Master's degree in therapeutic psychology from Norwich University, Vermont College, in Montpelier, Vermont, in 1994. Throughout this time she has continued to study Zen, while living it in her work at community mental health centers where she helps people who suffer from serious illness and in her private practice.

Zen and Psychotherapy

Integrating Traditional and Nontraditional Approaches

Christopher J. Mruk, PhD
with Joan Hartzell, RN, MA

SPRINGER
PUBLISHING COMPANY

PAPERBACK

Springer Publishing Company, Inc.
11 West 42nd Street
New York, NY 10036

Acquisitions Editor: Sheri W. Sussman
Production Editor: Jeanne Libby
Cover design by Mimi Flow

06 07 08 09 / 5 4 3 2 1

New ISBN 0-8261-2035-0 © 2006 by Springer Publishing Company, Inc.

Library of Congress Cataloging-in-Publication Data

Mruk, Christopher J.
   Zen and psychotherapy : integrating traditional and nontraditional approaches /
Christop[h]er J. Mruk ; with contributor Joan Hartzell
              p. ; cm.
       Includes bibliographical references and index.
       ISBN 0-8261-2034-2
       1. Meditation—Zen Buddhism—Therapeutic use. 2. Psychotherapy—Religious
aspects—Zen Buddhism. 3. Buddhism and psychoanalysis. I. Hartzell, Joan.
II. Title. [DNLM: 1. Buddhism—psychology. 2. Psychotherapy. 3. Spiritual
Therapies—psychology. WM 460.5.R3 M939z 2003]

RC489.M43M785 2003
616.89'14—dc21   2003042827

Printed in the United States of America by Bang Printing.

Contents

Foreword

PART I (CHRIS)

Between us, Joan and I have been in the mental health field in one way or another for some 80 years now. We have worked with many mental health disciplines and we have done that in a large number of settings, as we describe in the book. Although we certainly have not seen it all, we do have some sense of what the typical clinician, supervisor, or clinical educator is likely to encounter. Perhaps more important, both of us value the willingness to look at mental health work from different perspectives. For instance, I was first exposed to the field as a young bystander who witnessed a family member go through many lengthy periods of psychiatric treatment in the 1950s, when large state hospitals, electroconvulsive therapy (ECT), and first-generation psychotropics were still mainstream. Undergraduate school at Michigan State University exposed me to behavioral psychology and going on to work in medical settings also introduced me to the biological perspective. Both perspectives emphasize an empirical approach to understanding and treating behavior. During graduate school, however, I trained in Existential-Phenomenological Psychology at Duquesne University, which took a nearly opposite point of view because it emphasizes meaning, human experience, and the possibility of free will. In between those two periods, I also explored such things as working in automobile factories, landscaping, Transcendental Meditation and Tai Chi, and writing. Today, I have learned that I am known as a professor who seems rigorous to students, although I may not appear to be that way to some colleagues in nonclinical areas of psychology.

In a certain sense, this background gave rise to the book. For one thing, I have always been caught by the push and pull of the empirical and the experiential approaches to helping and healing. Most of the time, I want to say something like "science is best" because its insights can at least be argued and supported by evidence. But at other times, I know that science is not everything, that it may largely miss the most important things about being human. This desire for some sort of balance between the body and the mind, the head and the heart, or realism and idealism is probably the primary motivating force behind the desire to write this book, because it is an opportunity to explore these issues with others who care about them, too.

For another thing, the older I become, the more I realize that no one discipline can do the job on its own. For example, having trained in psychology, I once thought that we had the "privileged perspective" and looked somewhat less than enthusiastically upon other approaches. But working with people from other disciplines, as well as the experiences resulting from directing an interdisciplinary-oriented degree program in Human Services at Bowling Green State University, have taught me otherwise. I now know that each discipline brings something important to the table and that when it comes right down to it, one's training background has very little to do with whether a person is an effective helper or healer. This theme, which has also run throughout my career, is also a major aspect of the book.

Finally, like Joan, I am saddened by the crush of managed care, especially by its emphasis on gatekeepers, minimum treatments, and a very murky partnership between the pharmacological industry and health care today. Having a wife who is responsible for delivering quality mental health services to six counties in north central Ohio, I know that managed care is a fact of our times. However, her dedication, as well as that of the staff at the Firelands Regional Medical Center in Sandusky, Ohio, where I consult, also show me that mental health workers of all types struggle very hard to find ways to be compassionate in spite of such current social, economic, and political realities. Thus, it should not be surprising that concern for those who do this work is the third theme of the book.

In addition to giving the reader a sense of the background and motivation for the book, there are two other things I would like to address in my portion of the preface. The first one concerns the process of writing the book with my coauthor, Joan. Most of the material I have written over the years, which includes another book in its second edition, several chapters in other books, and the usual number of professional articles a professor is expected to produce, I have written alone. Coauthorship is a much more complicated process. It is like a dance, because it means blending together two personalities, styles, preferences, and so forth, to the same score. Imagine the kinds of difficulties that arise when a somewhat obsessive-compulsive, slightly anxious, well-intentioned but occasionally rigid professor encounters a highly independent, free-spirited, practitioner of Zen! Then, add the ingredients of living in different parts of the country and a history of one of them being the teacher for the other at one point in their relationship, only to have the roles reverse in another part of it. Toss in a little love and a lot of good will, and you have what we went through: a process of very hard work, lively discussion, deepening understanding, real care, and personal growth.

In many ways, then, both Joan and I struggled with the very themes of this book right as we wrote it, which is why we see it as a dialog and set it up that way. I think that this approach gives our book more authenticity than either a strictly academic or purely clinical approach might have yielded: We really do struggle with both sides of the issues we discuss here and maybe that takes us farther than we could have otherwise gone. In addition, working together in this way, which sometimes involved sitting on benches in the beautiful parks of lovely Savannah, Georgia, with tape recorder in hand, helped us to experience what Joan calls a sense of "connection." This connection transcends backgrounds, disciplines, genders, and even generations. It will also touch us both for some time to come, for I believe that if I can manage to incorporate even a small portion of what Joan has to say into my clinical, academic, and personal lives, they will all be much richer than I have a right to expect.

The other thing to do before closing my portion of the preface is to express my appreciation to people who have helped with this project. First come my editors. Karen Page Osterling is a colleague and friend of mine at the university. We have known each other for a long time and even worked together on a book before this one. However, this time she went way beyond the call of duty. Not only was Karen extremely patient in reading and correcting many revisions, but she also had a hand in helping Joan give language to many of the concepts and stories she describes. In a word: Karen did not just edit; she contributed. Sheri W. Sussman, the Editorial Director of Springer Publishing, ranks at the same level for at least two reasons. First, she found herself saddled with this project when she first stepped into her position, because the book was based on a commitment made with her predecessor. Second, as if playing "catch-up" were not enough to ask of someone who just took over an entire set of new responsibilities, Sheri was also generous enough to stay with us when we missed the first contract deadline due to unexpected complications. Similarly, it is important to thank Jeanne Libby for her assistance as Senior Production Editor and Jean Hurkin-Torres for executing her final copyediting duties well above and beyond the call.

It is also a pleasure to thank several other people. Family usually comes first, which means that this book stands in honor of my mother, Veronica

Mruk, my father, Joseph Mruk, and my brother, Steve Mruk, all of whom have, sadly, passed on. I have already mentioned my wife Marsha and how much I respect her work, but it never hurts to do that more than once in a partnership! Thanks for just being, Marsha; it has been some 20 years now! In the same loving sense, it is important to acknowledge Dee Mruk, Pam and Curt Pawloski, Chris Waid, and Brandi Savage, who now constitute my living family.

Three of my colleagues also need to be thanked because they helped in various ways. Dale Schnetzer is a philosopher and friend who helped make sure that my discussion of idealism and realism would not offend too much those who really study such issues. William Liu is a colleague and mathematician who read the entire manuscript over time. His knowledge of Zen will keep me thinking for many years to come, perhaps even to the point of a second edition! Tatiana Panas, a fellow psychologist and partner at work is next. I am extremely fortunate to have a colleague whose philosophy of education is similar to mine. Even more, she volunteered to do the one thing from which colleagues shrink the most: Instead of being asked to read a chapter, she actually offered to do that and in so doing helped make the dreaded introductory chapter a better one than it would have been without her. I must also thank David Hartzell, Joan's son, who taught Joan how to use a computer, its word processor, and who shuttled countless files back and forth between us over the Internet.

Of course, I will always feel a debt to Dr. Ursula Springer, my publisher, especially for her confidence in my first book many years ago, as well as for continuing to be interested in my work today. The academic and professional value of such scholarly presses can only rise each day that corporate giants continue to swallow up independent voices. One last thing needs to be said. In the book, Joan talks about how, from a Zen perspective, pain and suffering can be embraced as a valued teacher. In fact, she even goes so far as to recommend to clients upon occasion that they write a "Thank-You" note to the source of a particularly grievous injury, but only after they have come to accept it, learn from it, and move beyond it. I hope that all of us, particularly our clients, come to the point in our development where we may appreciate the wisdom inherent in this bit of Zen. Perhaps this book is my way of doing just that.

PART II (JOAN)

When I hired Chris in 1974 to work with me and the other therapists in the Emergency Service I could not foresee that we were to keep in contact with each other all these years. One may say we had connected on a level that went beyond time and distance. The 28 ensuing years took Chris and me on paths that would become the backbone of this book. Eventually, he furthered himself in academics while I stayed in clinical settings. I lost a position in midcareer, which turned out to be an event that led to tremendous personal growth. Although I would never advise anyone to deliberately get fired, when it happened to me, like a Zen proverb concerning an ox that got mired in the mud, I had to either sink further or learn to struggle with what "is." Eventually, I got hired elsewhere, but it was during this time I decided I would go back to school, where I completed a Master's degree in Therapeutic Psychology. The word "therapeutic" resonated with what I wanted to continue to be a part of—humanity, compassion and sensitivity. I always loved the work I was hired to do before and after this time, and whatever position I found myself taking always seemed to bring new learning to me.

After completing my Master's degree I asked Chris if he would read my thesis. He did so, commenting that he thought a book could be developed from the work. I was delighted when he told me he would be interested in coauthoring one based on my experiences and philosophy of care for patients and staff. In turn he would write about the relationship between traditional and nontraditional approaches to helping and healing. After some discussion we made plans for this book. What I found humorous and fascinating was that this meant Chris and I reversed roles. However, I must say that it was a very easy transition because, in retrospect, I never felt I was "more" than he was when I was his supervisor; nor was he more than I was while learning how to develop a book as he was now sharing his knowledge with me. I learned a lot about myself through this process and the teachings are invaluable.

For example, I became aware of how important the teachings of the Buddha have been for me personally, as well as professionally, while writing this book. Ironically, I believe the teachings are so uncomplicated that a person could misunderstand the Dharma. The value we place on thinking and how we devalue feelings, at least in the field of academics, have been addressed in the book. I am not jaded with academia, but I am aware of the enormous impact this profession has on our society, especially the role of the professor who has the power to shape students' attitudes toward themselves and the life's work they have chosen. I feel education is full of obligations that have the potential of draining the students' creativity instead of furthering spontaneity and curiosity. But good teachers can always inspire students to "wake up." Griffith O. Freed, PhD, was one of them for me. His willingness to spend time with me, to listen and to question with me, was such a gift that even to this day, I still do not take it for granted. He was the epitome of what I thought a teacher ought to be. Hopefully, what he instilled in me has been communicated to the clients and staff I have worked with. Carrying on his legacy will be my way of thanking him.

Over the years, the people who have had an impact, directly or indirectly, upon the completion of this book are too numerous to mention. Specifically, I owe a special thanks to Margaret Blanchard, PhD, my core professor from Vermont College. If she had been different, meaning unyielding or single-minded, I question if I would have completed my Master's degree. She patiently listened to me whenever I needed to speak with her about a problem. I am very grateful for her support and encouragement. She became as much a friend to me as she was my professor.

From the beginning, my son, David, provided me guidance about how to use the computer. He also served as the person who communicated with Chris through the Internet. I can't imagine having been able to accomplish this feat without his help. I feel indebted to my daughter, Sara, and her husband, Tom, for their understanding. Even while visiting them I worked on the book. I always felt their support. My granddaughters, Jacqueline and Morgan—you are my spiritual gurus. You were very patient with me throughout this process. Every time I see you, I am refreshed. To all of you, with love and a very grateful heart, I say "Thank you."

To Karen Osterling, the wonderful person who edited my work and encouraged me to use my own words, I give special thanks. Karen, you possess all the attributes of a loving teacher. I also want to say thanks to Marsha, Chris's wife, for being interested and patient with Chris and me during the time it has taken to complete this book. I have not taken for granted what your contribution has been in making this project successful. I must also mention David Pond, a dear friend, who provided unflagging encouragement and indispensable help throughout this entire endeavor. When I felt discouraged he would settle a disquieted heart with his understanding and gentleness. I could always count on his steadfastness.

Of course, I am indebted to the patients and colleagues I have worked with all these years. I wish they knew that without them, this book would not have been written. In a very real sense they have been my most significant teachers. It is a humbling experience to listen to a person talk about their pain. They may be grateful that I am accepting of them, but it also works the other way; I am equally gratified that they trust me. Respectfully, I have changed the names of patients and other identifying facts to protect their privacy.

Naturally, I wish to convey my deepest respect to the Dharma teachers who have influenced me over the years. Thanks to Michael Toms, host of *New Dimensions* (1984), who unknowingly set me on a path of the Buddha's teachings through his interview with Lama Sogyal Rinpoche so many years ago. In spite of the time that has gone by, I feel like I have barely touched the surface of what the Buddha has offered all sentient beings; I will always be a "beginner." The Dharma is the most unsettling thing in my life.

Finally, I want to thank Chris from my heart, for the opportunity to work with him on this book. First, he saw something of value in my thesis. Next, he was willing to coauthor a book, something he had not done before and was somewhat hesitant to do with a novice because of the additional work. Third, he was willing to learn something about Zen Buddhism for himself. And last but perhaps the most important, he helped me to write about something that is very dear to my heart. Ultimately, I hope we have presented our thoughts, experiences, and opinions clearly that they might be helpful to all. As Dogen said,

> *To be thus enlightened is to remove the barriers between one's self and others.*
> (Farrer-Hall, 2000, p. 9)

CHAPTER 1

Traditional, Complementary, and Alternative Psychotherapies

INTRODUCTION

There are many currents swirling through the waters of the mental health field today that affect each one of us who works in it, regardless of our particular discipline, type of job, specific work setting, or personal inclinations. Perhaps reflecting a very serious dissatisfaction with traditional health and mental health care, one of them is the relatively recent fact that many patients, and growing numbers of practitioners, are turning toward complementary and alternative approaches. As we shall see, the numbers are astonishing in terms of medical health care and the same pattern seems to be occurring in mental health care, especially as indicated by an explosion of interest in what might be described as the religious, spiritual, or meaning-centered needs of our patients.

Another rapidly expanding tributary in mental health care, as well as health care in general, is the increasingly interdisciplinary nature of our work. Although most of us train as a physician, psychologist, nurse, social worker, counselor, or case manager, the fact of the matter is that many hospitals, most social service agencies, and almost all community mental health programs require us to work together, just at a time when we are also competing for diminishing slices of the mental health pie! All too often, however, we fail to educate clinicians about this new reality and how to embrace it rather than to be resentful or fearful of it.

Similarly, almost everyone in this field, clients, therapists, and administrators alike, feels the steadily growing undertow of managed care. Although most of us acknowledge this fact and often complain about the burden it creates, we have yet to see much in terms of helping the individual practitioner find ways of navigating these treacherous waters so that they can continue to look forward to meeting the challenges of their work. Finally, all three of these currents interact with each other to add considerable complexity to work that is already challenging enough. Under these conditions, it is no wonder that so many of us experience stress and even burn-out: The wonder is that so many of us are willing to sustain our commitment to our work, and to those we try to help, as long as we do!

Instead of trying to stem this tide, which is probably impossible, we maintain that it is possible to set a fairly steady course in this setting by integrating certain aspects of Zen into our work as clinicians, supervisors, and educators. At the same time, however, we are not saying that one must embrace Zen as a philosophy, religion, or way of life in order to benefit from it in this fashion. Rather, we maintain that the judicious application of Zen makes these three issues (nontraditional approaches, interdisciplinary activities, and work-related stress) easier to live with intellectually, professionally, and personally. Of course, we realize that this order is a tall one to ask of Zen. Therefore, the approach we take in this book is to first understand the issues involved in integrating traditional and nontraditional approaches and then show how Zen can do that by presenting its basic principles, which includes illustrating them in various clinical, supervisory, and academic situations. In this way, readers may evaluate for themselves whether or not there is value in Zen and whether or not it is possible to integrate Zen into a traditional clinical or academic framework.

The issues that give rise to this book and our response to them may be of interest to mental health practitioners, supervisors, and educators in at least three ways. The first one concerns the main topic, which is the question of whether it is possible to integrate traditional (scientifically based) approaches to helping people deal with various problems of living with nontraditional ones and, if so, is that desirable? More specifically, we will explore how basic Zen principles may complement traditional therapeutic practices that are based on more scientific research. For reasons that will become clear in this chapter, interest in the psychotherapeutic possibilities of Zen has increased substantially in the past decade (Brazier, 1995; Kopp, 1988; Rosenbaum, 1998), along with a rise in investigating religious, spiritual, or meaning-oriented nontraditional therapies. Therefore, it may be helpful to distinguish our approach from the others before we move on to the next issue.

Even a cursory examination of online booksellers reveals that there has been an explosion of popular interest in Zen during the past twenty years, including what is becoming known as "Western Zen" (Goldstein, 2002), which is a term used to describe how traditional schools of Zen are being modified in the process of translation and adoption. Some books on Zen and psychotherapy focus primarily on helping the reader to understand what Zen is. Since this task is a very considerable one in itself, such an approach leaves it largely up to the reader to think about how to apply Zen concepts in clinical settings. Others tend to present an overview of Zen and then move directly into how it may be applied to the psychotherapeutic enterprise, usually by attempting to show how Zen is compatible with a particular psychotherapeutic perspective, such as the psychodynamic, humanistic, or even cognitive points of view. Rather than attempting to convince the reader of the merits of Zen and instead of presenting ourselves as masters of it, *we are more interested in helping clinicians, supervisors, and educators understand specific Zen principles that seem to hold significant therapeutic value, and how they are compatible with traditional, empirically oriented, scientifically based education and training, regardless of one's particular academic or disciplinary orientation.* The support we offer for this position is both academic and clinical. As such, our argument consists of analyzing the relationship between traditional and nontraditional psychotherapies and the use of clinical case studies.

The next feature of this book that may be of interest is its method because the way we go about the project reflects and addresses the interdisciplinary nature of our field. In other words, the authors come from two mental health disciplines, in this case psychology and mental health nursing, which gives an interdisciplinary quality to our look at contemporary psychotherapy and to Zen. We think this approach is valuable because, on one hand, the typical mental health professional acquires his or her training in what might be called a "mono-disciplined" fashion: medical practitioners are trained primarily in biological therapies by medical practitioners at medical settings, psychologists are trained largely in psychological therapies by psychologists at psychological settings, social workers are typically trained in social systems by social workers in social services settings, and so forth. Consequently, although they may all work with similar types of clients or problems, each group tends to learn different (and sometimes conflicting) theoretical views, specific (and sometimes jargonistic) technical languages, and certain (as well as sometimes opposing) preferences in terms of how to go about helping others. Indeed, differences between perspectives in our field can be so great that Fancher (1995) describes them as reflecting distinct "cultures of healing," a metaphor that we feel fully captures this important dimension of mental health care both historically and today.

On the other hand, however, as soon as we graduate, most of us find ourselves coming into regular contact with other disciplines in our work. For instance, we may encounter various specialties in the hospital setting, interdisciplinary teams of professionals in community mental health centers, and gatekeepers from different backgrounds in managed care, some of whom are more business than clinically oriented. Eventually, many of us come to find that the privileged perspective we thought our particular discipline had to offer may not be as special as we once thought: Over time, the complexity of our work and experiences with mental health professionals trained in disciplines other than our own usually forces us to realize that there are a number of legitimate ways to understand and treat mental illness, each of which has its own strengths and weaknesses. Given this reality concerning our work, it is very surprising that our formal training often does not prepare us very well for the increasingly interdisciplinary nature of our work. At best, mono-disciplined education is simply outdated and at worst, it is an impediment to all involved, especially to the patient or client. By contrast, an interdisciplinary approach is helpful because it builds bridges between practitioners, and, ultimately, this climate may create a better environment for our clients. This aspect of the book may be especially important for educators and supervisors to think about, because they shape future clinicians and are obliged to prepare them in the best ways possible. Giving only cursory attention to the interdisciplinary aspect of our work is certainly a disservice to our students and it may even be an ethical issue.

Another aspect of this book that may be of interest to readers, especially clinicians and supervisors, focuses on the personal level of our work, especially its impact on us as individuals over time. Although tremendously satisfying, it is well known that, at times, mental health work is very difficult, extremely demanding, or just plain old "hard." The greatest challenge we face, of course, is that of helping clients who are experiencing acute distress, in whatever form it may take. Given the nature of our work, what clinician has not encountered situations where traditional training seems to fail? Who among us has not wished for something toward which to turn in a crisis situation when all that we have done so far to help seems to be of no avail? Which one of us has not reached an impasse with a client, supervisee, or student that we cannot seem to break? It is precisely at such times that the clinician, supervisor, or teacher begins to appreciate the practical value of an alternative approach. We will also see that it is at this point that the wisdom of Zen may be just enough to make a welcome and positive difference.

Our work can be challenging in another way, too, because it deals with human suffering, again and again. The stress of dealing with so much pain day in and day out, year after year, can take a toll all of its own. Couple that kind of stress with the pressures of growing caseloads, increasingly severe client problems, as well as the incessant demands of managed care, and it is no wonder that so many clinicians or supervisors long for occupational change, may appear to become less caring over time, or sometimes burn out of the field altogether. In this sense, it is important to realize that Zen is concerned with human suffering, and with becoming free of it, too. Moreover, Zen has been doing that for many, many centuries, whereas traditional therapies are just moving into their second one. Even if Zen does not have the empirical appeal of more scientific perspectives, it has been working on similar issues for so long that it is likely to have something to teach us about what causes suffering and what may reduce it. Indeed, we will see that Zen may even show us a way to transform the pressures we face as clinicians and supervisors into tools for becoming better at our work, as well as for helping us to continue to look forward to it much longer than otherwise is likely.

Now that we have identified the major themes of the book and why they may be of interest to clinical and academic audiences, we can introduce the form of our investigation and the course it will take. The first step concerns how to go about integrating traditional and nontraditional therapies, with Zen as a case in point. Thus, chapter 1 describes the contemporary interest in nontraditional approaches to health care today. It also focuses on why there is a need for therapists trained in the various mental health traditions to consider this issue in their own work and why Zen may be of value to most of us in this regard, no matter what our clinical training or orientation may be. The next step is to understand the basic characteristics of Zen, so in the second chapter Joan provides us with a clinically oriented understanding of the heart of this particular approach to helping and healing. She begins with discussing The Four Noble Truths, which includes understanding the inevitability of human suffering, the causes of suffering, cessation or the process of reducing suffering, and the Eightfold Path, which leads to the way out of suffering. In addition to describing each of the classical "four pillars" of Zen, Joan illustrates their clinical relevance through various case studies and examples. Next she identifies six more Zen principles that have demonstrable therapeutic potential: acceptance, fearlessness, truth, compassion, attachment, and impermanence. In each case, Joan begins by identifying a particular principle, then describes what it means in Zen literature, and ends by giving actual examples of how she uses the principle to help her work. In this way, we present Zen in theory and in action.

In chapter 3, I endeavor to show where alternative approaches to under-standing and treating mental health problems fit into the general therapeutic continuum that spans traditional social and behavioral sciences. The first part of the chapter briefly presents the basic concepts, strengths, and weaknesses of the biological, learning, cognitive, psychodynamic, and humanistic per-spectives. The next part involves following a client who suffers from an interpersonal betrayal resulting in depression as he goes through treatment with a therapist who works from each point of view, including one based on Zen. The goals of this chapter are to provide a context for understanding alternative therapies in relation to traditional approaches and to establish the theoretical foundations for using Zen to help reduce human suffering in clinical practice.

The final two chapters are more practical. For example, in the first part of chapter 4, I ask Joan a number of questions concerning how Zen might help me deal with client-related issues that any clinician is likely to face. They include how Zen might help me to listen better, to deal with a difficult client more easily, or, most important, what to do when my traditional training fails me. She responds by identifying which of the 10 Zen concepts (The Four Noble Truths and the six general principles) may apply best to such a situation and then illustrates how that is so with a clinical example from her many years of psychiatric experience. The other section of the chapter follows the same format, but the direction of the questions changes to the other side of the therapeutic coin: This time I ask Joan how Zen could help me, the traditionally oriented therapist that I am, with various issues that concern the clinician as well as our clients. These themes include such things as how Zen can help one deal with making a clinical error, avoid falling prey to countertransference, and better tolerate the stresses of the work we do as clinicians. Again, she responds by identifying a relevant Zen concept or principle, discussing how it can be therapeutic, and then presenting a case study example that shows how the concept or principle may be applied in a practical setting.

In the fifth and final chapter we talk about how the principles of Zen may be integrated conceptually into the theory, practice, and teaching of psychotherapy. We begin with discussing in dialog form how Zen stands in relation to such issues as the medical model and evidence-based therapy, which dominate the mental health care scene today. Then, we take a look at how Zen can be incorporated into other aspects of our work, especially teaching students to become therapists and supervising them afterward. Next, we return to our original question and talk about the possibility of integrating Zen and psychotherapy by understanding Zen as a complement to our work.

This activity involves examining the progress that has been made on integrating psychotherapies in general. In particular, we look at Zen in regard to the three major ways that people try to bring different psychotherapeutic approaches together today, which are called "Theoretical Integration," "Common Factors," and "Technical Eclecticism" (Wachtel & Messer, 1997). In each case, we ask what the particular approach might have to say about integrating Zen into the traditional scientific picture. We then conclude with a look at how clinicians who find themselves interested in more advanced Zen concepts or in more Zen training can further their personal or professional development.

Next, it might be helpful to say an introductory word about the interdisciplinary nature of the book and why it is important here. One thing that an interdisciplinary background brings to any book is a broader range of experience than is usually otherwise possible. Ours includes working in psychiatric hospitals, staffing acute emergency psychiatric services, doing drug and alcohol work, offering outpatient community mental health services, engaging in private practice, as well as teaching and writing in the academic setting. In addition, this experience also involves clinical, supervisory, and teaching responsibilities, as well as interacting with a wide range of mental health professionals. At one point in our careers, we even had the good fortune to work together as a part of the mental health team in the same psychiatric setting. This one happened to be a "24/7" emergency psychiatric service that Joan created in the middle 1970s at St. Lawrence Hospital in Lansing, Michigan. This program was recognized by the National Institute of Mental Health as an "exemplary system" (Freedman, Kaplan, & Shaddock, 1975, p. 2,318) and was one of the first comprehensive systems in the country.

This familiarity with the various traditions, disciplines, and practices of the field creates a rich common ground for our work for this book. At the same time, however, interdisciplinary activity also involves appreciating differences, such as differences in training, in theoretical orientations, in preferred practices, in levels of professional status, and in administrative reporting lines, for example. Here, differences are important because they help us to understand and remember just how challenging the task of integrating different approaches really is: it is not just a case of "theory smushing" (London, 1986). On one hand, for instance, as a psychologist and professor, I have a clear preference for using and teaching about therapeutic theories and methods that have good empirical support. After all, we are dealing with the lives of others in our work and it is only ethical to give them the best we have, which is to say theories that have support and techniques that can be shown to work. Only the scientific method can provide us with this kind of information, so I value it highly. Moreover, although I have worked in a number of mental health settings for a number of years before becoming a professor, most of my career has been in the academic setting, which has something of a research focus. Thus, in a certain sense, my training and orientation is geared more toward "helping the mind," which is to say more characteristic of traditional therapeutic approaches.

On the other hand, Joan began her work as a psychiatric nurse and then earned an M.A. in therapeutic psychology much later in her career. She has over 50 years of acute psychiatric care experience that ranges from inpatient psychiatric work, through supervising an urban-based 24-hour emergency psychiatric service mentioned above, to working with the severely and chronically mentally ill in community mental health settings. In addition, she is still working almost full-time in the field today, at age 74, and does so out of a sense of choice, dedication, and joy that few of us have. In a word, Joan has seen it all, or at least most of it. During this time, she also witnessed a good portion of the evolution of traditional approaches to helping others. Therefore, in addition to its progress, Joan has also encountered the limits of traditional mental health care; from the brutality of psychiatric insulin shock therapy, through the many fads of the 1970s, to the neglect that seems to happen all too often with managed care as it is practiced today. Out of necessity as much as curiosity given the state of our field during this time, she became interested in alternatives long before that became popular. After exploring such diverse possibilities as counseling and Native American shamanism, Joan found a home in Zen and has been practicing some form of it in her work longer than most clinicians have been practicing their entire careers! Appropriately enough, then, she represents the nontraditional view, or the "healing the heart" aspect of this book.

In a certain sense, our respective backgrounds provide a rather balanced foundation for a dialog between traditional and alternative approaches, or for "helping the mind and healing the heart" as we like to think of it. For instance, when Joan asked me to describe my vision for the book in the early stages of writing it, I admitted that I was a little leery, because I didn't want to become involved with one that talked mainly about Zen as a religion or a philosophy, or with one that tried to persuade clinicians to become practitioners of "the vision." Rather, I hoped that we could develop something that the typical mental health practitioner, clinical supervisor, beginning student, or instructor could sit down and read with a reasonable degree of comfort, which is to say without a lot of mystical or philosophical jargon, and be able to apply to their work in a practical fashion. Much to my relief (and to her amusement), she enthusiastically agreed, pointing out that Zen can complement our work as clinicians and that she had been doing just that for years. Then, with typical Zen ambiguity, she added that she would never presume to be a teacher of Zen anyway, only a student, so I had nothing to worry about! In other words, our interdisciplinary degrees and backgrounds influence our writing, but in a way that provides a balance of perspective and practice that is helpful in attempting to integrate traditional and nontraditional approaches. Further, such an appreciation of similarities and differences means that we are not asking readers to give up their particular perspectives or practices, but only to think about possibilities that might complement their work. Which of us cannot benefit from that?

The final introductory word concerns the literary style we have chosen for this investigation and why it was selected. The book takes the form of a dialog between partners who share a mutual interest, but who also come from very different points of view in terms of disciplines, backgrounds, and orientations. The overall tone of this discussion moves from one that begins as rather academic and formal to one that is more personal and spontaneous at the end. This format was chosen for two reasons. First, we talk about things, and to each other, about matters that are both academic and personal. On one hand, integrating traditional and nontraditional psychotherapies is a theoretical challenge. As such, it involves dialoging traditional premises and points of view with alternative positions, which requires more formal description and argument. On the other hand, the work that we do is a very interpersonal endeavor and it is fitting that we address each other at that level, too.

Second, dialog is one of the earliest methods of inquiry people have used to learn more about life and living it well. Plato used this philosophical method with his students, one of whom was Aristotle, who then went on to set the foundations for the scientific method. The Buddha did the same with his disciples and created the other major branch of knowledge that is important for our project. With such a tradition already pointing the way, it is difficult to see how we could go wrong by thinking of the book as a dialog! Of course, conversations must have at least two participants. My voice will generally represent the traditional scientific approach to psychotherapy because that background is more a part of my history than it is for Joan. She will speak for the nontraditional part of the picture, especially from a Zen perspective because that is her orientation. Together we will be asking the question of whether or not it is possible to integrate Zen and psychotherapy and, if so, would it be desirable for the individual practitioner, supervisor, or educator to do that? Although we may become quite animated in the last chapter, the general tone of the conversation is one of mutual respect and shared curiosity.

We trust that the reader's participation in the dialog that follows will share these essential characteristics.

By the end of this book, we hope that readers find themselves able to do at least three things reasonably well. The first is to understand the theoretical issues concerning the possibility of using complementary and alternative techniques in clinical practice. The second is the ability to identify 10 basic concepts and principles of Zen that have therapeutic relevance and to see how they may help augment clinical work. The third is to appreciate how important it is to develop strategies for using at least some of those principles to help educate, train, and supervise clinicians in an interdisciplinary world. It should be said that since the book is a conversation, it could be joined from a number of junctures. The most logical one is to start at the beginning and simply follow the chapters in order, which is the way we intend them. However, those who are largely interested in Zen may want to jump in with chapters 2, 4, and 5. Similarly, those who have primarily an academic interest could do the same thing with chapters 1, 3, and 5. The rest of chapter 1 addresses five issues that may be unavoidable when attempting to integrate traditional and nontraditional psychotherapies. They are: a modern health care paradox; the problem of defining traditional, complementary, and alternative approaches to health and mental care; a Gordian knot in the field of mental health care; the historical roots of a paradigmatic problem that haunts integrating traditional and nontraditional approaches in the West; and a discussion of why we have selected to examine Zen as a case in point.

SETTING THE STAGE: A MODERN HEALTH CARE PARADOX

Integrating traditional and nontraditional psychotherapies is not an easy task. Nor is it one that occurs in a social or intellectual vacuum. Rather, both approaches are couched in a context of several larger issues that affect health care in general and it is important to spend some time identifying and exploring these issues before investigating Zen, its relationship to psychotherapy, and its practical applications for our field. To begin, one of the most important developments in modern health care and mental health care today takes the form of a curious paradox. On one hand, we are now witnessing some of the greatest advances in traditional approaches to diagnosing and treating physical and mental problems to ever occur. In terms of physical illnesses, for instance, it seems that we hear or see the announcement of some new diagnostic technique, treatment breakthrough, or research advance almost every day. Although progress in mental health care may not seem like much in direct contrast, considerable strides have been made in Western approaches to diagnosing and treating mental illnesses, too. For example, in some very real ways, the development of the *Diagnostic and Statistical Manual, Third Edition* (American Psychiatric Association, 1980), or *DSM-III*, parallels advances in physical diagnostics in that for the first time in human history, a reliable system for identifying, researching, and learning about mental health disorders was developed.

By contrast, both Joan and I are experienced enough to remember working with the *DSM-II* (American Psychiatric Association, 1968) and what a radical change the new system brought to our field when compared to that earlier one. For example, I saw one patient in an emergency psychiatric service setting who mentioned that she had been there four other times during the past year before she saw me. After she left with my diagnosis and treatment suggestions, I examined her "chart" and was struck by the fact that during the past 12 months this woman now carried five major mental health diagnoses, some of them quite severe. Yet, she did not seem this troubled when I saw her! The possibilities for there being a complete lack of agreement between five evaluations (and four clinicians) are very limited: either the individual was extremely ill, the diagnostic skills of the clinicians were very poor, there was something fundamentally wrong with the diagnostic system, or some combination of the above.

A few years later when I was attending a *DSM-III* training session led by its lead author, Robert Spitzer, I saw for myself what the problem was back then. There were about 200 psychiatrists, psychologists, counselors, and social workers attending the two-day workshop. On the morning of the first day we were shown videos of intake interviews with real patients by actual clinicians. Then, we were asked to make a diagnosis of the presenting problem using the *DSM-II* and turn them in to the conference officials by noon. In the afternoon, we were trained in using the *DSM-III* system, were shown more videotapes, and were asked to make diagnoses and turn them in, as well. The next day, we were shown concordance rates on all the diagnoses that were made using both systems. I was astonished to learn that there was less than a 50% agreement rate among the clinicians concerning what a given patient suffered while using the *DSM-II* and well over 70% agreement using the *DSM-III*! Another remarkable thing to consider was that this dramatic change occurred as the result of only one workshop. This kind of data made the point to all of us in a way we could not deny: The new *DSM* system does, indeed, create a diagnostic approach that we can all rely on regardless of our particular theoretical orientation or disciplinary background. Today, some two decades later, it is now clear that this new approach created the first universal or standard language for the field, and that it did so just at the time when more and more mental health disciplines were moving into it.

However, it is important to appreciate the fact that the story of the *DSM-III* is much larger than a clinical one alone. The idea of using behaviorally oriented, criterion-based, operationally defined diagnostic categories of abnormal behavior may actually constitute a "second revolution" in the field. In certain respects, this development parallels the one that occurred in the early 1950s with the discovery of psychotropic medications. What makes the current system so important in this regard is that, in addition to offering standardization for practitioners, the system was also conceived of as being a teaching and research instrument, or as its authors say in the newer *DSM-IV,* the system is a classification of mental disorders that was developed for use in "clinical, educational, and research settings" (1994, p. xxii). The point is that since it covers all three of the major areas involved in our work, this system offers a degree of reliability that touches the entire field at the deepest levels. It means, for example, that for the first time in human history, we have a system that allows clinicians to talk with patients, teachers to talk with students, and researchers to talk with each other with a reasonable degree of empirical reliability concerning the most elusive and varied thing in the universe: human behavior. Moreover, like many revolutions, the timing of other historical events was crucial. In this case, the revision of the diagnostic system that led to the *DSM-III* and continues today started just at the time when the field began to emphasize the importance of research on therapeutic outcomes as a major priority.

For example, think about what treatment research would look like if we did not use some operationally defined guidelines to meet the minimum scientific standard for developing relatively homogenous pools of subjects. There is little doubt, for instance, that studies which show that cognitive therapy, interpersonal therapy, and medication therapy are all relatively equally effective ways of treating many forms of depression are of tremendous value and importance (Clinician's Research Digest, 1999; Durand & Barlow, 1997; Nathan & Gorman, 1998). But if this body of research were done without using a reliable definition of depression, then we would really have no findings at all because comparing studies using different definitions of depression would be like comparing proverbial apples and oranges. A similar case could be made for the progress we have seen concerning anxiety disorders and with some of the more severe forms of mental illness (Clinician's Research Digest, 1999; Durand & Barlow, 1997; Nathan & Gorman, 1998). The slow but steady accumulation of knowledge that is the hallmark of the scientific processes would not be possible without a reliable way of categorizing, identifying, researching, and communicating about problematic behavior. The *DSM* also has problems, especially with validity and labeling (Durand & Barlow, 1997), but at least it provides a "common scientific tongue," which is no small achievement given the history of how often we have misdiagnosed behavior in the past.

On the other hand, and this is what creates the paradox, just as the empirical, scientific, or Western approach to physical and behavioral medicine has made its greatest advances, an explosion of interest and activity has taken place simultaneously in what is generally known as "complementary and alternative medicine." Indeed, according to various calculations, in 1998 alone Americans spent some 27 billion dollars on alternative care; the number of visits to such practitioners is estimated to have risen by over 200 million from 1990 to 1997; and the lifetime prevalence for turning to alternative care may be as high as 60% of the general population (Crone & Wise, 2000)! A secondary explosion of similar significance seems to have taken place in the professional community. Congress established the Office of Unconventional Medicine to research alternative approaches in the early 1990s, but soon changed the name to the more acceptable Office of Alternative Medicine. Interest in this area mushroomed once again, so that the name of the organization was changed to the very respectable sounding title of the National Center for Complementary and Alternative Medicine. Likewise, funding for this office expanded at a similar rate and reached some 50 million dollars during that time, and the organization itself grew from one office to the point where it sponsored some 13 research centers in 1998 (Crone & Wise, 2000), most of which will continue to do their work for some time to come.

More recently, popular interest in alternative and complementary medicine seems to parallel professional interest. For example, more than 46,000 *Consumer Reports* readers responded to a survey on alternative care conducted by that organization just two years ago. As they say it,

> The Berlin Wall that has long divided alternative therapies from mainstream medicine appears to be crumbling. Acupuncturists, hypnotists, massage therapists, and meditation instructors are now working at new complementary centers attached to major hospitals. And many conventionally trained doctors have learned to be sympathetic, not scornful, when their patients say they're trying alternative therapies. (Consumer Reports, 2000, p. 17)

A month later Juan Williams took the topic to the country in general through a series of broadcasts hosted by National Public Radio's "Talk of the Nation."

> In larger numbers than ever before, Americans are turning to alternative medicine. Whether it is acupuncture, meditation, herbs, or the Chinese exercise regimen of

tai chi, alternative therapies are changing the way Americans take care of their health. A national survey conducted at Harvard's Department of Health Care Policy found that Americans increased the use of alternative medicines by nearly 50 percent in the last decade. That makes the use of alternative medicine the fastest growing trend in medicine today. Demand for alternative medicine has grown so much that doctors and drug companies, who once dismissed it as so much hocus-pocus, are now studying alternative approaches to healing. . . . But alternative medicine is about more than herbal remedies. It's also about a different approach to health care. Alternative medicine focuses on wellness or keeping healthy people healthy. Traditional medicine is centered on the diagnosis and treatment of illness. (Williams, 2000)

Of course, much of this interest and work focuses on treating physical problems through the use of herbal medicines and various forms of homeopathy, as they are of potential interest to both physicians and pharmaceutical companies, both of which have huge economic stakes in whatever outcomes that may arise. But a good deal of what is included in alternative medicine involves mind-body interactions more familiar to mental health practitioners, such as hypnosis, meditation, massage therapies, as well as a small but growing interest in how alternative therapies may be applied to various mental health disorders. These trends do not even include how various alternative therapies are being sought out by those who simply want a better, healthier, longer, or more meaningful life, all of which are "outside" of the concerns of a health care system that deals primarily with "diagnosis and treatment of illness."

Various authors offer different reasons for the emergence of so much interest in complementary, alternative, or "nontraditional" approaches today. Most of them can be grouped into one of three major types: dissatisfaction with current health care, an increasing degree of self-direction, and money—lots of it. Although it is not possible to say which of these sources is the most important in stimulating the current explosion of interest in alternative health care, it is likely that some form of dissatisfaction plays a central role when people turn away from traditions. There are several ways that this type of motivation can stimulate people to seek alternatives and simple dissatisfaction concerning the way traditional health care is offered is one of them. It is probably not coincidental, for instance, that interest in alternative care has been increasing at the same time that waiting rooms have become ever more crowded, that 15-minute "conversations" with the doctor have become the norm, that obtaining reimbursement seems to be pathological itself, and that endless referrals to specialists have been growing dramatically. In other words, people sometimes turn to other approaches and professionals because they are looking for various "intangibles" that seem to be missing in traditional health care, such as a sense of being connected to the process or of having a personal relationship with one's health care provider.

In contrast, nontraditional helpers and healers often seem to be good at these things in large part because they tend to be more willing to spend time getting to know their clients on an individual basis. Consider, for example, the different way that the intimate act of touching and being touched occurs in typical traditional versus alternative health care settings. Who has not experienced the poking of this and the prodding of that while lying half naked on a physically and metaphorically cold examination table? Compare that form of touch with that which occurs with the "healing hands" of the chiropractor, the soothing rub of a skillful therapeutic masseuse, or the calming presence of a gentle Reiki expert! Although it is tempting to dismiss this "warm and fuzzy" dimension of health care, good rapport with the patient can facilitate the diagnostic process in that the patient can open up more and be more honest with their helpers. Similarly, a greater sense of partnership between provider and recipient can facilitate increased compliance with the health care plan. Indeed, research shows that physicians who take the time to do these things suffer lower rates of malpractice suits than those who do not (Moore, Adler, & Robertson, 2000)!

Often the dissatisfaction that turns people toward alternative modes of health and mental health care comes from a more serious source, from a search for some form of mastery (Muskin, 2000). Cold clinicians and alienating conditions are inconvenient but tolerable: Most of us have learned to live with them. However, the limits or failures of modern medicine can seem intolerable, especially in regard to two kinds of situations. The first one involves illnesses that are, or that can become, chronic, especially if they involve pain. Rheumatoid arthritis, fibromyalgia, chronic fatigue, and so forth, are all conditions that attack the psyche as much as, if not more than, the body. In fact, the three most frequent reasons that people seek out complementary and alternative care appear to be "chronic musculoskeletal disorders (e.g., osteoarthritis, back pain, and joint disorders), mental disorders (e.g., substance use, anxiety, affective disorders, fatigue, stress-related, problems), and metabolic diseases (e.g., diabetes, cancer, HIV, and endocrine metabolic and nutritional disorders)" (Peeke & Frishett, 2002, p. 185).

Even if they only turn out to be only palliative in nature, nontraditional therapies, including complementary and alternative psychotherapies, offer some relief from the suffering. Sometimes such health care alternatives can even help a person find a way of "living with" their conditions, such as by changing their life styles. For example, I happen to suffer a chronic pain condition associated with relatively serious back injuries and surgery. Although traditional medicine did help with certain aspects of the problem, alternative methods, in this case acupuncture, helped with others. The combination has allowed me to manage the condition in ways that minimize its interference in my life. Indeed, sometimes alternative methods may even help people "transcend" their condition by finding meaning in their pain or by using it to redirect their lives toward more important goals than they had before (Vash, 1994). This kind of psychological work is hardly a part of 15-minute office visits or technical discussions about the mechanics of the body.

Another more serious situation that often prompts people to turn toward nontraditional alternatives because of dissatisfaction with what traditional care offers involves illnesses or conditions that are, or that can become, incapacitating or even fatal. Although there are many other diseases that can motivate a person in this way, the terror and hopelessness associated with many forms of cancer seems to be the most common one. In this case, an individual may turn toward an alternative because it seems to offer more of one crucial element than does traditional care: *hope*. After all, an unproven practice is also one that has not been proven wrong, and taking an alternative view of an illness cannot make things much worse once the condition is already identified as hopeless. Moreover, once in a while miracles do seem to happen, which only reinforces hope.

Another source of dissatisfaction with traditional care is based on a different vision of what good health care is to begin with. As Juan Williams (2000) indicated, this approach involves a different philosophy than that which is characteristic of traditional, which is to say Western scientific, perspectives and practices. The most basic distinction is that where traditional health and mental heath care focus on gathering information about symptoms of disease or disorder, making a diagnosis of the condition, and then treating or managing the condition, many forms of alternative health care concentrate instead on reaching a state of general health, which includes mental health, and then maintaining it. Thus, in addition to treating illness, alternative health care is also concerned with avoiding it, which means that, unlike traditional approaches, prevention is an important part of the health care process. This emphasis requires much more time than traditional practices typically allow, because it involves doing such things as understanding the client as an individual, learning about his or her life style, identifying areas that need to be addressed, and doing follow-up on whether or not recommendations are effective. Reaching and maintaining a state of health often takes more time and effort, especially if it involves teaching the client how to manage stress more effectively, educating him or her about proper nutrition, helping the person to develop an individualized exercise or meditation program, and so forth, very little of which is included in standard health care packages.

In addition, where traditional health care largely tends to react to an illness or a condition, alternative health care seems to be more proactive in its approach to both illness and to health. Where traditional health care dedicates its energies toward the reduction of symptoms or of stress, for instance, some alternative health practitioners actually focus on the possibility of developing and maintaining what might be called "optimal health." In this case, and for those who can afford it, clients and practitioners are more explicitly concerned with what might be considered to be the highest level of nontraditional health care goals. This kind of health care partnership may focus on helping the client to increase their productive energy as well as reaching a more harmonious balance of work, interpersonal relationships, and play in life. Not only is mental health seen as being necessary for physical health, but the holistic orientation of this kind of alternative care can even include an active concern with the individual's spiritual well-being, something which is not usually even on the radar screen of traditional health care concerns.

Dissatisfaction with existing systems is one reason that people seek out alternatives, but another one seems to arise from various sociohistorical conditions of our times. One of them is a set of forces that encourage, and sometimes force, the individual to become more active in the health care process. One reason for this change is that we have reached the point where being a passive recipient of health care no longer fits with current social and economical reality, because today people are much more self-directed than they have ever been before. In fact, our entire American, if not Western, culture seems to promote such things as individual choice, self-determination, and free access to information, all of which carry over into our health care practices for both provider and consumer. Some of these factors come from external sources, meaning that people often cannot do much about them. For example, instead of socialized, government directed, one-size-fits-all, physical and mental health coverage, we expect the individual to find his or her own health care plans through employers, HMOs, PPOs, private insurance, and the like. Indeed, unlike any other industrialized nation on the planet, we even let some 44 million (Kaiser Commission, 2000) of the working poor "choose" to do without comprehensive health care altogether!

However, some of these forces emerge from the individual. For example, our higher educational levels (which involve some 24% of adults over age 25 having acquired a college education today, according to the U.S. Department of Commerce, Economic & Statistics Administration, 1998) and easy access to medical information fostered by the Internet and other services, allow us to become educated consumers of health care. The final effect seems to be that we are departing from a traditional health care system where patients passively accept medical opinion, advice, and treatment, and are embarking on a more active enterprise, which includes individuals researching various forms of treatments and care, because we are becoming socialized to do that.

Of course, money also influences the growing interest in nontraditional approaches. Today health care, including mental health care, is very big business, a business so big that even in the later days of the 20th century it consumed some 14% of our Gross National Product (Koudsi & Costa, 1998) and is still growing! Thus, alternative medicine and care means alternative sources of potential profit. Think of all the potential money to be made, for instance, if pharmacological corporations, which are gigantic players in the health care industry, had control of such alternative health care possibilities as herbal remedies and supplemental nutrients (Valenstein, 1998). Indeed, for better or worse, the comparatively smaller supplemental nutrients industry is struggling for its very survival against a movement to regulate that business that would clearly benefit the pharmaceutical corporations (Wagner, 1998). Similarly, one must wonder how many of those office visits to alternative practitioners represent actual losses or potential gains for the individual medical practitioner or health care system? Lest we seem one-sided, it should be pointed out that there is no end to those who are well meaning, but who can offer little evidence for the treatments they provide and thereby do a dangerous disservice to those who are seeking alternative forms of care, which is not even to mention those who seek to profit from human suffering through outright greed or fraud.

Although much nontraditional care focuses on physical dimensions of health, it should not surprise us to see the same forces at work in regard to mental health care. Indeed, we can see important parallels in our field today. On the one hand, we see many advances and a great rise in the research and number of publications concerning research on psychotherapy and treatments that work during the past two decades that parallel similar advances in physical medicine during that period. For example, the American Psychiatric and the American Psychological Associations have been involved with establishing and publishing guidelines on such treatments for some time now (Nathan & Gorman, 1998; Soldz & McCullough, 2000). Bolstered by managed care's interest in manualized, short-term, disorder-specific treatment, scientific interest in clinical efficacy is sure to continue at a high rate for the foreseeable future. On the other hand, just as we are making more progress in the science of treating mental illness than ever before, the past decade also includes the appearance of articles and books concerning nontraditional or alternative approaches to such conditions in unprecedented numbers, as I will document momentarily. Two major themes in this regard concern rising interest in the psychology of religion and an explicit focus on integrating what is usually called "spirituality" into the therapeutic process.

In addition, this development seems to be powered by the same factors that have created the interest in nontraditional and alternative physical health care. Large numbers of people, for example, are turning to complementary and alternative mental health care approaches in record numbers (Peeke & Frishett, 2002). In addition, many of those who endure chronic anxiety, suffer endless depression, or face periods of overwhelming psychosis often encounter the limits of traditional psychiatric care and eventually look for alternatives to conventional treatments as well. In reviewing the literature on the use of CAM (Complementary and Alternative Medicine) approaches with mental health problems, for example, Peeke and Frishett (2002) report that,

> Of special interest to psychiatrists and mental health workers is that many of these individuals continue to seek conventional treatments for their mental problems while also using CAM therapies. One survey of 2,055 patients found that over 60% of patients who visited conventional mental health providers also used CAM therapies. Moreover, 65.9% of the respondents seen for anxiety attacks and 66.7% of those seen for severe depression also used CAM to treat these conditions. Patients felt that CAM therapies were just as helpful in treating anxiety and depression as conventional therapies. (p. 186)

A related problem concerns the fact that far too many people who suffer a mental health problem become just as desperate as those who run into the limits of traditional physical health care. Unfortunately, little is known about the consequences of this aspect of severe or chronic mental illness, other than that it is likely to be associated with very negative consequences, such as acquiring a substance abuse problem in an attempt to cope with the despair, becoming homeless as a result of the failure to stay in the system, being marginalized by a society that values productivity and independence, or by turning to suicide in a last desperate attempt to feel that one has some "say-so" in life. I must say that it seems to me that we should know more about how such conditions wear down the psyche over time if we want to be of real help to the chronically mentally ill, because they, after all, need and deserve our attention the most. To the serious researcher or dedicated clinician, this concern involves exploring what, if anything, nontraditional approaches may offer when traditional treatment "fails," if only out of a sense of compassion if not scientific interest.

Indeed, as I think of the individuals I have known whose lives have been devastated by such illnesses as severe schizophrenia, it seems to me that we are ethically obliged to ask such questions as a matter of course. Simply giving people enough medications to reduce symptoms to levels that are socially manageable is not enough. Although in theory addressing this dimension of mental illness is a part of case management in mental health care, I can say as an individual who trains such practitioners that this aspect of the job is seldom prioritized. In spite of all our good intentions, case managers are usually assigned a client load that is far too large to allow them to develop the kind of relationship with clients that is needed if this dimension of their lives is to be a part of treatment. Moreover, it is saddening to find that we pay those who are willing to do this kind of very hard work much less than we do someone who puts tires on a car in a factory for a living.

Another parallel that affects our field reflects the self-directed patterns we saw in physical care. For example, we went through a period of radical experimentation with alternative approaches in the 1960s and 1970s, which was a time when the psychodynamic perspective dominated the medical community and nonmedically based treatment was ruled by the learning theories, particularly behaviorism. Humanistic psychology emerged in response to this situation, thereby bringing a "third force" into the mental health picture as an alternative to the traditional medical and academic communities (Goble, 1971; Misiak & Sexton, 1973). Abraham Maslow (1968) and Carl Rogers (1951) directed us to look at human experience and development in terms of the future rather than the past. Alan Watts introduced oriental mental health disciplines to occidental ones in his book, *Psychotherapy East and West* (1961), and Benson's (1975) groundbreaking work at Harvard on meditation seemed to give empirical support to this nontraditional approach. Those who are familiar with psychology's third force know that it has always been distinguished from mainstream approaches by such things as a methodological openness to individual experience and an acute interest in the development of well-being, including optimal functioning and self-actualization. It is less known that this movement also involved other social sciences, such as anthropology, which broadened the distinction between traditional and alternative approaches to include theories and practices based on different cultural paradigms of physical and mental illness or health (Castaneda, 1968).

The 1960s are history now and some would say, "Thank goodness." However, as I just mentioned, more recently people seem to be looking toward religion and to spiritually oriented psychotherapies in an attempt to find something that traditional approaches do not seem to provide. In addition to the forces just described, this longing for alternatives may also be tied to what David Myers (2000, p. 257) calls a "spiritual hunger in an age of plenty." In other words, these longings are, in part, a reaction to such forces as the emptiness of materialism as it feeds into a consumer-oriented life style, the creeping doubt of excessive skepticism associated with a mechanical view of the universe, and the loss of direction that may be the logical conclusion of postmodern philosophy.

In addition, these and the forces that pay far too much attention to the individual and to social relativism may result in a "culture of narcissism" (Lasch, 1978), where "looking out for number one" or "getting all the gusto this time around" and "he who has the most toys when he dies, wins" are *not* what they are promised to be. Finally, perhaps as Myers (2000) suggests, the interest in searching for deeper values and nontraditional sources of meaning reflects some sort of a collective mid-life crisis the boomers are experiencing as their mortality becomes a central psychological issue. The sheer statistical size of this group may be more than enough to push society toward considering values other than those which can be provided by a material view of the world and the vision of health care that comes with it. At any rate, all such factors have one thing in common: the lack of satisfying meaning and the search for it. If this is the case, then it is possible that nontraditional therapies can augment our current therapeutic armamentarium, because many nontraditional approaches focus explicitly on meaning and meaning making. If so, then we clinicians and social scientists would do well to learn about them and to incorporate what we can support into our theories of behavior and the way we train people to become clinicians, as long we do not violate our scientific foundations.

These issues are very much alive at the theoretical and practical levels of mental health today. For example, the field of the psychology of religion seems to have exploded during the 1990s and has done so to the extent that it now generates a steady stream of empirically oriented studies on religion and mental health (Pargament, 1997; Schumaker, 1992; Shafranske, 1996; Spilka & McIntosh, 1997), as well as ones that focus on how it may be possible to integrate spirituality and psychotherapy without becoming completely unscientific (Cornett, 1998; Cortright, 1997; Emmons, 1999; Miller, 1999; Wong & Fry, 1998). Similarly, when I did a database search on the topic of psychology and spirituality over a decade ago, I found less than a hundred citations in scientific publications, and only a few of those were clinically oriented. But, repeating that process with PsychINFO during the summer of 2002 resulted in over 1,200 citations, at least 100 of which seemed to address the topic at the clinical level! Moreover, it should be noted that until fairly recently, work in these areas was limited primarily to popularistic presses and religious publications. Yet, today, many authors whose scientific or clinical credentials are well established are addressing these themes, and mainstream publishers are printing their work. In addition to being one of those publishers, for instance, the American Psychological Association is now regularly sponsoring many workshops and forums on religious and spiritual issues, including integrating spirituality and psychotherapy, and Zen and psychotherapy. To paraphrase Shafranske and Malony (1996), the research seems to be telling us quite clearly that religion is an important variable in mental health and in psychological treatment. If so, then it is also necessary to take it seriously in the academic, clinical, and training settings. Otherwise, we are not being good scientists, clinicians, or teachers.

In addition to general interest, the same literature reveals that there are a number of key themes upon which researchers and clinicians focus in this area. One of the most striking of them concerns a huge gap between the attitudes shown by mental health professionals toward religion and those of the general public, the very people with whom we work. For example, Shafranske (2000), one of the pioneers in this field, found in a recent national survey of psychiatrists and psychologists that 38.2% of psychiatrists and 26% of psychologists rated religion as being "very important." He contrasts this number with that obtained through a Gallup poll done with a national sample during the same period. It revealed that some 58% of the general population feels religion is a very important part of their lives! Such a discrepancy requires one to wonder about just how effective traditional psychotherapies are addressing the needs and concerns of our clients when the gap between clinicians and clients is so great on such an important aspect of life.

Another important theme concerns a growing body of research that shows important links between religion and mental health as well as physical health. Religion may turn out to be an important, albeit complex, mental health variable in regard to such issues as "physical health, mortality, suicide, drug use, alcohol abuse, delinquency and criminal behavior, divorce and marital satisfaction, well-being, health outcome, and depression" (Shafranske & Malony, 1996, p. 567). In addition, this body of literature is not just oriented to research and theory. It even includes work on such practices as developing formats for assessing a client's spiritual life in the first series of clinical interviews. Other work focuses on researching the effectiveness of various forms of religious intervention techniques in psychotherapy, such as prayer or meditation (Richards & Bergin, 1997). Given these statistics, it certainly seems striking that such sensitivity and training is not typically found in traditional clinical programs. Instead, we continue to churn out thousands of therapists annually who are not trained to fully explore and utilize, let alone appreciate, a client's religious or spiritual background. Failing to include this central aspect in the development of a client's treatment plan would appear to be both clinically short-sighted and ethically questionable given the magnitude of the numbers involved.

Finally, it is important to think about how money affects a growing interest in alternative health care. Of course, this issue also affects nontraditional mental health care, but since the mental health dollar is not nearly as large as the physical health one it seems to be a weaker force in the movement toward nontraditional mental health care. For example, many forms of nontraditional or alternative counseling services are offered free or at markedly reduced rates through churches, temples, mosques, and so forth, not to mention other forms of "faith-based" activities that offer considerable social support as well. Suffice it to say that this part of the mental health care picture parallels the one for physical care, too, but that it occupies much less space.

TRADITIONAL AND NONTRADITIONAL APPROACHES: DEFINITIONS

It is probably safe to say that every health care system in every culture throughout human history has consisted of traditional approaches to helping, as well as less popular, relatively unsanctioned, nontraditional ones. Traditional approaches are, of course, those that enjoy the support of the culture in general, but there are two ways in which that occurs. First, such practices are traditional in that they reflect health care customs, beliefs and practices that have become ritualized or standardized over time. As such, they form the role expectations that shape the reciprocal social interaction that occurs when one "goes to the doctor" (or shaman, or healer, and so forth). Second, there is a deeper, more important way that traditional approaches are traditional: they fit into the larger historical, social, and philosophical values and beliefs of the culture itself. In other words, traditional approaches to health care are grounded in the way that a particular culture understands the nature of the world and life within it.

For example, in one culture, the physical world may be seen as being "alive" and animated by various kinds of forces; whereas in another society, the world is perceived as being "dead" in that it consists of "mechanical" matter, such as atoms. The first society might understand people as being largely "spiritual," as in American Indian or Hindu cultures, and the second might understand them as being "physical entities," such as might be the case with an evolutionary scientist or a dedicated Marxist. Likewise, the first group might regard the relationship between causes and effects in terms of fate, karma, or some other form of determinism, while the second might put forth concepts such as self-determination, free will, and so forth. All of these beliefs and values are incorporated into their respective culture's approach to health care as well. One upshot of this cultural dimension of care is that what is traditional in one environment may be nontraditional in another and vice versa.

In addition, no matter how a society establishes its particular traditions of care, interesting ironies inevitably appear within as well as between cultures. For example, chewing the bark of certain trees while in pain, or thinking that invisible organisms invade our bodies, or believing that behavior could change by merely talking about it, were all at one time "alternative" forms of medicine in Europe. Yet in time, they helped give birth to pharmacology (aspirin), allopathic medicine (germ theory), and psychotherapy (analysis), respectively. Similarly, the use of herbs, acupuncture, and meditation seem to be alternatives in our Western system of health care today, because they are not based on logical positivism, empirical science, or advanced technology. In many parts of China, however, herbal medicines, physical manipulation of life energies, and contemplative meditation stand as traditional treatments, while merely treating symptoms or prescribing brain altering drugs might stand as alternatives upon which to draw when tradition fails (Moyers, 1993).

Although it might be tempting to argue that this situation occurs only because modern Western techniques are often not available in the East, such a criticism may reflect a Eurocentric bias. In many instances, non-Western practitioners simply prioritize a person's physical, cultural, and mental or spiritual needs differently. They may even place them in reverse order of what we are used to doing in the West and work from the top down rather than the bottom up as our allopathic medicine typically does. In other words, Western medicine tends to focus on one's physical body first and then on other dimensions of life, such as the mind or spirit. However many alternative approaches move in an opposite fashion, where physical problems are often seen as the result of spiritual issues, which means that treatment must focus on this aspect of a person's life in order to deal with their physical health. I often wonder what we would think about Western medicine if we somehow found that there actually is a soul or something like that. In such a case it would mean that our approach might be inferior *in principle* to those that include the spirit as the central focus on health and illness!

The careful reader will note that so far, I have used the terms alternative, complementary, and nontraditional rather interchangeably. Although that practice is very common, it also can be confusing when talking about integrating traditional and nontraditional psychotherapies. The field of medicine attempts to clarify the convergence and divergence of traditional and nontraditional approaches by using three terms: traditional, complementary, and alternative medicine (Muskin, 2000, p. xv). We have already identified what is meant by traditional, so let us clarify distinctions between the other two approaches, because there are a number of ways to differentiate complementary and alternative and they are all filled with limitations and overlap. Carolyn Clark (1999), for example, offers a definition that is based on energetics, which is a very common approach among those who advocate complementary and alternative medicine.

> What are complementary health practices? Under this umbrella is found a wide range of therapies. These include such practices as massage, homeopathy, biofeedback, acupuncture, yoga, chiropractic, breathing, and therapeutic touch. These may or may not be used in combination with traditional treatments.
> What do all of these therapies have in common? They all involve some aspect of energy. (p. 5)

Still others use the terms interchangeably, or at least collectively, and refer to them both as simply CAM, which stands for "complementary and alternative medicine." For instance, Muskin (2000) points out that,

> Much of the difficulty involved with defining CAM has to do with the large number of practices encompassed within this term. CAM refers to familiar therapies such as hypnosis, acupuncture, meditation, chiropractic, and nutritional supplements. Less popular approaches include energy healing, ayurveda, naturopathy, and Native American practices. Even support groups and psychotherapy/counseling are considered CAM treatments by some authors. (p. 200)

However, even this very careful approach to defining the difference between traditional, complementary, and alternative medicine turns out to be problematic. For two years after it first addressed these issues, National Public Radio came back to them. They began this program with a very telling discussion of the results of the various research activities that were just beginning at the time of the first show.

> Two years, 10 Washington-area meetings, four town-hall meetings and several site visits later, the commission issued its report. Among the recommendations: more research. The commission recognized that most so-called complementary and alternative therapies have not been scientifically studied, and that we need to separate the safe from the unsafe and the effective from the ineffective. The commission also said that the very terms 'alternative medicine' and 'complementary medicine' need to be defined more clearly. (Silberner, 2002)

In other words, we still seem to be stuck at step one: defining exactly what we mean by traditional, complementary, and alternative care.

The problem of creating useful definitions is well recognized in science, but Joan and I think there is considerable conceptual value in attempting to make a distinction between complementary and alternative mental health care. One way to differentiate these concepts that might prove useful is to regard complementary care as consisting of those views and practices that do not necessarily contradict the prevailing medical and behavioral theories of the day, but which simply lack a high enough degree of evidence to allow them to be included in the traditional framework. Herbal medicines, and chiropractic medicine or massage therapy may fit here. Similarly, complementary care occurs when a traditionally oriented practitioner uses nontraditional techniques that have been shown to be helpful, but the techniques are helpful for reasons which are still largely unclear, such as the case may be with hypnosis or certain uses of acupuncture in controlling pain or helping with addictions.

If one uses the concept of complementary mental health care in this way, then alternative therapies would refer to ideas or practices that are grounded in points of view which lie outside of the parameters of the tradition involved, in this case modern Western medical or behavioral science as it is usually practiced, or which may even contradict the traditions in some fundamental fashion. Some culture specific healing "ceremonies," many shamanistic rituals, and most past-life regression therapies would, for example, all fall under the rubric of "alternative" health care using the definition being presented here, because they all involve concepts that conflict with the scientific model in very basic and irreducible ways. In other words, it is possible to think of a continuum of health care that ranges from views and practices that are consistent with cultural patterns, which we would call traditional health care, and those that either contradict the culture or those practices and which, therefore, would be alternatives to them. In this framework, complementary views and practices would lie in the middle and would tend toward one end of the continuum or the other, depending on such things as how much evidence is currently available to support them and how open the culture is to uncertainty.

Even then, however, there is still a large degree of variability in defining what actually constitutes an alternative approach and whether or not a particular technique should be thought of as being complementary or alternative in nature. The use of meditation, which actually stands up pretty well in terms of some empirical support (Benson, 1975; Muskin, 2000), is a case in point. The fact that meditation does seem to be useful in treating some physical or mental health problems whether or not the participants subscribe to its underlying philosophical or religious tones, seems to make it a complementary practice. Yet, it may also be true that stronger effects, or even different effects, may occur the more both clinician and client embrace and practice the underlying concepts and principles from which the practice of meditation stems. For example, it is possible to use meditation to help relieve some effects of having a stressful job or life as a complement to treating a person for high blood pressure. But think of all the other things that might happen if the individual adopts the nonmaterialism of the Eastern philosophies upon which meditation is based! In this case, we might see the client quit the frantic search for material wealth that is slowly damaging the body, eroding a sense of being connected to friends and family, or both. Again, the most sensible way to deal with the problem of conflicting definitions is to offer an operational definition of what is meant by traditional, complementary, and alternative health care and to use the terms consistently, while keeping in mind that it is possible to use the same terms in different ways.

For our purposes, then, traditional psychotherapies are defined as ways of helping others that emerge from, and are clearly tied to, at least one of the five major scientific perspectives on human behavior, namely, the biological, learning, cognitive, psychodynamic or humanistic points of view. These approaches are traditional in both senses of the term we encountered earlier: each one of them offers longstanding rituals, traditions, and institutions for researching and changing behavior which are practiced in ways that are acceptable to the larger society, and each one of them is very grounded in well-established philosophical traditions that embody the values of Western civilization itself. Thus, for our purposes, the question of whether a particular nontraditional therapy or technique is to be considered as being a complement or as an alternative depends on whether or not the approach or practice is used in a way that can be incorporated into one of these five major perspectives without violating its most fundamental principles.

Christian-based prayer might also offer another good example of what is meant by complementary versus alternative mental health care, because it is very relevant to the mental health scene in America today, and because many Christian-oriented counselors can use their faith to complement their work. For example, saying to the client something such as, "We should pray on this matter," could be a way of using a nontraditional therapy or technique to complement traditional work, providing that the practice is meant meta-phorically or as a way of supporting the traditional therapeutic goals such as insight or behavioral modification. But prayer can also be used as a genuinely alternative practice if it is offered in a way that is tied to a body of thought about behavior and changing it that lies outside one of the five major scientific traditions mentioned above. Using prayer to drive the "demons" out of a person who suffers from schizophrenia, for example, is a very different kind of prayer indeed! What makes this use of prayer very different from the first example is that it is based on an underlying metaphysical paradigm that conflicts with the traditional scientific one.

Lest we seem to be singling out a Christian point of view, it should be pointed out that the same distinction can be made with the use of prayer as a helping or healing technique from a Jewish or Islamic perspective as well. Indeed, the same distinction may be drawn in regard to non-Western approaches and practices, which is especially important to note for our purposes since we will be considering Zen. In this case, for instance, if a therapist includes Zen meditation techniques into treatment in order to assist the client in his or her attempts to decrease stress by reducing states of physiological and psychological arousal, then meditation is being used to complement therapy. If, however, the clinician is suggesting the use of meditation in order to achieve satori or higher states of universal enlightenment, then in this case Zen is being offered as an alternative therapy according to the definitions we are using. Although these distinctions have their own degrees of uncertainty, they can at least help us to communicate with others about what we are doing in theory and in practice.

A GORDIAN KNOT IN MENTAL HEALTH CARE

There is another related but much more complex definitional problem that inevitably occurs when considering traditional, complementary, and alternative approaches to health care, especially mental health care. Most complementary and alternative approaches tend to be holistic, which means they, in essence, give more equal emphasis to the body and mind in understanding, diagnosing, and treating illnesses than does their more traditional allopathic counterpart. But there is a serious difficulty that occurs when using the word "mind" with which we must contend: it concerns whether or not "mind" includes that which is usually meant by the word "spirit" or "spiritual," particularly whether or not those words refer to natural or supernatural characteristics, processes, and realities. As might be expected, this territory is filled with ancient puzzles and problems.

On one hand, the mind or "the human spirit" can be taken to mean the totality of our mental processes, such as individual consciousness, the capacity for reasoning, the development of social awareness, and so forth, that result from having a human brain and living in human societies. This view of the mind or spirit is naturalistic in that these qualities are seen as developing uniformly, that is, with the evolution of our brain and our cultures. Therefore, although this use of the terms mind or spirit refer to something that is tremendously complex, perhaps the single most complex thing in the known universe, it is still referring to a "thing" nonetheless, which is to say it is a natural phenomenon subject to physical, and not metaphysical, law. It is important to realize that there is considerable merit in this position because, for one thing, it allows us to accept the existence of such phenomena as transcendent values or behaviors and to consider them in a secular fashion.

For example, in this framework it is quite possible for someone to learn about and to adopt values that motivate him or her to transcend personal satisfaction, or even personal existence, for the love of another person or for the greater good of a group. A case in point might be that of a mother who sacrifices herself for her young, which is easily understandable in a scientific way in terms of evolutionary thinking. For a more sophisticated example, we might think about the dedication to the poor and downtrodden that certain nonviolent Marxists exhibit. In addition to giving up materialistic values, they sometimes may even sacrifice their very lives for the class struggle in which they see themselves engaged. A Marxist, logical positivist, or nonreligious social scientist would agree that this act involves a commitment to that which allows the individual to transcend personal survival. However, they would not agree that such selflessness is the result of metaphysical values. It is "spiritual," but in the naturalistic sense as meant by the "spirit of man" or the "human spirit."

On the other hand, mind, spirit, and so forth can also be used to mean something altogether beyond physical, personal, or social reality. In fact this is the more common use of the terms religious and spiritual. While this meaning can involve phenomena related to self-consciousness, it is also seen as being connected to transcendent realities which exist outside of the physical and cultural dimensions of the universe, and is somehow more true than them. Mother Teresa, for example, could certainly be considered as a spiritual person in the metaphysical sense. After all, she belonged to a religious faith and she lived out its most transcendent values in a way that stands as a beacon to us all.

To some degree, traditional approaches to physical health care can avoid this problem by leaving the question of whether or not there is a genuine, metaphysical level to this dimension of human life in abeyance: All that must be done instead, is to accept that there is a "mental" dimension to' human life. In this case, we can talk about such things as the "power of the mind" or the "human spirit" as they occur in such phenomena as the placebo effect, or the desire to overcome obstacles in order to survive. Anything more than that is regarded as being possible but unknowable, or at least beyond the realm of science. However, it is more difficult to take such a position when dealing with mental health and its care, because this endeavor emphasizes the mind more than the body, and that focus inevitably pushes us toward facing these issues more directly.

The result of this pressure is that each of us must address the question of what we mean by the mind, spirit, or soul and how far we are willing to extend such terms, because the consequences of how we do that are great ones for our work. If we understand the person as consisting of body and mind in the secular sense, for instance, the knottier problems seem to disappear. However, there is a danger to such a position. If there actually is a metaphysically transcendent dimension to human life and we omit it from our thinking, then whatever understanding of human behavior we are left with about human beings and human behavior is, at best, incomplete. Indeed, such a view may even miss the most important aspects of being human, which is something that could negatively affect our work as healers if not helpers. Yet, if we admit higher realities into the picture, then we are in the situation of either having to prove their existence or of saying that we simply believe them to be true without offering evidence for it. Either stance is untenable because they conflict with a scientific foundation for our work.

Of course, it is important to realize that we are talking about science in the deepest sense of the term here, which means to understand it in terms of the positivism upon which it is based. This distinction is important because it is tempting to use the scientific method without accepting its historical philosophical foundations. We see this all the time in science and social science, such as in the case of a deeply religious person who tries to reconcile creationism and Darwinian evolution. In this case, the argument would be that they are not incompatible, because the first notion can account for the second. In other words, as long as one is not committed to a literal interpretation of creationism, someone of this persuasion might say that it is compatible with what we know about evolution because it is possible for God to have created the universe mysteriously, but to have allowed for His creation to "work" in such a way that man emerged as a key part of the original plan. The contemporary school of "Intelligent Design" might serve as another example. However, although it may seem desirable to hold that both can be true, we shall see in the next section that such a solution is actually a form of Cartesian dualism and that cannot sustain itself under closer scrutiny. At bottom we simply cannot escape the problem.

Today, both researchers and clinicians in disciplines that study or help the person are divided as to whether there is value in making a distinction between the words "religious" and "spiritual," and if so, how to define them (Pargament, 1997). Many of us, for instance, know people who are very religious in that they adopt a particular faith, practice the appropriate rituals of worship at the proper times, train their children in these beliefs and yet behave in ways that contradict the most fundamental principles of their religion. In the extreme case, we even have a name for this way of being religious: it is called hypocrisy and it *never* involves what is meant by spirituality, no matter how that term is defined. However, most of us also know people who practice their religion in a way that embraces its deepest, most transcendent, metaphysical values, and who try to live them faithfully. Although it might be possible to describe this way of living a religion as "being religious," that approach fails to distinguish between the two examples just mentioned because they both involve religion. However, no one would regard the former way of being religious as also being spiritual and most would agree that the latter is, so Joan and I feel that it is necessary to distinguish between the terms religious and spiritual instead of using them interchangeably.

Yet, this distinction does not go far enough. For example, simply designating the first group as people who are *merely* religious and the second as those who are *truly* religious (or religious and spiritual) leaves out another group altogether: people who do not identify with, or partake in, a formal religion, but who nevertheless believe in some form of metaphysically transcendent values or meanings. Those of this group who actually live by such values can also be said to be spiritual, but they may not be religious. Indeed, it is conceivable that some of them may even be opposed to institutionalized forms of religion or even to religion in general.

One way to distinguish between these three possibilities that does seem to have some acceptance in the psychology of religion is to regard the first group as being composed of individuals who are "extrinsically" religious and the second one, those who are religious and spiritual, as being "intrinsically" religious (Masters & Bergin, 1992; Miller, 1999). Using this distinction, people who live their religion extrinsically are those who do not act in accordance with the deeper spiritual values of their faith, and people who are consistent with their faiths live their religion intrinsically. If the distinction between extrinsic and intrinsic religiosity is to be regarded as standard language in the field, then Joan and I would also consider the third group, those who live life spiritually but who do not embrace a particular religious orientation in doing so, as expressing a certain form of intrinsic religiosity. We would also point out that it is necessary to work from this perspective because, as we shall see, certain practitioners of Zen are spiritual in this sense but would take serious exception to being called either members of a religion or to being understood as practicing religion in any way, even intrinsically.

Although we favor this approach, it is only fair to point out that most researchers in the field seem to prefer to link spirituality to religion. According to Pargament (1997, p. 38), for instance, most people fail to separate being religious and being spiritual, which can make such a distinction, "overdrawn." Indeed, for many such people, it may even be that it is their religion that allows them to live a spiritually oriented life in the first place. In this case, their religion and commitment to it are so intertwined with spirituality that one gives rise to the other, meaning that they cannot be untangled even if they see some problems with their religion and its misuses. However, there may be a "selection factor" at work here in that the majority of work in this area concerns research on Christianity and most of the studies done in the work on psychology and religion involve subjects who identify with this particular form of faith because it is intrinsic to our culture. I have little doubt that this same kind of bias would be true in studies of devout Muslims or Hindus done in a culture in which these faiths are dominant, too. However, it is fairly clear that such a claim would not necessarily apply to Zen, because it can be seen as a religion, a philosophy, or as neither one (Brazier, 1995). The position that there are two ways of being religious (one "genuine" and one not) and two ways of being spiritual (one religious and one not) does not make the issue disappear, but it does seem to describe the possibilities more realistically than trying to impose one view or the other.

Cornett (1998) attempts to solve the issue of whether there is a distinction between religion and spirituality at the clinical level by operationalizing six specific elements that characterize spirituality, no matter how one defines it, that can be of value in psychotherapy. They are: a focus on meaning in life, attending to values, grappling with the issue of human mortality, finding some underlying organization to the universe, understanding the role of human suffering, and dealing with the possibility of transcending death. Of course, this kind of openness to a person's experience does not resolve the underlying issue of defining what is meant by mind (whether it includes a connection to metaphysical phenomena or not) or by spirituality (whether it requires religion or not). However, being open is important for two reasons. First, accepting both possibilities is good science: unless one can disprove either position, it is necessary to keep one's mind open to both possibilities. Second, unless a clinician limits his or her work to a particular group of clients where God or metaphysical realities are defined and accepted by both parties, most of us can expect to deal with clients who are religious but not spiritual, religious as well as spiritual, and spiritual without being religious, as we are using these terms. Although those who work in strictly religious settings may be able to do otherwise, most of us cannot afford to use such narrow definitions in our work. Therefore, there is implicit therapeutic value in remaining open to both possibilities, because this stance allows us to have the "profound respect for spiritual, religious, and cultural diversity," which *does* seem to matter therapeutically (Miller, 1999, p. 12). Yet, such openness is not to be taken lightly. In fact, it may even be the most difficult position to maintain because, while there is certainty in being a "true believer" and clarity in being a "real skeptic," the middle path, as we shall see, requires constant vigilance.

HISTORICAL ROOTS: CONFLICTING KNOWLEDGE PARADIGMS

The conflict or split between what we have been calling mind and spirit actually reflects a deeper problem that is as old as Western civilization itself. Philosophers and historians generally agree that this tension has its origins in the West about 2,500 years ago (Hunt, 1993; Miller, 1992). In other words, some of the problems with integrating traditional scientific, complementary, and alternative approaches to helping and healing can be traced back to ancient Greece, probably to the 6th century B.C. Of course, we cannot review here the complete history of how these two positions form the backbone of Western thought and how that pertains to how we understand behavior today, nor do we have to, as that kind of work has already been done by intellectual historians (Hunt, 1993; Miller, 1992). What we can do is to appreciate how this problem gives rise to much of what we are facing in the dialog between traditional and alternative health and mental health care today. In addition to showing us what we are dealing with at the most fundamental levels, such an appreciation will also help make it clear why we have chosen to focus on Zen.

Ultimately, the primary difference between traditional and alternative approaches to medicine or psychotherapy in the West seems to occur in the larger historical context of the eternal conflict between idealism and realism. On one hand, the best-known depiction of idealism is probably found in Plato's famous Allegory of the Cave, where he argues that as long as we try to grasp the world in physical terms, or one that is based on material objects and our senses, we will always be trapped by mere shadows of real understanding. Truth, according to this position, only occurs in terms of eternally existing ideals or "forms," which are pure or spiritual in their character and not physical or material in nature. Since all physical objects are imperfect manifestations of these ideal forms, they are only accessible to and through the psyche, which in the Greek world is composed of both mind and soul. The pathway to knowledge, then, lies within, not without, which means that knowing thyself is not only good psychological advice, but it is also the key to understanding in the highest sense possible.

On the other hand, the other major knowledge paradigm developed by Aristotle just a few years later in Greek history describes the process of gaining knowledge as the opposite. "Sensation brings us perceptions of the world; memory enables us to store those perceptions; imagination enables us to recreate from memory mental images corresponding to perceptions; and from accumulated images we derive general ideas" (Hunt, 1993, p. 31). From this perspective, the route to understanding is external, not internal, and based on observation, not introspection. I always find it stunning to realize that Plato was Aristotle's teacher, and that he presents an equally powerful vision that takes issue with almost every major point his mentor makes. As a psychologist I find it curiously ironic that the chasm created by these two powerful positions arose from two people who were so closely related to each other in time and in space. In any case, it is undeniable that Western philosophy seems to have been greatly affected by the gap between these two points of view because, as we shall see, it seems to have been concerned with trying to bridge it ever since.

Although Aristotle's logic formed the basis for philosophical discourse, various forms of idealism seem to have prevailed during the early part of Western intellectual history. One reason for such dominance is that this view, which holds that there is an unseeable but transcendent reality of ideals, is compatible with a Christian view of the universe. After all, in a very basic sense, the "Earth" or the reality that surrounds us, is flawed by Evil and "Heaven," which is perfection itself, is the ideal toward which we aspire. Medieval Christianity was very stable for hundreds of years, in part because it did not tolerate competing views particularly well. Thus, historians of intellectual development generally seem to agree that the next pivotal moment in the unfolding of the paradox created by these equal but opposite views seemed to occur in the 17th century when René Descartes tried to resolve it. He attempted to do that by dividing the world into two separate spheres, one of mind (which can be seen as Platonic, "soft," or intangible to the senses) and one of matter (which seems Aristotelian, "hard," or present to the senses). Although each such dimension was seen as having its own distinct qualities and laws, it was also argued that they could interact with each other in orderly ways. Human beings, of course, represent the epitome of such interaction, because we consist of both mind and matter.

At first it might appear that the areas where both realities interact with each other would present unsolvable problems. However, Descartes' solution suggested that resolving potential conflicts was "simply" a matter of understanding the particular laws of each sphere, knowing how they worked in their own respective domains, seeing where they came together in a particular phenomenon, and then untangling how each sphere influences events in a given instance. In the case of human beings, for example, our minds are governed by the spirit, while our bodies are governed by matter. The two systems are connected through a zone of interaction or an interface where both worlds overlap, which Descartes hypothesized to be the pineal gland because of its location in the brain. From this view, then, the key to understanding behavior lies in understanding the laws of mind (which includes those of God or the ideal world), the laws of matter (or those of the physical or material world), and how they interact with each other via the inner workings of the pineal gland. The idea is that although this challenge might prove complicated, in theory, it is only a matter of time because the more we understand about either world, the more we could understand how they work together in the person. When difficulties did arise, they were thought to be due to the stresses associated with two worlds colliding rather than a basic incompatibility that separates them. In other words, although things might seem tangled at times, they are consistent and comprehensible, providing one keeps in mind the fact that there are two realities at work, both of which follow orderly processes.

There were advantages to this approach, some of which were not even apparent to those of that time. For one thing, separating mind from matter may have placated the Church and all of its powerful forces just when that was most needed. The rising interest in the material world that was beginning to emerge at the time was a real threat to the existing social and political order. However, placing such things as God and souls in a high or ideal world meant that the Church was still the supreme power on Earth. At the same time, freeing matter from the mind also allowed the natural world to be explored on its own terms, which is to say rationally, empirically, and, eventually, scientifically. In essence, Descartes found a way to say that the Platonic and Aristotelian knowledge paradigms were not necessarily incompatible, which also means that neither are spiritual and material views of the world: they are both right, but right about different worlds. Given the historical conditions of the time, which involved a strong but weakening Church and a small but growing interest in an alternative (naturalistic) view of the world, such a solution may have been the only way out of a number of intellectual, social, and political tensions without risking great instability and perhaps even revolution.

On the one hand, he taught that a person was a machine, capable of being studied by the methods of natural science. On the other hand, he taught that the most valuable and unique human attribute, the soul, was beyond the reach of scientific method and could be understood only by rational reflection. And then finally the interaction between body and soul was said to be deducible through a combination of anatomical inference, psychological introspection . . . and logical analysis. (Hunt, 1993, p. 68)

However, instead of solving the problem of the paradigms, Descartes' mind-body dualism seems to have only disguised it, for as Hunt goes on to say, Descartes' analysis is "peculiarly empty," which means that it only begs the question. In other words, Descartes' argument promises to solve the dilemma, but does so by shoving it into the hands of the future, of the someday that will unravel the innermost workings of the pineal gland. Although certainly useful at the time, the consequences of this approach were much greater than met the eye. Even though we know that we are unlikely to unravel the universe by studying such a relatively small part of the brain, we still act as though it is possible to divide reality into two somehow overlapping independent spheres.

Despite the logical difficulties with parts of Descartes' position . . . most people—at least in the West—continue to think of their minds and their bodies as separate but somehow interacting aspects of themselves. This is a tribute to the power of Descartes' theory. Whatever its faults, his interactive dualism captured the Western imagination to such an extent that it became accepted almost as a matter of course. Few theories, in any discipline, can claim equal success. (Hunt, 1993, p. 68)

Thus, although trying to separate the mind and the body may have solved various problems of the day, it resulted in a split between the physical and mental worlds that we still see today. Instead of approaching health care, especially mental health care, in an integrated or holistic fashion, for instance, traditional medicine treats the body like a machine and splits off the mind, especially in regard to what is meant by the spirit. Although a person somehow may dwell "in" his or her body, the two are seen as being somehow separate, like the inhabitant of a house who comes and goes according to an unknown schedule. Similarly, traditional approaches to mental health and mental health care focus on the mechanics of the mind: all too often, we seem bent on researching the inner workings of the brain and consciousness without admitting that, ultimately, we might be obligated to include the spirit as well.

In more modern philosophic times, Immanuel Kant attempted to open a pathway out of the conundrum by taking two steps. The first was to acknowledge that there are, indeed, two separate worlds, each with its own qualities.

The world, according to this view, is composed of various physical realities that exist in and of themselves. Similarly, the world of the mind is characterized by certain essential capabilities that are intrinsic to it, and not to nature, called "categories." The second step lies in understanding the relationship between the mind and the world, which is based on the idea that the categories of mind are capable of being receptive to the qualities of the world. In other words, our bodies respond to the physical properties of the world through our senses and our mind organizes the sensations according to its own unique capacities for perception and understanding. As Morton Hunt (1993) so nicely says it, " . . . For the human mind is not merely blank paper upon which experience writes, and not a mere bundle of perceptions; it actively organizes and transforms the chaos of experience into sure knowledge" (p. 92). For example, because the mind has the inherent ability through one of its categories to recognize cause and effect, we are capable of seeing connections between events that occur in the physical world and recognize them as involving the phenomenon we call "causality." However, although we see causality in the physical world, it does not share that appreciation, because matter has no categories of mind with which to engage in the process of understanding and follows those rules unknowingly.

Unfortunately, however, Kant's solution turned out to be less than successful. Today we see the same ancient paradox between the two most powerful social and intellectual movements of our times. On the one hand, we find the logical positivists and their contemporary descendants seeing the world and all things in it, including people, as natural phenomenon, governed by natural laws. These laws are consistent, which means that they are best approached and understood empirically and rationally, that is, scientifically. Allopathic medicine and sociobiology, a school of biological thought that advances the position that *all* behavior is biologically based (Wilson, 1998), represent this position in the medical and behavioral sciences today. Even if the forces of culture and history are added to the picture, then we still end up with what is called evolutionary psychology. If we go on to say that all human reality is socially constructed as postmodern thinking does, then we must conclude that it is not necessary to even consider the possibility of absolute truths or transcendent realities of any type when trying to understand human behavior. At this level, truth becomes a matter of perception, not actuality (Gergen, 1991), relativity reigns, and if so, there is no truth at all, except for that one.

On the other hand, just when it looks as though realism may have overcome idealism in the 19th and 20th centuries, it also looks like the 21st is showing signs of a major resurgence in idealism, this time in the form of an interest in religion all around the world (Myers, 2000). For example, just as the hard evidence for Darwinian science becomes overwhelming to most scientists, we see such things as a renewed interest in forcing creationism into the classroom, the emergence of a substantial interest in the psychology of religion, and the upsurge of extreme fundamentalism as seen through horrific acts of terrorism on September 11, 2001. The point is that not only does a religious point of view insist on an absolute reality that transcends such things as matter and culture, but it also holds that this reality is found in the world of ideals, not objects.

Reconciling the conflicts and differences between these two contemporary and competing systems is just as difficult as resolving the fundamental Western paradox because they stem from the same origins. Thus, whatever else it is, the contemporary dialog between traditional, complementary, and alternative approaches to health and mental health care is actually a part of a much older and much more complex conversation between idealism and realism. For example, we can see similar trends in the social sciences, particularly in psychology. Early in the 20th century, for instance, the behaviorists virtually banned the mind from mainstream psychology in favor of understandings of behavior that could be based on scientific, which was to say observable and measurable, methods (Gardner, 1985). Today, the wheel has turned, largely because of two forces in the social and behavioral sciences.

One of them is the development of cognitive psychology, which has brought consciousness back to the social sciences. The other occurred at nearly the same time and is found in the emergence of humanistic psychology, which also includes a focus on consciousness. Although it is very possible to reconcile behaviorism and cognitive psychology because they both have deep roots in the realism of logical positivism, humanistic psychology is incompatible with the determinism of such a position because it emphasizes free will, which is decidedly idealistic. While cognitive and humanistic approaches to understanding human behavior did give psychology back its mind, so-to-speak, they still struggle as to the nature of its soul. As we shall see in chapter 3, they do so in a way that brings us right back to the fundamental clash between realism and idealism. Apparently, it is impossible to escape the fundamental paradox of knowledge paradigms, at least for the West.

It is also important to appreciate the fact that the behavioral sciences, including psychiatry, face this classical problem much more acutely than do most other disciplines, because we are charged with understanding and treating the mind, and all that we have seen it to entail, but must do so through the methods of science! Thus, it is not surprising that the same tension shows up in the social and behavioral sciences right from their beginnings. It is well known, for instance, that William James referred to this problem through his famous distinction between "tough minded" and "tender hearted" approaches to knowledge. However, many people do not realize that the first several chapters of his greatest work, *The Principles of Psychology* (1890/1983), explicitly address the mind-matter problem. Since this work is often regarded as the first American psychology text, it can be argued that the mind-body problem has always been central to the way we understand behavior. In fact, we shall see in chapter 3 that all the major modern traditional approaches to researching, understanding, and treating human behavior span the gap between realism and idealism created by the Greeks. The surprise turns out to be that the biological, learning, cognitive, psychodynamic, and humanistic points of view that characterize the behavioral sciences today stretch across realism and idealism in a complex but wonderfully orderly fashion.

While theory is one thing, practice is another and we see a similar problem at this level as well. On one hand, we psychiatrists, nurses, psychologists, social workers, and counselors genuinely embrace the value of an empirical or "objective" approach to human behavior, because we need to know how to help others in ways that "really work." In addition, much of what passes for a complementary or an alternative approach can be useless or even harmful. Therefore, we are actually obliged to approach such things with a strong measure of scientific skepticism. On the other hand, the practice of our respective disciplines, no matter how empirically based, sometimes takes us to the very limits of our scientific training and beyond. Even the rather straightforward therapeutic challenge of helping someone deal with an ordinary "adjustment disorder" associated with a "typical" divorce may take client and therapist into a full blown "crisis of meaning" that medication or standard therapies do not address well. Similarly, how many times does the real work of helping someone deal with schizophrenia only begin after they have been "stabilized" with the latest neuroleptic? Sometimes healing the heart of a shattered existence, or finding a pathway to meaning in the face of overwhelming suffering, is just as much a part of therapy as is helping people to stay on medications or out of the hospital, if not more so. Finally, it is to its credit that the *DSM* system now recognizes that such conditions exist with its new diagnostic category for religious problems in the "Other Conditions" section of the manual. However, I wonder how many therapists are trained to even recognize what is known as a "spiritual emergency," let alone how to deal with one.

The contemporary interest in complementary and alternative care seems to have brought us full circle once again, which means that the next question is what to do now? Certainly, we must continue to train clinicians scientifically (i.e., empirically, methodically, and systematically) and strive to give them tools that can be shown to work as our first priorities. At the same time, it should also be clear that we must take care to prepare our mental health professionals for the times when traditional approaches and techniques are not enough. One way to deal with this mental health paradox is to ask if it is possible to find nontraditional approaches that can be integrated into traditional clinical, academic, and supervisory frameworks without undermining their scientific foundations. Obviously, Joan and I think that Zen can offer something important in this regard, and that it does so in a way that is ethical, conscientious, and reasonably rigorous.

WHY ZEN?

In general, there are at least three good reasons that practicing mental health professionals, as well as those who educate or train future practitioners, should look at complementary and alternative approaches to mental heath care. The first and perhaps most important one is to simply supplement current clinical practices. If there are techniques that are available or potentially available that we are not using but which can help others, then we are ethically bound to know about them. Here the focus would be on asking what kinds of nontraditional techniques can be of use and is there any evidence for them? The second reason for considering alternatives is to give therapists tools for dealing with matters and issues that do not respond well to traditional techniques. Can, for instance, nontraditional approaches or techniques be used to offer anything to those whose lives have been ravaged by severe mental illness? If they can, then we are also obliged to know about such possibilities, how to use them, and when to use them, not to mention the need to recognize that many if not most of our clients also have a religious or spiritual life. The third reason to examine nontraditional therapies concerns an issue our field does not address often enough: can they help therapists to take better care of themselves? It has long been known, for instance, that the occupational hazards of the field include such things as countertransference, stress, burnout, even suicide, and that was before managed care was added to the mix. Under such conditions, it would behoove all of us to know whether complementary or alternative approaches may be of help on this side of the couch, too.

Most therapists have some inkling of these concerns, even as students. For example, I remember in my own training when I kept pestering a professor,

Tony Barton, along these lines. He was describing how he handled a particularly difficult clinical situation involving the possibility of suicide. It was clear that he had done a masterful job of resolving the crisis and of helping the person to move beyond it. At the end of his presentation, I asked something like, "But professor, what would you do if the client had done this?" and gave a reasonably possible scenario that he had not covered. He replied, "Well, Chris, I might have tried . . . " and then offered an equally reasonable technique for me to use in that kind of situation. But then, being a bit of a worrier, I asked further, "Well, what if that didn't work and the client got worse?" Again, the good doctor responded with a reasonable suggestion, along with some patience for his slightly obsessive student. After continuing in this fashion for quite some time, the professor realized that what I was really asking about was not a particular event, but what a clinician can do when he or she seems to have exhausted their training and things have not gotten better.

Upon that realization, he said, "Well, Chris, at that point, you just do the very best you can." Although this answer could seem like it was somewhat vague, I realized that it was actually a very good one. What he meant, of course, was that life is unpredictable, that all of us will face situations which seem to have no ready solutions, and that a good therapist will rely on his or her training, experience, and capabilities to find a creative and helpful response. The answer is also an honest one that has stayed with me all my clinical and academic life, especially when dealing with my own "persistent" students. However, through my work with Joan, I now realize he was also saying "Doing the best you can" may also involve doing the best you can to keep an open mind about your work. In this case, that would mean being willing to examine some nontraditional therapies, especially those that do not emphasize control and that are more open to the processes of living. Perhaps Zen offers the therapist some help in terms of reducing his or her own anxiety and thereby increase their chances of being helpful to the clients. In fact, doing even just that much may allow a therapist to better model to the client how a person can face uncertainty in a healthier way than they might have otherwise shown. After all, we know that modeling by the therapist is an important factor involved in the therapeutic process (Bednar & Peterson, 1995).

Of course, there are many nontraditional approaches to dealing with the three types of issues and problems just mentioned (identifying useful alternatives, being able to help the client when traditional techniques are not enough, and easing the therapist's own burden). Every native culture, each major religion, and several philosophies of life offer possibilities to consider, such as American Indian healing ceremonies, faith-based counseling of whatever orientation, and ideological systems, including postmodern ones, respectively. But there are at least four good reasons why Zen should be considered as a "first choice," especially the 10 basic concepts and principles of it that Joan will be discussing in the next chapter.

First, Zen offers what can be seen as a "middle path" between science, religion and philosophy. David Brazier portrays what is known in Zen as the Middle Path in his reference to the Buddhist monk Punnagi who discusses the psychotherapeutic aspects of Zen.

> Of course, the Buddhists of . . . Buddhist countries don't look upon Buddhism as a psychotherapy. It is mainly understood as a form of religion. Of course, those scholars who study the teaching of the Buddha . . . tend to regard the teaching as a philosophy. Now as I see it, these two ways of thinking . . . can be seen as two extremes. . . . Avoiding these two extremes, I would like to take the Middle Path, which is to treat the teaching of the Buddha as a form of psychotherapy. . . . I would say that if Buddhism is introduced into the modern world as a psychotherapy, the message of the Buddha will be correctly understood. (1995, p. 20)

Appreciating Zen as a Middle Path is extremely advantageous in that it solves several problems that religion-based alternatives may not. For example, Zen does not force us to believe in or dispute a particular version of God, which means that therapists and teachers are not forced to deal with religious dogmas while treating or teaching others. As such, we do not have to worry about the dangers of either fundamentalism or mysticism, either of which could easily take us out of the realm of scientific psychotherapy and into all kinds of trouble. At the same time, the openness of Zen allows us to be receptive to more types of issues and possibilities, including spiritual ones no matter how that term is used, which seems to be becoming a more frequent part of our work today. In addition, and unlike many other approaches that are sympathetic to religious or spiritual issues, the Middle Path does not require us to dismiss them, believe them, reframe them, or do anything at all with them, except, perhaps, to "let them be," which is sometimes the only respectful thing one can do. Upon occasion, such gentleness also turns out to be exactly the right thing to do for helping to occur.

Moreover, Zen is practical: It is relatively easy to incorporate the concepts and principles we will explore into what we already do without making a commitment to particular religious practices, specific rituals, or culture-bound customs. The only thing that Zen does require from us is a willingness to be open to experience and to meditate. No therapist should have difficulty with this aspect of the approach, as long as it is not presented as the only strategy to use in one's work. Similarly, by focusing on the practice of Zen as the Middle Path instead of seeing it as a formal religious or philosophical *system*, we avoid the vexing questions associated with determining how much of it should be adopted by the practitioner or how much we should influence another's life toward adopting such a philosophy themselves.

Second, unless one practices it as a religion or philosophy, which we have just said is not what we are advocating, the Middle Path does not necessarily conflict with standard, scientific approaches. Again, there are several ways to illustrate this advantage, but the chief one is the fact that at least some of Zen is compatible with various aspects of the major traditional approaches to understanding and treating abnormal behavior. For example, the physiological and psychological benefits of meditation are already accepted by biological, learning, cognitive, psychodynamic and humanistically oriented psychotherapies for working with certain types of problems. Similarly, at least three of the major perspectives, namely the cognitive, psychodynamic, and humanistic approaches, include insight and the development of self-awareness as therapeutic processes or goals, just like Zen. Likewise, it will become clear that, at the very least, these principles are compatible with the standard literature on what are usually called the "nonspecific" or "common factors" aspects of the treatment process, which although difficult to measure, seem to be an important part of effective therapy (Hubble, Duncan, & Miller, 1999; Wachtel & Messer, 1997). Indeed, as we shall see later, because of its openness to the world, self, and others, the Middle Path may even enhance a given clinician's ability to facilitate such basic aspects of the therapeutic process. Indeed, Zen has already been incorporated into some standard treatments, such as Linehan's (1993) dialectical-behavior therapy for the Borderline Personality Disorder, a number of aspects of the psychodynamic approach (Christensen & Rudnick, 1999; Epstein, 1995; Rubin, 1999), and even with some cognitive work on depression (Segal, Williams, & Teasdale, 2001).

Third, in addition to being reasonably compatible with standard therapies, providing one is judicial in their application, the Middle Path found in the 10 concepts and principles we will be covering can be used in conjunction with most traditional clinical teaching and supervisory arrangements. It is necessary to be more cautious here because there is some theoretical conflict between the more passive "let it be" attitude of the East and the more aggressive "fix it" approach therapies of the West. But this kind of tension also exists between various traditional approaches, such as when we compare the invasive techniques of biological treatments with the "other-centered" orientation of the humanistic approach, as we shall see in chapter 3. Nevertheless, if one respects the science behind "treatments that work," teaches them first, and then offers the concepts and principles of the Middle Path as a complement when standard techniques are not enough on either side of the couch, then most supervisors and educators ought to be able to find it useful. At the very least, this approach would certainly help them to deal with well-meaning but anxious students as I mentioned earlier!

The last reason to consider Zen might be the most interesting one of them all: the concepts and principles we will consider have been used to address problems of living for many centuries now. Not only has this been time enough to discard many things that do not help, but such a lengthy period of development also allows for considerable refinement, which is something that scholars, helpers, and healers in the East are just as concerned with as those of the West. In other words, although all of these techniques have *not* been supported by controlled studies to the extent that evidence-based therapy might demand, they *have* passed a test of time that Western techniques would be hard pressed to match! In addition, there are striking similarities between Zen and Western approaches to consider. For example, they share certain common goals and values: both are concerned with reducing human suffering as compassionately as possible; and both emphasize individual freedom from the tyranny of suffering, whether it takes the form of the emptiness of a materialistic culture, interpersonal conflict, or personal distress. Of course, it must be pointed out that there also are ways that Zen is incompatible with traditional science-based psychotherapies. However, these characteristics usually arise when considering Zen as a religion, a philosophy, or as a genuinely alternative approach as we have defined that term. Fortunately, we can avoid such problems provided that our focus is on a complementary use of Zen.

It is necessary to make one final point before turning to the next phase of our dialog. Like all great world religions and philosophies, it is inevitable that various, sometimes even competing, schools of thought will arise over time. As ideas spread, they are influenced by key personalities, different cultures, and new times, each of which embraces certain aspects of the original ideas, modifies others, and adds new ones to the old. For example, we saw such a pattern in the development of Western philosophy as it grew from Plato, to Aristotle, through Descartes, on to Kant, and then to the postmodernists. The same kind of transformation occurred with Christianity as it moved from Christ, to the Gospels, through St. Augustine, Thomas Aquinas, Martin Luther, and so forth. Therefore, it should come as no surprise that Buddhism has its own rich history. Like the others, it begins with a founder and is characterized by the emergence of several major branches, each of which involves the development of various schools that reflect the temperaments of their leaders, the particular cultures in which they arose, as well as those cultures to which they spread over time.

While it may disturb purists, there can be little doubt that as it reaches the Western mind, Zen will again undergo new transformations, probably major ones. As Joseph Goldstein (2002) so aptly describes it,

> What makes this time unique in the development of Buddhism is not only that East is meeting West, but also that isolated Asian traditions are now meeting for the first time in centuries, and they are doing so here in the West. Emerging from the fertile interaction of these ancient teachings is what we can now begin to call Western Buddhism. (p. 2)

He makes two more points that are relevant to our discussion of Zen and our focus on the Middle Path of this branch of Buddhism. First, Goldstein describes Western Buddhism as focusing more on practice than on theory (which includes scriptures and traditions). Perhaps such an emphasis reflects our pragmatic orientation, but it is clear that this emerging approach is more concerned with "what works" (p. 2) than it is with either building up or defending a particular set of beliefs or dogma. Second, he reminds us that there are "many paths, but only one way" (2002, p. 9): no matter what a particular school may say about Buddhism, there is one "truth," or *Dharma*, and that is suffering, the causes of suffering, liberation from suffering, and how to do that, or The Eightfold Path. With these points in mind, let us now hear from Joan as she introduces us to Zen in relation to psychotherapy.

CHAPTER 2

The Basic Principles of Zen and Their Psychotherapeutic Implications

FINDING A PATH

This chapter introduces Joan, the coauthor of this book, as well as the basic concepts, practices, and principles of Zen that form the basis for our approach to using Zen in therapy. After Joan tells her story of how she came to adopt a Zen perspective, she will then focus on developing an appreciation for what are referred to as the Four Noble Truths as taught by the Buddha. In order, these are: life is suffering (*dukkha*), the cause of suffering (*samudaya*), ending suffering (*nirodha*), and the Eightfold Path (marga). Next, we strive to understand the central role of meditation in Zen. Finally, Joan will present six additional Zen principles that have the potential to assist therapy. In each case, the format for this look at Zen will be to identify the particular Zen concept, practice, or principle that is to be considered, describe what it means in traditional Zen literature, and then show how it can be used in various clinical situations through examples of Joan's clinical work.

Take a moment to reflect on your own career and its development. When did you decide to become a therapist or a teacher? Can you identify what life experiences and people influenced you in making that decision? How did you become the kind of therapist or teacher you are now? Where are you going next in your development as a person who helps the mind or heals the heart? Now imagine having done this kind of work for nearly 50 years and trying to describe it to someone else in a few pages! That is the task I face here, but it is a necessary one if you are to know enough about me to understand how important Zen is in my work.

When I was a student nurse, my exposure to psychiatric patients was relatively limited. There were three rooms designated for mentally ill patients on the medical unit in which I trained, and the only treatment to which I was intimately exposed involved electroshock. The treatments were given in a room that had no windows; it seemed as if it was the size of a large walk-in closet. Patients would be lined up in the hall on gurneys to wait their turn to receive electroconvulsive therapy (ECT). I felt very uneasy being a part of this treatment, because I innately felt that something was wrong with it. The aftermath of this procedure was at times devastating to observe; the confusion and disorientation of patients was disturbing to me.

From the early sixties until the seventies I saw this treatment used repeatedly on patients, at times in an almost relentless way. I vividly remember a lovely, genteel, depressed, and troubled woman who was subjected to a series of six ECTs every time she was admitted, at least twice a year over a three-year period. As the time went on, this lovely lady seemed to lose much of her personality. It was a painful observation, one that made a lasting impression on me. Of course, I am fully aware there have been improvements in the technique, and that it is beneficial under certain circumstances. However, I still have some reservations about the treatment in general because it seems to take something away from the person.

As a student nurse I spent several months learning the techniques of scrubbing in surgery, a service I loved. For two and one-half years I worked in surgery at the hospital where I graduated. The nun who was responsible for surgery, Sister Adelhaides, R.N., gave me an unexpected gift that is still important in my work as a therapist today. She was a wise, shrewd, and loving woman who did not conceal her mission to have her service as perfect as it could be, but she also had confidence in me that I did not. An example of this trust took place when I was a student nurse. A man was brought up from the Emergency Room on a gurney. Earlier that morning he had fallen in between railroad cars and both legs were injured to the extent that they had to be amputated. The Chief of Surgery would perform the operation without his usual crew because they were finishing up a previous operation for him. It also so happened that the experienced nurses were busy assisting doctors. I was the only one who was available to scrub along with the doctor!

I soon became aware I could be told to scrub and I was scared. When Sr. Adelhaides notified me that I would be scrubbing, there was no room to even discuss the situation. She knew I was petrified at the thought of assisting the Chief of Surgery alone. She didn't find fault with me and indicated to me, "You can do it" nonverbally. The Chief of Surgery was patient and kind with me and we performed the surgery successfully. Afterwards I felt I had passed a kind of test related to fear. It was like sticking your fist in a bucket of water; for a split second there is a space and then the water rapidly fills in that space. In that moment I faced the fear and then reality flooded in to take my mind off of it.

Like many others who do our kind of work, the beginning of my path in this field started with my own therapy. I married and the first four years of that relationship were spent at the Chicago Lutheran Theological Seminary in Maywood, Illinois. After my husband John had completed his three years of theological education, he made a decision to apply for admission to earn a Master's degree in Pastoral Care at the seminary under the professorship of Charles A. Sullivan. John was accepted into the program with a few other students. This particular decision of my husband's, which was unknown to me at the time, had an affect on my future both personally and professionally.

John and three single male students were invited to live with Professor Sullivan and all of us accepted without hesitation. Sully, as he liked to be called, used his living room for a classroom in the evening when he taught the graduate course of study. Quite frequently, I would sit on the stairs listening to them talk about psychotherapy and practicing psychotherapy. Fortunately for me, the discussions that took place in his living room usually extended to the kitchen where they took place on a more informal, though just as enlightened, basis. I literally sucked in all that I heard; being exposed to this information, the mutual exchanges with the students and Sully, was a true blessing. I don't really recall what moved me when I asked Sully to be in therapy with him, other than the fact I had a feeling of incompleteness. At that time I was the only seminarian wife who did that and it was sometimes painful and at other times embarrassing for me to live with my "therapist." However, his kindness and patience, along with my trust in him, allowed me to have the courage to face some anxieties I had harbored for years.

During the next four years my husband was an associate minister in a Midwestern church. He decided to go back to school in 1960 to earn a Ph.D. in Clinical Psychology and was admitted to a major university in Michigan. Soon after, I was hired as a staff nurse to work one day a week on a psychiatric unit of a local hospital that would soon be affiliated with the university. My husband and I divorced in 1965, so I began to work full-time as a staff nurse on the unit. Eventually this position led to being asked to be the Head Nurse for the psychiatric unit. Several years later, I was promoted to the position of Assistant Director of Nursing in Mental Health. Perhaps the first signs of being willing to step outside the traditional bounds of the system occurred here, because one of the first things I did was to get permission from administration to allow all staff, no matter what their position, to wear street clothing. I wanted to decrease the division between the patients and the staff as much as possible. My next step was to unlock the unit. After a lot of work and even more talk, I convinced the administration it would be safe; the unit was eventually open like any other service in the hospital.

In the meantime, the hospital was negotiating with the Department of Psychiatry of the university's School of Human Medicine and the local county mental health center to work under the same umbrella. This merger was completed in the late 1960s, and my clinical responsibilities increased to include maintaining the In-Patient Unit, Day Treatment Program, and the Partial Hospitalization Program. Later, when an Emergency Service was being developed, I was reassigned to be the 24-hour Emergency Service Coordinator. The coordinators of the various programs for the mental health center were given appointments as Assistant Clinical Professors in the Department of Psychiatry at the university. Being appointed to the faculty, even in an adjunct fashion, gave me the opportunity to be a part of the university and to learn and know what takes place behind the academic and training as well as clinical scenes.

To me, the typical way that teaching occurs in a classroom in the West tends to be based on the mind. But in the East, the heart can be seen as an important tool for learning, too. In the 1970s there was a movement in medical education to help students interview patients in a way to obtain information, but to do so in a manner that would be attentive and express interest in them in order to promote a good nurse-patient or doctor-patient relationship. I had mixed emotions about this trend, only because it seemed so completely obvious to me. It seems to me that if a person has to be taught in a classroom how to relate and listen to others, then maybe the medical school's admission procedure needs to be expanded to really knowing something about the personality of the prospective student before admitting them. In fact, I often wonder how the Office of Admissions would revise their criteria for prospective students if they understood that they are selecting the caretakers of the future. For example, contrast this academic or "head" approach with one based on the "heart" that a great physician, Dr. William Osler, Chair of Medicine at John Hopkins Hospital in the late 1800s, envisioned.

> Dr. Osler put the man, his personality and character first; and he felt sure that given the power to work and the desire, sufficient brains were probably there. . . . The practice of medicine is an art, not a trade; a calling, not a business; a

calling in which your heart will be used equally with your head. (Reid, 1959, pp. 519–520)

Which kind of student or physician or therapist would you prefer?

In order to have the Emergency Service (ES) run smoothly, the staff and I met once a month to discuss the month's coverage and any issues that needed to be resolved. We saw each other as kindred spirits. For example, the hospital published a newspaper every two months and it included a column called "Inside the Departments." The March/April, 1979 edition wrote a piece on our service. The caption read "Common sense and decency provide the cornerstone to CMH Emergency Service." The article described the ES as an "around the clock service, seven days a week and holidays, with night staffing covered by therapists working under contract." It went on to say that the service operates under a simple philosophy: "provide a service based on common sense and decency with as little paperwork as possible to get in the way of humane care." I was quoted as saying "I believe in relying on instinct. It's not always foolproof, but it's very useful in caring for a patient." One of my therapists described my expectations of the staff: "Do Good, Be Good, and Document." This philosophy has been with me from the start, although I did not think of it as a philosophy until much later. Actually, from a Zen perspective, I wouldn't call it anything; it is simply being with people just as you would have them be with you, otherwise known as the Golden Rule.

I see documentation as an important part of our work, but not necessarily for the usual reasons. I urge the staff to write about a person as if the patient was looking over their shoulder so that the report was both accurate and sensitive. They were to paint a picture of the person through the assessment form and the title of the picture would be the diagnostic impression as it applied to this particular individual. Some of our clinical work involved doing psychiatric consults on all the services of the hospital. Typically, the patients I was asked to see were difficult patients from the standpoint of being moody, depressed, terminally ill, unmanageable and "noncompliant." But they were treated in the same way.

Partly because of the ties of the hospital to a major university, I was exposed to many fine teachers and was blessed through my association with one in particular: Dr. Griffith O. Freed. This professor was also the Chief Psychologist assigned to the hospital from the university, so I worked closely with him. In addition, I met with "Griff" for one hour every Saturday morning at his office on campus for ten years. I learned about being clear with others and ourselves through our exchanges, especially the value of questioning when something was unclear and the importance of humor during such times.

I also began to audit his graduate courses, which I did for eight years. However, I must say that a lot of the time I felt out of step with the students, because what took place in class seemed foreign from the real world; what took place on the unit seemed a far cry from academia. After a bit of trepidation, I spoke about this sense of disconnect with Griff. Much to my relief, he seemed to welcome my comments and we embarked on a discussion that lasted many years into the future. I will always be indebted to his friendship and the wisdom of clarity that he showed to me in both words and deeds.

One of the textbooks used for his class was Wilhelm Kaiser's book, *Effective Psychotherapy* (1965). Kaiser wrote about the struggles he went through in questioning therapy and how he slowly developed a sense of what he perceived as being most helpful in therapy. "It seemed that the patient's improvement depended much more on the personality of his psychoanalyst than on the amount and so-called depth of the insight acquired" (p. 166). Kaiser also noted that, "The universal symptom is duplicity in communication. The universal therapy is the communicative intimacy offered by the psycho-therapist" (p. 207). Between the teachings and wisdom I received from my mentor and the approach outlined by Kaiser, I came to learn two things that still stand me well today: an appreciation of the power of listening to others and realizing that being as clear as I can be with myself allows me to offer some degree of clarity to others. In retrospect, Griff reminds me of a Buddhist teacher who offers healing kindness by being patient, truthful, and attentive. Looking back like this, it seems as if some of the teachings of the Buddha have been with me throughout my work without my knowing it.

At the same time, even though my background was in organizational theology, I felt a spiritual void and emptiness in my work and in my life, but could not identify what was missing. One night in 1984 a chance decision made all that change. I was driving home that evening and turned on the radio to a program I had not heard before on National Public Radio. The show was called "New Dimensions" and was hosted by Michael Toms (1984). The format of this particular program was to interview scholars, artists, theologians, and others who are involved with change in all areas of life. That night Toms was interviewing a Buddhist monk, teacher, and author named Lama Sogyal Rinpoche who was born in Tibet. The program was, of course, on Buddhism.

That discussion of Buddhism resonated with inner beliefs and inner needs I could not speak about but felt the need to explore and live. The teachings of Buddhism I heard that evening seemed to make instant sense to me. My life opened up to them and I wanted to hear and learn more about such an approach to life. Soygal Rinpoche spoke about the cause of insecurities, attachments, projections, dualities, fears, losses, and anger. He talked about these things and more with metaphors that were useful, not mere platitudes. Rinpoche went on to talk about the importance of developing a sense of compassion and friendship with oneself, and then used Christ's teaching that "charity begins at home" to emphasize the point. He also emphasized the usefulness of going deeper into oneself with the practice of meditation as a way of "taming the mind." This master talked about Zen teachings and of "discovering the self without the extra, the ego" (Toms, 1984). It was the first time I had heard anyone say, "The nature of life is pain" without making that a depressing thought; it is when you are not told that life is pain and it descends upon you that it is real pain. Soygal even talked about the Buddha saying that "All the happiness in the world comes from thinking of others" (Toms, 1984). I was intrigued by his words and knew what he was saying awakened something in me.

The next phase of my development as a therapist involved more formal education. When I started in this field, a basic nursing or undergraduate education was all that was necessary to work in it, unless one wanted to specialize in psychiatry. Psychologists, social workers, and counselors were not licensed then. However, with the passing of Act 54, the so-called National Mental Health Act, basic mental health services were mandated for all citizens across the country, thereby creating such a need for workers in the field that jobs were plentiful at all levels. The culture of mental health treatment and practices changed soon after that to focus more on credentials than experience, and for me it meant going back to school as an adult student. In 1994, I completed a Master's degree in Therapeutic Psychology. Not surprisingly, I took a different slant on things in graduate school, as indicated by the title of my thesis: *Alternatives to Psychiatric Treatment: Is it safe to be human on a psychiatric unit?* (Hartzell, 1994). This work focused on the aspects of mental health care I had seen over the years that made little sense to me humanistically. Much of the material pertained to patient care, especially the attitudes I saw expressed all too often by middle management, administration, and education: how the technical jargon of the field seems to disregard the uniqueness of the person and how alternative approaches don't seem to do these things.

Another chance led to the next step in my development as a therapist practicing from an alternative perspective. It occurred in the early 1980s when I purchased a lithograph called "Earth Man Spirit" in Jerome, Arizona that spoke to me on a spiritual level. Now I explored Shamanism and Native American practices as well as Buddhism as alternative ways of helping people who are emotionally troubled. At that time, I was also working in a hospital that admitted Native Americans on a regular basis for a number of problems, often alcoholism, and physical, emotional, and sexual abuse.

During this time, three people from South Dakota came to the facility to present a seminar to the staff about Lakota beliefs and what was being developed on the reservation. The following summer, I spent five days with them at the reservation. Living in a seminary for four years, being the wife of an assistant pastor, and being very much connected to organized traditional religion since the early 1950s, did not come close to the sense of spirituality and spiritual awakening I experienced in the time I spent with the Native American people on the reservation. I especially remember being invited to attend two ceremonies: the first was the *Inipi* or Sweat Lodge Ceremony and the other was the Sun Dance Ceremony.

My experiences of Native American healing practices show the difference between the concepts of traditional, complementary, and alternative approaches, so I asked and received permission to share one of them here. I will begin by sharing how those who are steeped in this tradition write about it.

> While the sweat lodge itself is simple to describe, it is beyond any mortal writer's ability to adequately convey the ultimate culmination of spiritual, mystical, and psychic expression of the Sweat Lodge Ceremony. Everyone that I have seen experience a Native American *Inipi* agrees wholeheartedly: the Sweat Lodge Ceremony is impossible to describe fully. You have to experience it to truly realize its fullness and depth. (McGaa, 1990, p. 61)

As the ceremony gets under way, it is clear that this process involves a complex intermingling of body, mind, social forces, and, spirituality.

> The four directions are called upon within the lodge. The misty, fire-heated steam covers you, bringing forth your own mist (your sweat). Your universal lifeblood comes forth and intermingles with the misty waters of your brothers and sisters around you. The waters of the world (the bucket of water), which have been brought into the lodge, join and mix with the air of the four directions when the dipper of water is ladled onto the hot stones, making steam. The four winds will carry the life blood out of the lodge to the four quarters of our planet. A part of your lifeblood will seep back into our Mother Earth. (p. 62)

The ceremony focuses on four endurances, meaning that people "endure" what they will be experiencing during this sacred ceremony. However, it is important to understand that compassion is involved as well:

> Anyone who becomes frightened or fearful should try to endure or try to summon courage to stay, but at times there are some who cannot take a Sweat Lodge

Ceremony. If this is the case, the participant should simply call out, and the ceremony will be halted temporarily so that person can carefully leave through the doorway. (pp. 64–65)

The First Endurance, *Wiyopeyata* (West) is the color black. "The recognition of the spirit world is symbolic of the First Endurance. For some, it is a time to ask the Almighty for a spirit guide" (p. 65). The lodge leader speaks certain prayers and, "At this point, a dipper of water will be poured upon the rocks. Steam will shoot upward" (p. 65). There will be more prayers and additional water, three dippers full, will be poured onto the rocks. This endurance is where the people introduce themselves to the Spirit World. After it is completed, the flap of the lodge is opened to allow cool air to come in. Praise is then given to the air; a practice that occurs after each endurance is completed. The Second Endurance, *Waziya* (North), color white, begins after the lodge's flap is closed and, "The cleansing steam and the recognition of courage symbolizes the second endurance" (p. 67). Again, prayers are said and led by the leader and the ritual begins with more water being poured on the rocks. "Enough dippers are poured to bring forth the steam throughout the lodge" (p. 67). The end of the second endurance comes after a time of contemplation.

"The recognition of knowledge and praying individually out loud symbolize the third endurance. All within look upon the stones in silence, viewing images upon and within the red glow. After a while, water is poured upon the rocks, and the leader begins" (p. 68). The leader begins to speak about the color red, which is the color of the east. This third endurance, *Wiyoheyapa*, is time for individuals to say prayers out loud, beginning with the person sitting to the left of the leader. I remember how awkward I felt at this time, for praying has always been a silent happening. The spirit and authenticity I felt within this group of people gave me courage to speak my prayer. It was a time I cannot describe: suffice it to say that I was in, and felt a part of, a sacred ceremony. Holding, smelling, touching, and smoking the pipe was almost like a surrealistic experience. I felt a great sense of humility to be in the presence of these Native American people and to be accepted even though I was a *wasicu*, a white person. The fourth endurance, *Itokaga* (South), "stands for healing and growth" (p. 70), and is the color green. "The leader may even point out some specific areas and ask for the Great Spirit's wisdom regarding them . . . the leader will usually offer a summarizing prayer, or one or several of the participants may pray out loud in respect to a particular area of healing" (p. 71).

At the conclusion of the ceremony, we left the Sweat Lodge, beginning with the first person to the right of the entrance. We were provided with cool fresh water to drink and served a traditional meal of vegetable beef soup and a dessert made from wogapi berries. I will never forget this moving experience sitting with these people, listening to the leader chant and sing, praying out loud, smoking this beautiful clay colored pipe, listening to others pray, becoming one of many, passing a dipper full of cool and delicious water to others after partaking of some myself, sweating, smelling sage and sitting on sage, being given a towel to protect my legs from the red-hot stones. All of it created a deep sense of peace, unity, and serenity. I did not want to leave the lodge even though at times I felt close to being unbearably hot; I felt safe and snug in this dwelling. Could it have been like going through a kind of birth process?

That night I had a *woihanbla* (dream) about the wife of the man who so graciously invited me to the *Inipi.* In my dream, she took on the form of Mother Earth, large, full-breasted, round, and nurturing. She was covered by an Indian blanket. Her skin was rough like the bark of an old tree, not like the skin of a human being. In my *woihanbla* she was vulnerable, wise and peaceful, yet a feeling of worry seemed to emanate from her. I found myself feeling a sense of kinship with Native Americans, for only the coldest observer could be unmoved by such experiences. It does not take much imagination to see how powerful altered physiological states, social ritual, and intense prayer could be helpful to anyone in need. As time goes by, the teachings of the Buddha and this spiritual ceremony affects my time with people, whether at home or at work.

Let me share some of my journey with you in this regard, but first, please note that I am not claiming to be a scholar of Zen. Rather, I have been studying Zen for some eighteen years while I have been practicing as a psychotherapist. Therefore, my words about Zen and how it can be helpful will not be written in a strictly scholarly tone. Instead, I want to share with you my understandings of Zen as it can apply to our work.

THE FOUR NOBLE TRUTHS

Earlier it was said that the Four Noble Truths are the backbone of the Buddha's teachings. As Huston Smith, a highly respected scholar, said, "A noble truth is a truth that can make a difference in one's own life. So the Four Noble Truths about life and existence are what his discoveries are encapsulated in" (Smith, 1995). The First Noble Truth speaks about truth of suffering. This truth is referred to as *dukkha,* a Sanskrit word that translates as "suffering" (Chah, 2001, p. 218). Suffering is pervasive in human life. It begins with the trauma of birth and it is seen each time we are ill. Suffering often appears to worsen as we age and approach death. Not only is suffering inevitable in these ways, but it is ever present in life: we encounter it in disappointment, loss, failure, humiliation, and strange as it may be, in our successes. We see it in the lives of our loved ones when they hurt, in strangers on television, in the sufferings of war, the tragedies of starvation, the devastation of natural catastrophes, and, of course, in mental illness.

Initially when I read about the First Noble Truth, it sounded grim, even disheartening, perhaps even absolutely pessimistic. Of course, that was before I realized that not only was it "the truth," but it was a "Noble Truth." In other words, suffering is the human condition and it cannot be denied or avoided without terrible consequence. A more contemporary description of suffering and its consequences is rendered by Huston Smith, (1991): *Dukkha* can also be seen as a "shopping cart we try to steer from the wrong end. . . . Life as typically lived is out of joint. Something is awry. Its pivot is not true . . . (blocks creativity and interpersonal conflict)" (p. 71).

I remember a clinical story of suffering that lasted from childhood through much of adulthood that stays with me to this day. It involves a white woman who grew up in poverty. At age five, she was severely burned by battery acid. The skin on the side of her face, neck, and part of her chest were badly scarred from the burn. The family, being poor and living in the country, did not get proper care for her. Although she recovered functionality, she was left permanently and severely scarred over the three areas. Imagine the pain she must have suffered! However, even after the wounds healed, her suffering did not end. Instead, she grew up as a girl who became the butt of jokes from other students and the recipient of humiliating comments from adults, including her teachers. As an adolescent, she also became an object of curiosity and stares so intense that she decided to hide herself whenever possible. As an adult, she took that to the extreme, frequently staying indoors, rarely venturing out, and socializing with men at a minimum. Mary eventually married a man who did not provide for her emotionally or financially. She separated from her husband and raised her two children alone. Her childhood accident conditioned her to be lonely and her contact with life was through her children.

Fortunately for Mary, she had a family doctor who was sensitive to her depression and advised her to seek therapy at a time when she was particularly depressed. She told me it was some time before she made an appointment because she was afraid of talking with a stranger. Initially she didn't talk about her scars; she verbalized how worthless and hopeless she felt. My intuitiveness told me that being physically present was all that she could tolerate for a while until she got to know and trust me. After two sessions Mary began to talk about the agony and loneliness created by the accident in her life. As a practitioner of Zen, I realized that unlike most of us whose suffering scars us only on the inside, hers were also visible on the outside. For me, this simply made her more fully present than most of us. Eventually, we were able to talk about her scars in ways that were new for her; together we came to see her scars as beautiful, unique, interesting, expressing character and courage. From that point on, her suffering seemed to become a source of strength.

Alan Watts says that the Second Noble Truth "relates to the cause of frustration, which is said to be *trishna*, clinging or grasping, based on *avidya*, which is ignorance or unconsciousness" (1989, p. 47). This truth is often discussed in terms of desire, which we can understand psychologically as a form of resistance, perhaps its ultimate form. "The Second Noble Truth says that this resistance is the fundamental operating mechanism of what we call ego, that resisting life causes suffering. Traditionally, it is said that the cause of suffering is clinging to our narrow view" (Chodron, 1991, p. 40). Smith writes about the lure of desire in terms of a wish or "desire for private fulfillment" (1991, p. 71) that inevitably leads to a dead end. In this case, our attachment to the world of objects and wants leads to a condition called *Tanha* (desire), in which "the ego oozes like a secret sore" (Smith, 1991, p. 71). As long as this kind of wound remains secret, it cannot be healed. In some sense, then, desire is a universal symptom, an impoverishment of the spirit that always leads to emptiness and loneliness.

Of course, we are all familiar with the traps of desire, both small and large. Being recognized for our work, winning at sports, getting a promotion, buying a new car or house, are all rather mundane examples of desire, especially in a consumer-oriented society like ours. But sometimes the stories of desire are more poignant. One time there was a client who came into the emergency room after being treated for ingesting "Vanish," a toilet bowl cleaner. He almost died, but because of a quick medical response he "only" suffered a damaged esophagus. While interviewing him, after establishing rapport and letting him know that I cared, I simply asked, "What happened?" He looked me in the eye with all seriousness and said, "Well, my girlfriend dumped me and I just couldn't bear the loneliness. I went to her house and explained that to her and begged her to take me back. While standing on her porch pleading for her to not send me into that blackness, she said, 'I wish you would just disappear!' I tried to do that to please her!" When exploring his history of relationships, it became very clear that this fellow was seeking relationships not out of love, but out of desperation. For him, being in a relationship was soothing to the wound. It made its pain go away like a narcotic, but required constant "doses" lest the pain return. Like an addict, he was doomed to suffer this desire until he realized the compulsion and emptiness of spirit it created.

The Third Noble Truth speaks directly to the second one because it concerns the healing process, the process of freeing oneself from *TANKA* or desire. In the book, *The World of Tibetan Buddhism*, the Dalai Lama writes, "Suffering originates from its causes and conditions" (Bstan-dzin-rgya-mtsho, 1995, p. 16), which is a way of saying that desire gives rise to suffering and the cessation of suffering comes from giving up desire. Note that Zen does not say we must give up all desires, because that is not humanly possible. Rather, it is excessive, unrealistic, desires that are the problem, things that we might call "attachments," the fixations of the ego or, in the largest sense, even our "selves." "The third noble truth says that the cessation of suffering is letting go of holding on to ourselves. By 'cessation' we mean the cessation of hell as opposed to just weather, the cessation of this resistance, this resentment, this feeling of being completely trapped and caught, trying to maintain huge ME at any cost" (Chondron, 1991, p. 41).

In order to see this concept in action let us consider two clients. In Mary's case, it is clear that she was able to give up the attachment to her scarred self. In other words, from a Zen point of view, it was her attachment to a desire to look "normal" that doomed her to a life of suffering. As long as she sought to soothe her wound through the fulfillment of a wish instead of an acceptance of reality, she could only continue to deepen her suffering. It was only after she could embrace her life and the uniqueness of her own life as expressed through her scars that she could resume living. Although perhaps an extreme case, Mary is not so different from you and me. Suffering is often tragic if not acknowledged. For instance, the young man mentioned earlier never did face his suffering and, as far as we know, still desperately lives his attachment or desire in a continual search for relationships that can't last, which makes him repeat the process again and again.

So far the Noble Truths have shown us the reality of suffering, the causes of suffering, and the way of ending suffering (or at least reducing it). The Fourth Noble Truth helps us turn theory into practice, which is to say turning suffering into nonsuffering. As such, it is the most complex and difficult practice, because it is one thing to have an idea and another altogether different matter to embody it in everyday life. Liberation from suffering comes from practicing the Eightfold Path. "Wherever the Noble Eightfold Path is practiced, joy, peace, and insight are there" (Hanh, 1998, p. 47). Hanh goes on to say that the Buddha's first *Dharma* talk (teachings) presented the

Noble Eightfold Path, which consists of Right View, Right Thinking, Right Speech, Right Action, Right Livelihood, Right Diligence, Right Mindfulness, and Right Concentration. Let us take a moment to understand what these terms mean in ordinary English and illustrate them with a clinical example. Before doing that, however, it is necessary to say a word on what is "Right." For Zen, something is right when it is "true," that is connected to the path of liberation. Each of the eight aspects of this Noble Truth is "right" because each one offers a unique connection to a healthier way of living, one that is based on freedom instead of bondage or suffering. Hence, each one can be seen as a certain kind of suggestion, hint, helpful reminder, or "technique" that can help us become freer.

The first one, Right View, concerns perception. To me, it is the key to the others because striving to maintain a Right View helps me keep my perceptions from becoming cloudy, unclear, or murky by "my own stuff." By my own stuff I mean my own limits, personal and cultural preconceptions, and most of all, my own attachments and their related forms of suffering, especially those that are not yet healed. Learning how to develop and maintain the Right View is especially important because it keeps one open to the world, to others, and to oneself.

An example of a Right View in action occurred in my work with a woman named Alice. I was warned about Alice before I met her; she was well known in the community as a Borderline Personality and extremely manipulative; she had a history of pressing people's "buttons." The first time I met her she was standing on top of a radiator in the day room looking as though she was taking on the world, as if she was challenging me to get her down. Instantaneously I liked something about her spunk and yet I wondered how I was going to get her down in a way that made sense to her without thinking that I was manipulating her.

For a while I sat on the couch beside the radiator looking up at her. The words that were exchanged were unimportant but the nonverbal interplay that was going on between us was almost electrical. In my head I was trying to figure the "right" way, which must involve some expression of what I perceived to be true in this situation. What I knew for sure was I did not want to succumb to her manipulations, I did not want to manipulate her, and that my neck was getting stiff looking up at her at this angle. So instead of trying to "do" anything, I simply told her the truth as I felt it, "My neck is getting stiff looking up at you." The truth set us both free. She laughed. I did too. Then she sat down beside me. Instead of the typical "Borderline-therapist" transference counter-transference entanglement, the Right View allowed our relationship to start out as equals.

Right Thinking is next. "Right Thinking is thinking that is in accord with Right View. It is a map that can help us find our way" (Hanh, 1998, p. 58). Hanh's analogy of Right Thinking as being something like a map is an excellent one to consider. Maps are helpful because they assist us in getting to a specific place. They show us the lay of the land and possible routes toward various destinations. A good map is one that is both clear and that corresponds well to reality because such a map allows us to choose a straight-forward route to a destination. A poor map can cause all kinds of difficulties, such as taking unnecessary detours, endless backtracking, or becoming hope-lessly lost. With Alice a poor therapeutic map could lead to anything as mild as mere histrionics, alienating staff further through yet another episode of angry acting out, or worst of all, the impossibility of a therapeutic relationship between us. However, if our mental map of Alice is accurate and clear, which means that we are really seeing her when we look at her and not just a diagnosis, and that we see ourselves as ourselves and not as "a therapist in charge of Alice," then it is more likely that we will strike out in the right direction. Apparently that is what happened with Alice.

The third aspect of the Path involves Right Speech, which is something that I feel should come naturally from a sensitive therapist. The classical definition of Right Speech is speaking truthfully. Instead of using my own words to describe this truth, I would like to simply quote one of my own teachers.

> Aware of the suffering caused by unmindful speech and the inability to listen to others, I am committed to cultivating loving speech and deep listening in order to bring joy and happiness to others and relieve others of their suffering. Knowing that words can create happiness or suffering, I am determined to speak truthfully, with words that inspire self-confidence, joy, and hope. I will not spread news I do not know to be certain and will not criticize or condemn things of which I am not sure. I will refrain from uttering words that can cause division or discord, or that can cause the family or community to break. (Hanh, 1998, p. 77)

Imagine the kind of speech encountering Alice with a poor map might have created. If I had spoken on the basis of the kinds of understandings offered to me by the nurses, the art therapist, or even her psychiatrist who should have known her best, it would have been a disaster for both of us. Words like, "You are being manipulative, acting out again, being loud, being de-manding, being unreasonable," and so forth, are likely to become self-fulfill-ing prophecies. How we speak to another person is important because language is powerful; it can be used to heal or to harm. As the interaction with Alice illustrates, Right Speech, which is based on Right Thinking, is much more likely to help than hurt.

Hanh says that, "Right Action (*samyak karmanta*) means Right Action of the body. It is the practice of touching love and preventing harm, the practice of nonviolence toward ourselves and others. The basis of Right Action is to do everything in mindfulness" (1998, p. 86). There are two characteristics of our actions that make them especially important. One is that they express who we are in a concrete way. Our actions reflect our self; they are manifestations of our perceptions, thoughts, and, in a certain sense, the ultimate form of expression. Our actions convey our uniqueness, our developmental history, and our own choices over time. Second, our actions have consequences. They are "real" in a way that perception, thinking, and talking are not: They have "weight" because they have "matter" in the world. As Hanh says, "My actions are my only true belongings. I cannot escape the consequences of my actions. My actions are the ground upon which I stand" (p. 116). What we do, then, really exposes who we are and that dynamic presence will have an impact on others, for better or for worse. If this is so, someone working from a Zen perspective might think the intelligent thing to do is to act for good or not act at all. As the Dalai Lama said, "You must help others. . . . If not, you should not harm others" (Farrer-Hall, 2000, p. 43).

Perhaps the best way to see the importance of Right Action in the situation with Alice is to look at how easy it would have been to act poorly. For example, I could have tried to control her behavior, out of my own fear, out of a desire to demonstrate my power, out of a sense of being challenged, or whatever. This kind of action would, of course, have had an impact on her behavior. A typical "Borderline" response might have been to see my attempts at gaining control as a threat, which would result in a defensive response from Alice, such as losing more control, escalating her disruptive behavior, threatening to harm herself, trying to embarrass me in front of the staff with her continued defiance, or any number of other strategies a person with this diagnosis is likely to demonstrate.

Actions cause reactions, meaning it is very important to exercise them cautiously. The question becomes one of how to know what to do. So far, the only guideline mentioned is to "do no harm," which is good advice because it tells us what *not* to do and that surely helps. Right Action, however, is not ungrounded action. Action always flows from perception, which is to say from thoughts and feelings, conscious and otherwise. It is at this point that we can begin to see how the Eightfold Path actually consists of eight aspects of the same thing. If I am practicing Right View, Right Thinking, and Right Speech, then my actions, which flow from them, will likely be Right, too, which is to say helpful! Of course, it is very important not to exaggerate or misunderstand this point. The teachings of Zen are not magic, although it may sometimes be portrayed that way, and they do not come with guarantees. In spite of my "Right Ways," there are no certainties of the outcome. Alice, for example, could have simply chosen to "fight" me anyway. All that the Eightfold Path promises is to help us move away from that which may be destructive and toward that which may be helpful.

The next part of the Path involves Right Livelihood, which concerns what one does for a living. Usually, when Zen authors talk about this part of the Path, they focus on how one supports oneself or family economically. But Right Livelihood applies to all of us, whether we are working outside the home or not, earning our own way through the world or taking advantage of our family's good fortune, facing a period of unemployment or taking the time to go to school. All human beings must be concerned about how they make their way through the world because how we do that affects other human beings. No matter what our current situation, all of us face the same basic choices: to choose a "Right" way of directing our lives, or not.

Let us consider this point by thinking about examples of "Right" and "Wrong" Livelihoods. The obvious examples of failing to maintain a Right Livelihood range from the extreme to the mild. Killing or stealing for money, excitement, power, and so forth are clearly not Right Livelihood. Being a neglectful or abusive parent cannot be Right Livelihood. Working for a company that pollutes the environment unnecessarily and not trying to do something about it is not Right Livelihood; so is neglecting your own development. Right Livelihood, by contrast, is both a personal and collective matter. At the personal level, Right Livelihood is doing work or engaging in activities that reduce our own suffering. Work or activities that allow us to grow, develop, and express ourselves, are certainly better for us than those that do not. Ideally, they can even bring a sense of joy and fulfillment, which, considering the fact that most of us will spend most of our time doing this particular endeavor with our lives, is a great and noble gift.

But Right Livelihood also goes beyond the individual: It is collective matter in that what we do inevitably affects others. For example, I have been practicing in this field for nearly 50 years now. Over that time, I have seen many things, including therapists who have burned out. Yet I've never experienced that kind of reaction to clients: Indeed, they "juice me up." The kind of involvement I have with them keeps me connected to humanity. In this way, being a therapist is a "Right Livelihood" for me at the personal level. That is good for me, but what about my clients? What we do with our livelihood always affects others, whether we mop floors, collect garbage, work in a bank, or write software. Our work as therapists just happens to affect others directly and visibly, which means, if anything, that our work has the potential of having far-reaching effect, touching people we don't know. Imagine, for instance, what might have happened if this person had been approached by a nurse who was not mindful of how she could exacerbate a fearful reaction from Alice. The point is that Right Livelihood always involves how our actions affect ourselves and others, a kind of psychological and social "karma." It has been said we don't get away with anything and I think that is true.

Right Diligence is somewhat similar to the Western concept of virtue, or perhaps conscience. It concerns the use of consciousness to foster wholesomeness in our minds, which helps us walk the Eightfold Path, and to limit unwholesomeness, which can create difficulty in seeing, or staying on, the Path. Right Diligence involves four practices:

> (1) Preventing unwholesome seed in our store consciousness that have not yet arisen from arising, (2) helping the unwholesome seeds that have already arisen to return to our consciousness, (3) finding ways to water the wholesome seeds in our store consciousness that have not yet arisen and to ask our friends to do the same, (4) nourishing the wholesome seeds that have already arisen so that they will stay present in our mind consciousness and grow stronger. This is called the Fourfold Right Diligence. (Hanh, 1998, p. 92)

Once again using Alice as an example, if I had let "unwholesome" seeds rise to my consciousness, such as listening to the stories the other nurses told me about her or trying to prove my competence to the professional staff, I strongly suspect the outcome of our first exchange would have ended in a different way, one where both she and I would have suffered. By practicing Right Diligence, such negative seeds could not grow, and my instinctive need to reach out to her, to let her know I was there to be "with" her, that I had no interest in complicating her life (which was already infested with pain), led to the fruition of Right Action. Note that just like anyone else in this situation, I had no idea what was going to occur and I had no idea what would make sense to her. The teachings of Zen seem to help because something happened between us that did not contaminate the future in a negative way.

Another word that might describe the quality of the interaction Alice and I had with each other is that we were living together in the "now." Right Mindfulness concerns being fully present to the moment. This kind of awareness requires two things. The first requirement involves using our awareness (consciousness) to attend to that which is before us in the "here and now," without being distracted by preconceptions, worries, or other thoughts that interfere with clarity of perception. When one is truly mindful, that is fully present to some thing or some one, this kind of orientation brings with it certain "gifts" that are of value for living "Right" and for such things as connecting with people. To paraphrase Hanh (1998), these gifts are: greater clarity of perception concerning what one is seeing, smelling, hearing, and so forth; the benefit of allowing the other to reveal itself more completely; the ability to nourish what or who is present by respecting or honoring it; the capacity to relieve suffering through appreciating the other more deeply; a greater appreciation for your own capacities and potentials as a living entity; a deeper understanding of the present movement that is the foundation of a loving attitude toward self and others; and last but greatest of all, transformation, or the ability to embrace suffering and move beyond it.

The other aspect of mindfulness that is especially important for Zen is a reminder that such gifts do not come overnight. "The Sanskrit word for mindfulness, *smriti*, means remember" (Hanh, 1998, p. 59). Thus, Right Mindfulness includes remembering the value of mindful perception and to seek it out as often as possible. Right Mindfulness, then, is an evolving process that is tied to all the other parts of the Path: Each time we do it, the significance of the others becomes more important in our lives. For example, Right Mindfulness allowed me to see Alice as a person who was suffering, who was in so much emotional pain that she had to "act out" to get even the smallest degree of relief. Right Mindfulness meant that I did not have to see her as being "manipulative," "challenging," or "scary," all of which could have led to "Wrong Action" instead of "Right Action." Moreover, remembering to be fully present to Alice gave me the freedom to be myself instead of trying to "be a professional." As such, I could simply share the discomfort in my neck with her and mean just that. Being the decent human being that she was, such clarity allowed her to respond to me in kind.

The last leg of the Path concerns Right Concentration. Hanh points out that Right Concentration concerns cultivating a mind (awareness) that is "one-pointed" (1998, p. 96), but there are two ways of maintaining such a focus: one that is active and one that is not. On one hand, active concentration is a one-pointedness of mind that is flexible or fluid in character. This kind of concentration allows us to be fully present to a series of events or an ongoing process. For instance, a master of judo may be fully focused on her opponent, but her opponent is always changing. Active concentration allows the master to keep her mind on the opponent's center of gravity, no matter where it moves. Thus, she is always attuned to him whatever might happen and can use his own force against him whenever she desires.

Selective concentration, on the other hand, involves attending to an object or person and staying more "passive," which is to say more receptive. By keeping our attention focused on one thing or person, our perception becomes more acute. Selective concentration is like a microscope; it narrows our attention and magnifies it so that we can see more deeply, accurately, and more intimately. Right Concentration has certain benefits in being with a person like Alice or in Alice's situation. Although I clearly did not see her as my opponent, I did see her as my dance partner. Active concentration allowed me to stay with her as she moved to the outer circle of our tango so that I would not be caught off guard by her next move. At the same time selective concentration helped me to look her in the eyes with my heart when she sat next to me. Once again, it is important to realize that Right Concentration is not magic: rather, it is a mode of being present to self, world, and others, that we can cultivate over time.

The careful reader may have wondered why I relied on Thich Nhat Hanh's characterization of the Eightfold Path so much. Although others have described this aspect of the Buddha's teachings quite well, I chose to use this approach for two reasons. First, Hanh's depiction of the Eightfold Path allows us to translate Zen concepts into clinical action, as seen in the story about Alice. Second, his approach offers a theoretical foundation for connecting Zen and psychotherapy. For example, he organizes the various aspects of the Eightfold Path into a dynamic circle. Beginning with Right View, each one of them is placed clockwise on the circle, suggesting that the practice of one fosters the practice of the next. At the same time, he notes that each part of the Path is connected to all the other parts. This arrangement makes it clear to us that not only does each part of the Path embody the others, but each time we practice one part of it, we are also practicing all the others. Hence, the Eightfold Path is a dynamic, evolving process that leads to cessation, which breaks the stranglehold of self's desire, and frees us from suffering. We can modify Hanh's circle to represent the role of the Eightfold Path, especially as it applies to therapists and therapy (see Figure 2.1).

At first glance, the Eightfold Path seems both beautiful and daunting. Each aspect of the Path appears to make sense; yet living this way might appear to be impossible for mere mortals. Therefore, it is also important to appreciate the fact that it takes a lifetime to walk this Path, which is why Zen is more of a direction than a destination. Fortunately, although a journey of a thousand miles does indeed begin with that famous first step, such a trek also builds up momentum. Like a circle, stepping on one part of the Path seems to direct us toward another so that after a while distance is covered. Although it is very difficult to reach higher levels of existence, such as those which a master may experience, it is not as difficult to achieve the more modest goal of simply developing a higher level of awareness one step at a time. For the

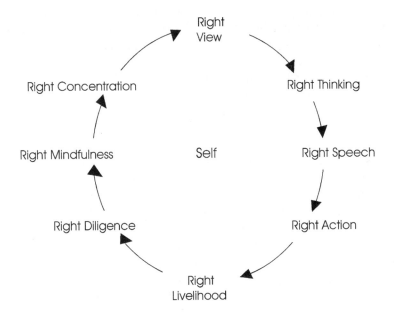

FIGURE 2.1 The Eightfold Path.

therapist, this means we do not necessarily have to become practitioners of Zen to benefit from it in our work. Although walking the Eightfold Path may lead one in such a direction if one so chooses, such a commitment is not necessary if we wish to appreciate Zen as a complementary rather than alternative approach as we have been using those terms.

MEDITATION

In 1974 Chogyam Trungpa, who founded Naropa University, the "only accredited Buddhist-inspired university in North America" (Chodron, 2001, p. 138), wrote these thoughts on meditation:

> Meditation is not a matter of trying to achieve ecstasy, spiritual bliss, or tranquility; nor is it attempting to become a better person. It is simply the creation of a space in which we are able to expose and undo our neurotic games, our self-deceptions, our hidden hopes and fears. (Farrer-Halls, 2000, p. 184)

This description of meditation may seem simplistic, but it is actually very humbling, just like the phenomenon of meditation itself. Meditation is not a mystical process. Rather, the practice of meditation is a way to grow both psychologically and spiritually. "But broadly speaking the basic character of meditation takes one of two forms. The first stems from the teachings, which are concerned with the discovery of the nature of existence; the second concerns communication with the external or universal concept of God. In either case meditation is the only way to put the teachings into practice" (Trungpa, 1996, p. 59). Meditation helps us to see others and ourselves with honesty and compassion.

The basic goal of meditation involves quieting the mind or watching your mind. This may sound simple, but is actually a difficult thing to do, because in our everyday life, consciousness is seldom quiet. We wake up to buzzing alarms, rush through a breakfast, weave through traffic, hurry to the work place, skip lunch, travel wearily back home to take care of the family until we collapse only to face the same challenge all over again in the morning. Instead of slowing down, the pace seems to do nothing but increase. Even though they do not have these same pressures, children of all ages are experiencing a similar crush of life in our modern society. At times the world seems to be spinning right before our eyes, as though modern life abhors solitude. But even before the modern age, this state of mind has often been likened to a monkey in Zen, because it is constantly busy, agitated, and moving from one thing to another.

> The Buddhist has an image for this, they say it is like a monkey jumping around in his cage, but, that doesn't do justice to it, it is like a drunk monkey all over the cage. But that doesn't go far enough it's like a drunk monkey that has St. Vitus's Dance, that's a disease where you just be in motion all the time, and they add, even that doesn't tell the story. The mind is like a drunken monkey with St. Vitus's Dance that has just been stung by a bumblebee. That is their testimony as to how restless the mind is. (Smith, 1995)

In order to understand this phenomenon and to come to terms with it, the Buddha is said to have sat under the Bodhi Tree in Bodh Gaya, India, meditating on truth, determined not to get up until he had found what he was seeking. It had been a long journey.

> To meditate is to make a complete break with how we "normally" operate, for it is a state free of all cares and concerns, in which there is no competition, no desire to possess or grasp at anything, no intense and anxious struggle, and no hunger to achieve; an ambitionless state where there is neither acceptance nor rejection, neither hope nor fear, a state in which we slowly begin to release all those emotions and concepts that have imprisoned us into the space of natural simplicity. (Soygal, 1993, pp. 57–58)

If truth is liberating, then meditation is the path we take to get there. As such, meditation is powerful; it is psycho-spiritual work.

By breaking the monkey of its habit, by quieting the mind from its distractions, we also increase its abilities, especially our ability to become single-minded. However, there is a certain irony to meditation. The more it is practiced, the quieter and more peaceful the mind becomes. The quieter our consciousness becomes, the more we are able to perceive and experience the richness of what is right there before us, moment by moment, whether it be a thought, another person, ourselves, or something as simple as a cool breeze on a warm summer day. This kind of presence is inherently therapeutic because sharpening our focus actually lightens our burdens. After all, if we are truly present to only one thing, then we cannot be bothered by all the others! At the same time, it is important to realize that, while meditation is beneficial, it is really "nothing special" because meditation itself can become an attachment for some people when it is not seen this way. In this case, meditation becomes an end and not a means to an end, which means that a person's progress may stop by attempting to pursue or perfect the practice instead of living life fully.

> If you continue this simple practice every day you will obtain some wonderful power. Before you attain it, it is something wonderful, but after you attain it, it is nothing special. . . . When you give up, when you no longer want something, or when you do not try to do anything special, then you do something. When there is no gaining idea in what you do, then you do something. In zazen what you are doing is not for the sake of anything. You may feel as if you are doing something special, but actually it is only the expression of your true nature; it is the activity which appeases your inmost desire. But as long as you think you are practicing zazen for the sake of something, that is not true practice. (Suzuki, 1970, p. 47)

Since meditation also allows us to observe our mind without struggling with it, meditation is good for us emotionally, too.

> Meditation is a process of lightening up, of trusting the basic goodness of what we have and who we are, and of realizing that any wisdom that exists, exists in what we already have. Our wisdom is all mixed up with what we call our neurosis. Our brilliance, our juiciness, our spiciness, is all mixed up with our craziness and our confusion, and therefore it doesn't do any good to try to get rid of our so-called negative aspects, because in that process we also get rid of our basic wonderfulness. (Chondron, 1991, p. 6)

In other words, meditation allows us to accept ourselves without judgment, and that is refreshing as well as liberating and not easy to do.

Although there are many ways to do meditation, none of them is the "only way." Some people use a concentrative technique that involves focusing one's attention on one's breathing, on an object, or on a single thought. Others use repetition, such as that found with a mantra as in Transcendental Meditation, or in chanting. One does not have to be in a zendo (meditation hall) or require a master to learn, but it is important to get instructions. Fortunately, there are plenty of good tapes and videos available that are made by fine teachers.

I have listened to Zen masters talk about sitting to help an anxious mind, to help fear and apprehension settle down like apple pulp will settle at the bottom of a glass. It is like our mind that goes bonkers speeding down the highways of our thoughts. The rapidity and fluidity of thought is difficult to control, like trying to change horses in the middle of the stream. At times, then, using the technique of sitting quietly almost seems impossible to do. However, it is possible to achieve this goal through perseverance, patience, and practice.

> Training the mind is a bit like training a young puppy to sit. You sit it down and a moment later it's jumping all over you, licking your face and hands. You sit it down again, "Sit, sit," and again in just a few moments it's up and running about. But with some gentle persistence and dedication, over time, the puppy does learn to stay and sit. Our minds are very much like this little puppy. (Goldstein, 2002, p. 83)

Tom, a client who knew nothing about meditation before coming into therapy, offers a good example of how meditation can be used to help people clinically. As a youngster, he was the epitome of what Winnicott described as a child forced into a "reactive mode" (Epstein, 2001, p. 30) because of early problematic experiences. His childhood was fraught with emotional and physical abuse. In addition he was separated from his family at a young age. Tom was the second child of four siblings. Until he was 18 years old, he lived in foster care homes, an orphanage, and, for a period of time, in a Juvenile Detention Home. His father was an alcoholic who abandoned the family when Tom was quite young. His mother left the children in care of an abusive maternal grandmother. He had experienced many psychological "threats of annihilation" (Epstein, p. 30) and his mode of reacting to these events became one of physical and psychological "survival" at any cost.

In spite of this impoverishment, he was able to attend a technical school when he graduated from high school. Yet, he was unable to fulfill his dream of working as a plumber. Feelings of inadequacies, or what might be called "defensive self-esteem" (Mruk, 1999) interfered with his work. For example, he did not get along with his colleagues, would become defensive, and at times his work was not satisfactory. These problems ultimately led to his being fired. Eventually he stopped trying to work. He entered therapy because he was getting to a point where he was having trouble functioning in almost all of his endeavors. For example, he had married shortly after high school and was now divorced, which is the event that gave rise to the feeling of needing to grapple with his chronic feelings of despair.

It was very apparent to me that Tom had great difficulty with trust and my first thought after hearing a portion of this story was to work on establishing the kind of rapport that would allow such a man to reveal, as best as he could, his inner most fears to himself as well as to me. For example, when he came into the clinic's waiting room, he would always sit in a corner to be as far away as he could from everybody in the lobby. Often times he would become distraught and leave the sessions early, so I felt that the first step had to be helping him learn and feel that he had nothing to fear from me, that he was in a safe place where he could talk freely about his self-doubts. He was obviously afraid and it was clear that in this state his mind was not his ally; it was a ruthless foe or an invisible prison. I brought up a way he could quiet his mind by suggesting that it might help to sit and be mindful of his breath by using the "counting technique." This simple method of meditation consists of counting each breath from one to ten, and then starting over. If one loses track of the number, he or she simply starts over, always bearing one's breath in mind, not concentrating on the number, so that there is no pressure to do it "right."

I had mentioned to him that since he lived in the country, going outside when he felt panic might help him relax because he might find the presence of Mother Nature to provide a nurturing or at least nonthreatening alternative. One day he was feeling anxious at home because he was feeling very closed in by circumstances. Rather than continuing to stew in his own mental juices, so-to-speak, he walked out to his yard where the chicken coop was located. He had a cell phone and called me. We talked about what was going on at that moment, why he needed to be outside. After a bit of reflection, he became aware that he felt less suffocated outdoors. As we talked I could hear the chickens in the background, so I asked him if he could concentrate on the sounds the chickens were making and try to immerse himself in the smells and sounds. He laughed. That seemed to stop the momentary sense of foreboding he had. Humor seems to create space. The next session he told me that being with the chickens, quieting his thoughts, helped bring him back to the "now" rather then getting caught up with the feelings of fear. He had learned to control the monkey, at least for a time.

As therapists, we have all had such insights with our clients and there is value in reflecting upon them regularly. *"The best of modern therapy is much like a process of shared meditation, where therapist and client sit together, learning to pay close attention to those aspects and dimensions of the self that the client may be unable to touch on his or her own"* (Kornfield, 1993, p. 244). It is always true that regardless of one's current level of awareness, if suffering is the nature of the human condition, and if freedom is found through walking the Eightfold Path in life, then meditation is the key to the process of liberation. We can represent this aspect of meditation and its relationship to the Eightfold Path in Figure 2.2.

In other words, meditation is the key to the Eightfold Path. Meditation allows us to access the Path at any moment, during any day, at any time in our lives. Although it is unrealistic to think that meditation will "cure" us of this bad habit or that problem attitude in a single or even multiple sessions, we can use it to improve the quality of our work as therapists. I will talk more about how to do that in chapter 4, but suffice it to say that, like Tom, there are many times during a week (or even a in day if it is a "bad" one) that taking even a few moments to meditate (quieting my mind) may calm

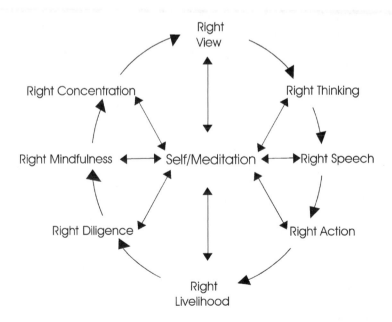

FIGURE 2.2   The Eightfold Path in action.

me down or allow me to see my client in a clearer, more soothing, nonjudg-mental light. Although it may be true that the fabled journey begins with a single step, it does not end there. Each milestone is marked by an expanding awareness and appreciation of the Eightfold Path. Meditation is important because it helps to keep us on the road to freedom from suffering, both for ourselves and our clients. The point I am trying to make is to try to meditate whenever possible, especially at the beginning, because Zen is a gentle path that is chosen, not a harsh one to be forced. Acquiring this skill requires patience, as well as practice and time.

SIX ZEN PRINCIPLES OF PSYCHOTHERAPEUTIC VALUE

So far in this chapter I have focused on the basics of the Buddha's teaching. To further this exploration, I will also show how his teachings are closely related to psychotherapy. To this end, I will focus on six Zen principles that have had an effect on me and on my clinical work with people.

ACCEPTANCE (OF SUFFERING)

Most of us who work in this field know that acceptance is an important part of the therapeutic process. Even those who practice medical psychiatry or behavioral therapy will usually concede that having an accepting attitude toward the patient or client is at least rapport building. Those who are inclined toward psychodynamic and humanistic practice will go one step further and appreciate how acceptance of self and others is itself therapeutic, especially since so many of our clients have had so little of this kind of nurturing in their lives.

However, the teachings show us that acceptance is much more powerful than establishing rapport or being nonjudgmental, because its deepest power comes from the fact that acceptance is related to the First Noble Truth, that in life there is suffering. Of course, there are two ways to respond to suffering in life: the first, which is our natural inclination based on the ego's desire to avoid pain, is to deny it, avoid it, or blame it on someone or something else. Existentialists might call this human tendency "inauthenticity." But the fact of the matter is that refusing to accept the basic fact that life is suffering dooms us to harboring a sense of fear towards life.

> Much of the practice life is about dealing with fear. Fear tells us to close down, not to go beyond the protective outer edge of our cocoon. But by giving in to fear,

we make it more solid. We strengthen our cocoon, contracting and limiting our existence. Fear has us avoiding some terrible imagined outcome, yet the substitute we experience by giving in to our fear is already a terrible outcome. (Bayda, 2002, p. 65)

Buddhism sees suffering in a very different way: instead of being avoided, it is something to be embraced in a certain sense and for two very complementary reasons.

First, acceptance of life and its pain allows us to minimize suffering or at least to avoid unnecessary forms of it. To deny suffering is a form of "ignorance" because the refusal to acknowledge and face pain keeps us trapped in it. Indeed, denial and self-deception can create more complicated forms of suffering, such as clinical neurosis, becoming or staying addicted, having a need to hold power over others, becoming greedy, and so forth.

It's difficult for me to say that you and I are ignorant without sounding dogmatic and repressive, like an old-fashioned fire-and-brimstone preacher. In Buddhism, the concept of ignorance refers to the age-old problem of delusions and confusions. Until we reach enlightenment, we are all at least a little bit ignorant of the truth or out of touch with reality. We don't perceive the truth of how things actually are directly, without distortion or illusion. Instead, we insist on seeing things as we would like them to be. We tell ourselves stories and we live in our fantasies. (Das, 1997, p. 59)

Thus, as ironic as it may sound, acceptance of life and its suffering is actually useful, perhaps even liberating. Although it never feels good to accept suffering as a valid experience, in the long run it prevents us from compounding our pain in ways that denial, deception, or avoidance inevitably end up doing. This aspect of acceptance alone makes it a position worth developing and helping others to develop. In a word, acceptance has practical therapeutic value.

However, there is another good reason that accepting suffering is important: Accepting our pain allows us to see and experience reality more clearly instead of manufacturing some face-saving distortion of it. By focusing on the here and now instead of what might have, could have, or should have been, acceptance allows us to be more fully present to the new and important possibilities of understanding and growth. In this sense, it is important to see that suffering can be a teacher as well as a foe. When suffering is accepted as a teacher, we can then learn from our pain instead of being trapped or chased by it, which means that we become freer than before.

Pain can teach us healthy and unhealthy ways of living, such as whether to take a drink or talk with a friend when faced with a problem, or trying something new rather than falling prey to the same old solutions that have already proven futile in the past. Perhaps most of all, we learn that suffering is like any other part of life if we care to see it that way, which is to say truthfully. When we do that, we also learn that suffering is transitory, impermanent, and eventually changes. In other words, suffering does not have to be avoided because even though it truly hurts, it, too, is an important part of being a person.

Another part of accepting the truth that life involves suffering is that it reminds us that we are all in the same boat. By understanding how hard but necessary it is to accept suffering in ourselves, we also have greater understanding and compassion for others who are suffering and struggling with it in their own ways, however that may be. This attitude toward suffering allows us to be more accepting of others, and of ourselves, at the deepest levels.

> We must first understand that both our pain and our suffering are truly our path, our teacher. While this understanding doesn't necessarily entail liking our pain or our suffering, it does liberate us from regarding them as enemies we have to conquer. Once we have this understanding, which is fundamental change in how we relate to life, we can begin to deal with the layers of pain and suffering that make up so much of our existence. (Bayda, 2002, p. 77)

For me, there is no doubt that suffering can be our teacher, even though it is very difficult to accept it.

For over three years, I had been working with Sandra, a woman who had been severely traumatized as a child by her mother and father. Her parents drank heavily and often when they were drunk, they would verbally and physically abuse her. Sandra's sister had committed suicide when she was a teenager, leaving a lengthy suicide note to Sandra explaining why she wanted to die. This was an additional trauma for Sandra from which she had not recovered because she felt that somehow she had failed her sister. Sandra kept the letter in her attic because she didn't want to be reminded of her sister's death. At one point, we spent considerable time talking about the impact this letter had on her. But I was surprised when Sandra actually brought the letter to a session. With some trepidation, she asked me to read it to her. As I read it out loud she sat huddled in her chair covering her face in her two hands. After I read the last sentence Sandra began to sob uncontrollably. I wanted to hold her in my arms but all I could do was to move my chair as close as I could and hold her hand. I did this until she stopped crying. We said very little; perhaps the silence brought us closer together and that may have been broken by words, even well meaning ones.

At the end of the session we held each other and I thanked her for bringing the letter.

As time went on Sandra spoke about the childhood of her parents. She revealed that they had been traumatized by their parents, too. For example, her father had been whipped, tied to trees, and threatened with bodily harm by his father. Her father's mother died at childbirth. Sandra's mother had been sexually molested by two uncles while she was between ages 5 and 14. At the age of 16 she ran away from home. Sandra described her mother as uncaring and frequently absent from home. She did not know where her father was and had little contact with her mother after graduating from high school.

As the sessions progressed, Sandra began to understand her suffering. One of the things she learned from it was that she was not responsible for what had happened to her or for the decisions her parents made. Instead, with much courage and effort she realized how powerless she was as a child and that she had been conditioned to think of herself as being bad. Like many abused children, she became an adult who had a pervasive feeling of worthlessness that resulted from parental abuse. When she could feel compassion for herself she was able to see her abuse, her parents, and her feelings of worthlessness in a different light. Acceptance of suffering allowed Sandra to make an important discovery that began to free her from an invisible prison. She developed new understanding of what she had gone through, and of her parent's behavior, too. "Maybe they didn't know how to love," she said, and along with this revelation she knew she would not place herself in the victim role again because she would be aware of how she could harm herself by forgetting the "truth." Sandra had experienced the suffering, she had been *with* the suffering of her parents vicariously, she now was not afraid to be vulnerable to life. In a word, she connected "with her soft spot" (Chondron, 1994, p. 48) and it was liberating.

This kind of awareness requires hard work and taking it to everyday life is even more difficult. I assured Sandra that if she faltered, it was okay; becoming free of suffering is a lifetime endeavor for everyone, not just her. What is important here is that in experiencing her fear in its fullest, the seed of enlightenment took root. Susan had been afraid of the letter because she thought that in some way its contents had the power to annihilate her. The fruit of facing the fear is that she began to see that she did not have to place herself in the victim role. She started to become mindful of how she had suffered by opening up and accepting the truth. By experiencing the truth of her suffering Sandra was not as vulnerable to life. As Padma Sambhava says, *"One does not err by perceiving, one errs by clinging; But knowing clinging itself as mind, it frees itself"* (Epstein, 1995, p. 157).

FEARLESSNESS (COURAGE)

Fearlessness is next. Fear, and all its manifestation, such as anxiety, dread, a sense of inability or incompetence, is something that most of us avoid whenever possible. Instead of facing our fear, we typically deny it, hide from it, bury it, or engage in some behavior that allows us to focus on something else. Sometimes the fear is very acute, such as in a state of panic. At other times fear is much more subtle or even unconscious. Either way, the anxiety fear creates is consuming, so turning away from fear in what ever way we do makes a certain psychological sense: Avoidance is "economical" to the ego, because it offers escape. Nevertheless, if we are unable to accept ourselves or another person or a circumstance of life because it scares us, then we cannot see reality, which means that we cannot respond to it effectively. The result is a state of avoidance instead of acceptance and the continuation of suffering instead of release from it. This means, of course, that overcoming fear, which is done through the principle of fearlessness, is a necessary part of the teachings.

We all know how to be fearful, but few of us know how to be fearless. "True fearlessness is not the reduction of fear; but going beyond fear" (Trungpa, 1984, p. 47). Rather, fearlessness is an act of personal or interpersonal courage, both of which are essential to therapy as well as life. Fearlessness is difficult because it is scary: It means standing still when all one wants to do is run; it means looking at what we have tried to bury in spite of its horror; it means being honest with ourselves and others instead of keeping up facades; but most of all, fearlessness means feeling the pain that has kept us trapped. In other words, fearlessness is like going through a fire in order to get to the water beyond it. A great irony of the teachings, and psychotherapy for that matter, is that most of the time, our fears turn out to be nothing more than that—ghosts instead of monsters. By accepting our dread, or disgust, or shame, or anger, we can see our fears for what they are, which is usually our attachments to the past and desires for the future.

I often wonder how much of resentment, anger, and even acting out have to do with fear and the avoidance of fear. While working as a staff nurse on the afternoon shift in a psychiatric unit, a young man, we will call him Mark, was brought to the unit. He had been confined previously in a juvenile detention institution. Mark was admitted because he had barricaded himself in the bathroom and ripped the sink off the wall (I do not know to this day why he did that). It took tear gas to remove him from the room. At the time of admission he was assigned to the "seclusion" room, in which the bed was bolted down to the floor and there was no other furniture. All was quiet during the early part of the evening and I had spent time with him to help him feel comfortable on the unit. I have always thought that entering a psychiatric unit was like going into an unfamiliar territory and feel that it is very important to try to calm any fears the patient may have about this event. After all, the language of the psychiatric unit is different, the staff is unknown, what might happen is unforeseeable, all of which has the potential to compound apprehension within the patient.

I don't know what triggered Mark off, but I soon noticed that he was changing from being friendly to becoming angry. I knew I did not want to call a "code Dr. Strong" and involve the orderlies or call the police again. But neither did I want the unit or staff be affected by his behavior. Instead, I felt that the best way to help him was to be alone with him, to stay with him until he was able to get control of himself in a nonthreatening way. Rather than responding to his outburst, then, I tried to keep in mind the person I met and talked with earlier that evening, not the one who was before me now. Although frightening, I still believe that this was the best way to react.

By remaining fearless instead of overreacting or jumping to conclusions, I was able to approach him, and ask in as steady a voice as I could (even though I was feeling tense inside) if he would come with me to his room. In his room was a large tubular punching bag hanging securely from the ceiling. I asked him if he wanted to use the bag and suggested he might find it useful. I gave him a set of gloves to protect his hands. He not only punched the bag, he also kicked it with his feet—hard! The punching bag swung wildly as I sat quietly on his bed, watching him take out his feelings on this bag. His intensity was so great that it seemed at one time his complexion turned to a pale, almost greenish tone. It was clear that Mark was a young man with plenty of rage.

After what seemed like a long time, he stopped and looked exhausted. Our exchange after this event was quite simple and pragmatic; I just asked him if his knuckles were sore, would he like a drink of water, and made simple, caring comments which had nothing to do with his anger. For some reason it made no sense to me to do anything but to make an effort to provide physical comfort for him. It seemed to be the "Right" thing to do because the remainder of the evening was peaceful. He followed me around like a puppy, wanting to be helpful to others. A connection had been made and it was transforming! As a result, I did not medicate Mark with any PRN medication. In the end, he seemed to have faced his fear, too, and no one got hurt psychically or physically. We had developed a special relationship of trust. As Chodron said, "This very moment is the perfect teacher, and, lucky for us, it's with us wherever we are" (Chodron, 1997, p. 12). This was a moment I had to rely on something that was a part of my inner self. I felt fear, but by facing it I also felt compassion. In spite of his strength and anger, I felt Mark was struggling for his very life in that moment and by facing my fear, I was able to be with him in his very dramatic mode of suffering. He never acted out again this way on the unit.

Mark was an incredible teacher for me and I am very grateful I was able to be with him that night so many years ago. Maybe both of us were in an unknown territory and became fearless together. At least he had an experience that validated his existence and I learned that patience and compassion is part of "being with a being" that is scared. It also seemed to be a turning point for both of us.

> How long does this process take? I would say it takes the rest of our lives. Basically, we're continually opening further, learning more, connecting further with the depths of human suffering and human wisdom, coming to know both those elements thoroughly and completely, and becoming more loving and compassionate people. And the teachings continue. There's always more to learn. (Chodron, 1997, p. 17)

TRUTH (ENLIGHTENMENT)

The opposite of truth is illusion. During my years working in the field of mental health, I have been privy to being with people when they wake up to a realization of a truth that has led them further into a path of freedom from fear. The relationship between fear and truth is a bumpy road, so it takes great practice and courage to pursue the truth over the comfort of illusion. From my perspective, when people have the courage to face their fear and pursue a truth, a kind of mystical force seems to guide them forward. By this I mean, under certain conditions, people seem to have an inner need to sense and experience their own truth. When an individual is in this state, they seem to have a willingness to face the dragons and tigers that appear to be waiting to devour them at any turn.

Fear, courage, truth, and enlightenment are all linked together in Zen. They are also connected in psychotherapy. For example, a classic Zen story concerns a man who is determined to break free of his negative emotions.

> He struggled against anger and lust; he struggled against laziness and pride. But mostly he wanted to get rid of his fear. His meditation teacher kept telling him to stop struggling, but he took that as just another way of explaining how to overcome his obstacles. Finally the teacher sent him off to meditate in a tiny hut in the foothills. (Chodron, 1997, p. 3)

As the story goes on, at one point the man finally settles down and begins to meditate.

> Around midnight he heard a noise in the corner of the room, and in the darkness he saw a very large snake. It looked to him like a king cobra. It was right in front of him, swaying. All night he stayed totally alert, keeping his eyes on the snake. He was so afraid he couldn't move. There was just the snake and himself and fear. Just before dawn the last candle went out, and he began to cry. He cried not in despair but from tenderness. He felt the longing of all the animals and people in the world; he knew their alienation and their struggle. All his meditation had been nothing but further separation and struggle. He accepted—really accepted wholeheartedly—that he was angry and jealous, that he resisted and struggled, and that he was afraid. (Chodron, 1997, p. 4)

As the story continues to unfold, the man stands up in the darkness, walks toward the snake, and bows. He slept after doing that. In the morning the snake was gone. The man didn't know if the snake was real, but it didn't matter, because the man realized that such intimacy with his fear caused his terrifying fantasies and imaginings to disintegrate. Once the illusions crumbled, reality could finally get through and he found that it was not nearly as terrifying as he had thought. I do not know how many times I have found that to be the case. As bad as it can be, reality is often more hopeful than our fears, perhaps because it is real and they are not.

This story is important because it makes two points. One is that many times when we do not avoid our fear, we often find that the situation resolves itself, thereby teaching us the value of facing what we are afraid to face. The other is that many times, if not most, facing fear is a difficult, stumbling, uncertain, and confusing process. Although courage may sometimes take on the character of a movie hero looking the so-called enemy in the eye, for most of us just getting through the event is enough. The recognition of the fact that I am only human, which is to say imperfect, coupled with the realization that often all I can do is to remain steadfast and persevering, is a great enough victory for me. I have passed this on to patients I have talked with and I can say unequivocally that such a truth usually seems very welcome to those who suffer. It even seems to affect many in a beautiful and compassionate way, because sometimes they realize that it is also true that they deserve happiness in life.

We need courage to see the truth in order to break out of our illusions and reduce our suffering; it is amazing to realize fear is the "juice" (stimulus) for growth and enlightenment. It takes time and patience to understand the value of fear, but to realize that these times are blessings in disguise is a very powerful truth. They are seeds of liberation. Although we will stumble repeatedly before we become masters of our fears, it is important to realize that each time truth prevails over illusion, no matter how imperfect the triumph may be, it takes us one step closer to peace. Fortunately, a Zen master might point out to us, there is never an end of these opportunities, so if we don't quite "get it this time" there is always a next time. As Chodron has said, "We don't experience the world fully unless we are willing to give everything away . . . not holding anything back, not preparing our escape route, not looking for alternatives, not thinking that there is ample time to do things later" (1997, p. 133). However, it is important to realize that we do not have to learn to do this all at once.

COMPASSION (TOWARD SELF AND OTHERS)

To many people in today's world, the word "compassion" conjures up a syrupy-sweet attitude with little substance. However, the word compassion is closely connected with the teachings of the Buddha, especially as he became aware that compassion and life are interrelated through suffering. In general, such things as projection, ignorance, illusions and desires bring about suffering. From a Buddhist perspective, mere feelings of compassion are insufficient, because true compassion includes action, especially the attempt to relieve suffering in others. "A beautiful word or thought that is not accompanied by corresponding acts is like a bright flower that bears no fruit. It would not produce any effect" (Bloom, 2000, p. 16).

Unfortunately, the word compassion seems so out of place in the modern medical and psychiatric settings that in the past, I have had some trepidation using this term while describing my work or clients to my colleagues. It wasn't until I began studying and attending conferences and retreats led by the Vietnamese Zen master Thich Nhat Hahn, Joan Halifax, and Ram Dass that my own experiences led me to the realization that the practice of medicine and mental health work are incomplete and perhaps even ineffectual without compassion: Although we may help the mind, we will never heal the heart without compassion. Compassion is the thread that connects all sentient beings, parent and child, teacher and student, as well as therapist and client. From my point of view, it is a curious thing that this word, which has such love and truth in it, both of which are important in helping and healing, seems to have such little value in our empirically driven health care systems. It is as though we are afraid to focus on the "soft spot" that is in everybody.

Like many therapists, I felt empathy and compassion in my heart, but I was reluctant to speak in such a way. I was afraid of letting people know that I had feelings for patients, that I was "getting emotionally involved" (which was frowned upon since nursing school days) and that I was not being "scientific." Yet because that was the truth for me, I have always felt a bit like a salmon going up the stream of my field. Fortunately over the years, the principle of compassion allows my actions to speak for themselves and now I share my thoughts and feelings more freely with clients and colleagues.

> When you begin to touch your heart or let your heart be touched, you begin to discover that it's bottomless, that it doesn't have any resolution, that this heart is huge, vast, and limitless. You begin to discover how much warmth and gentleness is there, as well as how much space. (Bloom, 2000, p. 66)

Curiously, I have also found that compassion can be liberating for the helper as well as for the one receiving help.

Compassion played a key role in my decision-making, even when I was responsible for hiring staff at the Psychiatric and Emergency Service units mentioned earlier. For example, if I felt the person did not have a sense of gentleness or was not in touch with his or her "soft spot," I did not hire the prospective candidate to work in the service. In my attempt to assess the person, I would ask myself if I would feel at ease with a potential candidate talking with a loved one of mine who felt troubled. Of course, such a position caused controversy among my more traditional counterparts. I recall a colleague that I had respected, for instance, who felt that such a criterion was way off-base. She felt that I should have concentrated on "clinical ability," by which she meant academic credentials and prior experience. I could not do that in spite of the fact I had self-doubts after my friend's remark, because when I was in the "now" with the candidate, my guts and heart took over.

Moreover, in higher level positions, most of the candidates have the proper credentials, but I feel that what is needed when they are facing human suffering, a person in pain, no matter how bizarre or scary the form, is sensitivity and gentleness; both are crucial. "Compassion is the desire that others be relieved of suffering" (Brazier, 1995, p. 93). Each therapeutic exchange is an opportunity to awaken both the therapist and client to the liberating power of compassion. There is a story of a Zen master whose student asked what was the best way he could help others? The master replied, "By helping yourself," to which the student said, "But how can I do that?" The master responded by saying that the way to help himself was to help others, or as Pema Chodron says, "What you do for yourself, you're doing for others, and what you do for others, you're doing for yourself" (Chodron, 2002, pp. 109–110).

The point applies to psychotherapy as well. We, too, insert ourselves in to the lives of others. In fact, that is the whole point of our work. In other words, our work involves opening ourselves up to another's suffering and anguish.

> In their work with clients Buddhist psychotherapists are directly offering to cojourney with them through their psychological and developmental experience and through their spiritual experience, spiritual anguish, spiritual struggle. . . . It is very important to emphasi[z]e the need to know another's suffering, another's anguish, as if it were our own. If we can do this we are not one step removed. We are being fully available. We are being as close to that other's experience as possible. We do this through the whole field of relationship, based on a profound understanding of equality in terms of spiritual journey. The therapist is not the boss. There is a profound equality and integrity of relationship despite the apparent deficiency, need or disturbance of the client. (Sills, 2002, p. 193)

Fortunately I acted upon my intuitiveness when I hired staff. Gratefully I can say this instinct did not fail me, nor does it usually fail me when I will take the time to listen to my intuitive insight, which is based on an unvarnished feeling. Intuition is not a very scientific concept. However, as the philosopher Huston Smith noted when asked about intuition in an interview with Michael Toms of National Public Radio, the insight that intuition is capable of providing can be an important part of life and, therefore, of clinical work, too.

> The answer is by intuitive insight. Now you can say that's vague and insight gives us different things, but this is where the test of a human being comes in and whether they have from their tradition or their experiences of life put in place a gyroscope. I'm reaching for metaphors, or a northern star, or something like that, a sense of judgment and discernment and which we find in the great philosophers of the great minds, the Great Spirit, throughout history. (Toms, 2001a)

I have an amusing story to share about using compassion as a criterion for hiring that makes the point here. When I was looking for a new therapist for the Emergency Service, which, remember, was recognized as an NIMH model program, we had many highly qualified candidates with extremely impressive credentials from major universities. One of them, an individual with less than average credentials compared to the others, stood out to me. He was dressed in what appeared to me to be an ill-fitting, light brown, tweed, sport coat with leather patches on the elbows. He had long hair, seemed kind of nervous, and did not smile a lot. He was not ingratiating as the typical candidate tended to be. However, I could sense his "soft spot." He seemed sensitive, decent, and honorable, all qualities that were important to me. So, he made it to the final round of interviews, which entailed interviewing the next patient who walked in to the Service for treatment.

This procedure was an administrative decision; I felt it was not necessary and, furthermore, I felt it was contrived and put pressure on the perspective staff member to "perform," however, there was also nothing I could do to change that practice at the time. Therefore, with the client's permission, the candidate was observed and evaluated by the entire staff as we watched the interaction through a one-way mirror. Although perhaps a "rigorous" hiring exam, I had already made up my mind. In spite of his dress and relative inexperience, it was a unanimous decision to hire this individual. Although knowledge and training were important for this position, only compassion could allow the therapist to be effective with all the varieties and degrees of suffering he or she would encounter in our emergency room. My own soft spot served me well once again and today this individual is coauthor of this book. He also dresses much better now!

ATTACHMENT (DESIRE)

A chief cause of suffering, and a major obstacle on the road to liberation, occurs in the form of attachments, which are akin to desire. The major difference between the Second Noble Truth and the principle of attachment is that, while the former is a general concept in the body of Zen, the latter concerns the particular ways that individuals become trapped by their desires. For example, materialism is a common form of attachment. In the extreme, the excessive pursuit of success, wealth, power, prestige, physical beauty, are obvious forms of attachments to worldly objects that doom us to unhappiness, because there is always more to possess and possession of such things is only temporary at best. Although these things seem to feel good and ease our pain, each step in such directions takes us further away from ourselves and, therefore, from our freedom.

Other forms of attachment take a different shape. Addictions to drugs, alcohol, sex, gambling, and many compulsive behaviors, such as an excessive dedication to one's job or hobby, also take over our lives and may lead us away from the truth and ourselves. In addition, other forms of attachment are much more subtle.

> The objects are not the problem. It is our attachment and our identification with what we crave that causes suffering. Tilopa, a wandering tenth-century yogi sang,

"It is not the outer objects that entangle us. It is the inner clinging that entangle us." (Das, 1997, p. 83)

These inner clingings can include what we might call ego attachments, such as an overly large investment in our professional identities, seeing ourselves as this or that kind of person, overinvolvement in our relations with our loved ones, and so forth. Moreover, ego attachments can also be unconscious and "neurotic," such as refusing to deal with pain in our lives and continuing the role of a victim, not seeing the need to let go of a painful past or a perceived injury and thereby keeping its pain alive, avoiding situations that might help us deal with our aloneness, anger, fear, or even clinging on to hopes or goals that are so unrealistic they can only keep us feeling miserable.

In Zen there are three Lords of Materialism that are used to capture all the forms of attachment: the Lord of Form, the Lord of Speech, and the Lord of Mind (Trungpa, 1973, pp. 6–7). The Lord of Form, for example, concerns the "neurotic pursuit of physical comfort, security and pleasure" (Trungpa, 1973, pp. 5–6). In this mode of attachment, there is an attempt to control nature and to avoid all irritations. Of course, such motivation is related to the fear of change: As a result, we live in a fantasyland that will protect us from what we don't want to face. However, such attachments turn out to be made of papier-mâché and often collapse around us, under us, over us, beside us, resulting in more pain.

The Lord of Speech "represents how we use beliefs of all kinds to give us the illusion of certainty about the nature of reality. Any of the 'isms'— political, ecological, philosophical, or spiritual—can be misused in this way. 'Political correctness' is a good example of how this lord operates. When we believe in the correctness of our view, we can be very narrow-minded and prejudiced about the faults of other people" (Chodron, 2001, p. 12). Of course, this kind of speech includes judging people instead of understanding them, finding fault with people in an attempt to elevate our self-perceptions or minimize our inadequacies, covering up our limitations instead of moving beyond them. This form of attachment may also occur in therapy. For example, when the therapist becomes too invested in a particular outcome, they cannot see the client for who they are or what they are actually doing.

According to Chodron, the Lord of Mind may be the most dangerous strategy of all because it is the subtlest.

The lord of mind comes into play when we attempt to avoid uneasiness by seeking special states of mind. We can use drugs this way. We can use sports. We can use falling in love. We can use spiritual practices. There are many ways to obtain altered states of mind. These special states are addictive. It feels so good to break free from our mundane experience. We want more. For example, new meditators often expect that with training they can transcend the pain of ordinary life. It's disappointing, to say the least, to be told to touch down into the thick of things, to remain open and receptive to boredom as well as bliss. (Chodron, 2001, p. 14)

Given the events of September 11, 2001, it is clear that religious fanaticism is an incredibly dangerous form of attachment, but the point is that there are many states of mind that can be abused in this fashion.

A poignant clinical example of attachment pertains to a young woman I will call Caroline. She buys "stuff" to avoid feelings that create uncertainty in her life. She describes her bedroom as her domain. It is filled with beautiful furniture, clothes, knick-knacks, and pictures that are special to her. Caroline projects her fears on almost everyone she comes in contact with by telling people her story of emotional neglect and finding fault with them when they don't respond as she wishes and believes she deserves. For reasons that will become clear momentarily, Caroline has not gotten rid of the past in her mind: she is attached to the desire for her life to have been different than it was, an attachment based on "if only" and the feeling that "it should have been," has prevented her from knowing her true self.

The background Caroline grew up in was based on money and the cliché, "children are to be seen but not heard." She was provided all things material but received very little attention or nurturing from her parents. She was not to own emotions, or talk about feelings, and certainly not to show them. As a child, she acted out in spite of the rules of the house, which mostly focused on attempting to treat her as an object, not a being. This unwanted behavior increased the alienation between Caroline and her parents as she grew into adulthood. Coming to therapy was not easy for her because the sessions had to deal with the illusions she created.

The turning point in Caroline's work came when she became very angry with me and I did not retaliate. The previous week Caroline had been invited to a social party where she overheard an endearment spoken to a stranger. She had been drinking to the extent that she was beginning to lose control. It was as though the remark, while not even directed at her, brought all the hurt of not being loved to the surface and Caroline projected her pain on this innocent person. Instead of feeling her pain, however, Caroline began to insult the woman for no reason that was apparent to others. She became so verbally abusive to this innocent individual that the host insisted Caroline leave the party. She did not express remorse then or now, "I wanted to hurt her!" and added that she felt she was entitled to say what she wanted. Moreover, she also hid behind her drinking at the time and felt that she should not be held responsible because of it.

When I spoke about the possible aloneness she might have been feeling, the sense of emptiness that dwelled within her, plus the affects the alcohol had on loosening her usual restraint against such forms of awareness, she swore at me and said, "You don't understand!" After that outburst she began to sob, covered her face with her hands and seemed to melt into the chair. In this moment of connection, Caroline's attachment to fear was being exposed. For a time she was touching her "true self" or perhaps the "soft spot" of openness that is within each of us. We worked on these issues the following weeks and, with courage, she faced her fears by recognizing how her anger helped hide the pain she had been feeling since a child. As long as she comes to therapy I will be there for her without any demands that she *should* be different than what she is. Now when we are in session, our primary focus is on the present and her current responses to life. She is facing the fact that her illusions are not providing her with a sense of satisfaction in any sphere of her life except, perhaps, when she is shopping and now that pleasure is only momentary. Her demeanor has changed from one of irritation and defensiveness to sadness and softness. The change is particularly noticeable in her voice, as it softens, and her facial expression is pensive rather than hard.

Attachment is a part of life, and all of us use something to avoid the painful realities of life until that attachment wears out its usefulness. However, attachment also needs to be understood for what it really is, which is a source of pain and an obstacle to being free of it. If we have the courage to walk the Eightfold Path, then it is possible to break free of our attachments, one by one. Although such work requires a lifetime, the Path is not as difficult as it might seem.

> Once we stop blocking it with ego's strategies, the refreshing water of bodhichitta will definitely begin to flow. We can slow it down. We can dam it up. Nevertheless, whenever there is an opening, bodhichitta will always appear, like those weeds and flowers that pop out of the sidewalk as soon as there is crack. (Chodron, 2001, p. 15)

In other words, when a client begins to understand the ways in which their individual ego attachments keep them imprisoned in their pain, it is like breathing in air that has been infused with the scent of sweet grass. Although we will find ourselves breathing in putrid air at another time in our lives, we now know that what we strive for is fresh, clean, and pure air. The realization that false gods, mistaken beliefs, or gratifying ego needs will never satisfy our deeper yearnings can be a turning point in life as well as in therapy.

IMPERMANENCE (AND LETTING GO)

In the 1970s I was given a popular poster that included a picture of a serene pastoral setting with a tree, a stream, a grassy meadow. The caption pointed out the fact that the only thing a person could count on in life was change. At the time, I didn't like the poster's message. Its implications were disturbing to me at the deepest level. I had worked hard at making my life meaningful, productive, and reasonably predictable. Like many Americans, I was happy with the way my life was going and I certainly didn't want to think about any modifications.

Change and the forces of change challenged the order and stability of my life and my identity or self. After studying Zen, however, I now find this poster to be a good friend. It helps remind me about the Zen principle of impermanence and to appreciate the transitory nature of experiences, situations, and life in general. After all, if things were permanent instead of impermanent, infants could not become children, children could not become adults, and adults could never change. More important, if it were not for impermanence, then suffering would never end. It never occurred to me that I had been living a state of "impermanence" ever since I was born! Although that realization may seem frightening at first because it can mean losing whatever we have or whoever we love, impermanence is also our ally because it means that pain won't last forever. Impermanence is the foundation of hope because, although we do not know what will happen in the future, we do know that the current situation will change and new possibilities will arise. In other words, "this too will pass."

Impermanence is a great liberator and it is extremely gratifying to be with someone who comes to this conclusion on his or her own during therapy. Emily provides us with an example of how the realization of impermanence can be freeing. She had been admitted to the unit because of a major depression associated with her family, especially her father, who was a domineering, rigid, over-achieving, physician. Her behavior troubled her dormitory advisor because Emily had become increasingly withdrawn, had stopped attending classes, and would have angry outbursts. She was admitted to our unit because of a suicidal threat. One morning when I went to see her for our daily session I found her in a fetal position, her body shaking with apprehension. When she spoke to me, she demonstrated a rare clinical phenomenon, something akin to aphenia, that involves speaking words, and sometimes even entire sentences, backward. I had never been with someone who manifested fear in this way before, so I sat on her bed and stroked her shoulder for a while, not saying anything. After a long period of time, she was able to speak to me. Her first remarks were about her fears; she felt uncomfortable in her room and did not want to go to my office because of having to go out in the hall.

After she expressed her thoughts, I excused myself, telling her I would return in a few moments. I went to the nurse's station, obtained two pieces of paper, and wrote on each of them "DO NOT DISTURB, THERAPY IN SESSION." I returned to her room and taped one of these signs to her chest and one to mine. I gently urged her to walk together with me in the hallway. With some hesitation she finally did as I asked and we walked together on the unit. As we walked rather slowly, holding hands, not talking something happened that was spontaneous and wonderful. We began to giggle. We had a connection, one based on trust. Moving from absolute dread and paralysis to strolling the halls and giggling in less than one hour is a good example of impermanence in our lives. Emily and I talked about how transitory emotions and experiences can be, even bad or negative ones. When we see experiences from the Zen understanding of impermanence, we have already begun to free ourselves from our attachments, whatever they may be, and the suffering they cause.

Each time I can help a client understand how impermanent experience can be, they seem to relax visibly and gain hope from the fact that their pain, or depression, or worry, or anger, or whatever torment afflicts them, does not have to go on forever. The wisdom of impermanence is that life will change. Learning to accept that fact instead of fighting it can only lead to gracefulness instead of rigidity. Cooperating with life in this way is not easy, but every time one practices this attitude, the event that causes difficulty or suffering is transcended to some degree and the negative impact it has on the individual is weakened. Eventually, when practiced long enough and when used with the other principles of Zen, especially meditation, one's entire view of the self, the world, and others changes. Once again, we see that the very thing that causes us pain, in this case fear, can be the same thing that liberates us from it. Impermanence takes away fear's punch and that can help us to break free of an attachment for a time. In short, the practice of Zen is a process, not a goal, and each step on the Eightfold Path we take already points us toward the next one.

We began this chapter by introducing the other voice of this book and her history in the field of mental health. This introduction also included how Joan came to walk the path of Zen in her personal and professional life. Then, we examined the Four Noble Truths of Zen: *dukkha* (life is suffering), *samudaya* (the cause of suffering), *nirodha* (the cessation of suffering), and *marga,* the Eightfold Path. While doing so, we spent considerable time exploring the nature of the Eightfold Path and how it applies to helping and healing. Finally, we identified six principles of Zen, namely, acceptance, fearlessness, truth, compassion, attachment, and impermanence, and how they apply to the process of therapy and to life. Now the question becomes one of whether Zen can be understood as a complement to our work? As we shall see in the next chapter, the answers to these and related questions can be found only by examining the teachings in terms of the major traditions of scientifically oriented psychotherapy, which consists of the biological, learning, cognitive, psychodynamic, and humanistic perspectives.

CHAPTER 3

From Realism to Idealism: Traditional Therapies and Zen

There are probably more religions than cultures, and each age produces several philosophical systems. However, there are just a few major scientific approaches to understanding and changing human behavior and it is important to understand them for at least two good reasons. First, the biological, learning, cognitive, psychodynamic, and humanistic perspectives and the connections between them constitute the larger scientific background against which we need to consider a Zen approach. Second, the various clinical disciplines and techniques that characterize traditional mental health care are also grounded in the five perspectives, so understanding how each of them addresses clinical issues prepares the ground for a consideration of whether and how Zen techniques can be used at the practical level.

There are several ways to examine the basic approaches to theorizing, researching, and altering human behavior. The most widely adopted one usually begins with presenting a set of key ideas about what is most fundamental in determining human behavior from a particular point of view. That information is often followed by a discussion of major theories or schools of thought that represent a particular perspective on behavior. Typically, the investigation includes a look at how behavior can be changed according to each position and usually ends with some kind of evaluation that considers the strengths and weaknesses of each major theoretical position. One thing that most such examinations do not take the time to do, however, may actually be crucial in developing a comprehensive appreciation for the field as a whole.

This issue concerns the philosophical dualism we encountered earlier, only now we must consider what it means in regard to understanding human behavior scientifically. As a student of mine once said on an exam concerning the relationship between these two disciplines, "Psychology cannot escape philosophy." In other words, each of the five major perspectives in the behavioral sciences lie along a continuum of theoretical possibilities that spans the gap between realism and idealism. Starting with an emphasis on physical reality at the left, for instance, we find that the "hardest" or most scientifically rigorous perspective in terms of using observation, measurement, and experimentation, is the biological point of view. Learning theories come next, because of their classical emphasis on the same scientific paradigm. Cognitive psychology occupies the middle position because, although it is founded on neuroscience and therefore prefers more classical scientific methods, it also includes consciousness, which is very problematic for the other two naturalistic points of view just mentioned. The psychodynamic perspective is clearly moving toward the "soft" end of the continuum, because most of its notions are difficult to research or support in a way that is compatible with science practiced from a naturalistic paradigm. Finally, the emphasis on free will, the individual, and the commitment to understanding the farthest reaches of human nature clearly places the humanistic perspective in another paradigm often called the "human science" approach (Aanstoos, 1984; Giorgi, 1971).

A PHENOMENOLOGY OF TRADITIONAL PSYCHOTHERAPY

There are several ways to approach doing what amounts to a brief phenomenology of traditional psychotherapies. The one we will employ, which is presented in Figure 3.1, is based upon the continuum mentioned above, because that method will help us understand whether or not Zen can be seen as a complement or alternative to traditional practice. The heading of "paradigms" in the diagram, then, represents the chasm created by realism and idealism. The Aristotelian or hard end of the continuum that spans the two different paradigms is characterized by an emphasis on the physical world and the forms of the scientific method that are used to study it. As such, this side of the scientific picture prioritizes observable data, measurable findings, the experimental method, and "objective" knowledge. The primary value of investigating human phenomena from this natural science paradigm is that the knowledge it yields is more reliable and valid: Findings generated from this way of doing science are relatively easy to test, duplicate, and

I. SCIENTIFIC PARADIGMS IN THE SOCIAL AND BEHAVIORAL SCIENCES

"Hard" <——-> "Soft"
(Aristotelian, measurable)   (Platonic, experiential)

II. PERSPECTIVES (Broad, long-standing, scientific approaches to understanding behavior)

Biological	Learning	Cognitive	Psychodynamic	Humanistic
-Evolution	-Conditioning	-Information	-Unconscious	-Free Will
-Brain	-Environment	-Representation	-Stages	-Self-fulfillment

III. MAJOR SCHOOLS (Major views or theories within a perspective)

-Sociobiology	-Behaviorism	-Cognitive	-Psychoanalytic	-Phenomenology
-Biological Psychiatry	-Social Learning Theory	-Constructivism	-Psychodynamic	-Transpersonal

IV. EXAMPLE: Depression

-Physiological Imbalance	-Negative Reward Ratio	-Thought Distortions	-Unconscious Conflicts	-Meaning Making
-Achieving Homeostasis	-Positive Reward Ratio	-Pattern Breaking	-Working Through	-Making Choices

V. EVALUATION

-Factual	-Factual	-Integrative	-Individual	-Individual
-Reductionistic	-Reductionistic	-Reductionistic	-Subjective	-Subjective

FIGURE 3.1 Information map of the five major scientific perspectives on human behavior.

verify. They also tend to be nomothetic in that they apply to behavior across the board for a particular species.

The other or "soft" end of continuum, by comparison, does not ignore naturalistic findings, but it also includes the data of human experience, which means that its methods are more descriptive and inferential or Platonic. Although less reliable and valid in the classical scientific sense, the value of this approach is that it is able to access dimensions of being human that are inaccessible to harder methods. Consequently, research and practice from this end of the continuum tend to emphasize the individual, which means that it is more ideographic. Gregory Kimble (1984) described the basic difference between these two paradigms as "psychology's two cultures," which I have always found an apt metaphor. He also found a number of different scientific values that distinguish the two groups and these theoretical and research priorities parallel the hard-soft distinction mentioned above. Of course, lest one become too biased toward either direction or "culture" right from the beginning, it is important to realize that each end of the continuum has strengths and weaknesses in terms of understanding and treating behavior. For instance, one is more concrete or factual, but the other is more holistic or comprehensive.

The second level of the diagram illustrates the relationships that the perspectives have to one another as they span the scientific continuum. There are a number of ways to characterize each view, but the key question is how much detail to include while describing them, which is to ask how many of the more important ideas characteristic of each perspective should be considered in order to understand its uniqueness. If we were doing a history of psychology, for instance, then we would present each view in great detail, beginning a discussion of the philosophical foundations of each perspective, moving on to identifying its ideas and their founders, and then tracing development of important lines of thought up to the present. Since we are not doing such an investigation, we can take a lesser course as long as it is still descriptive. Therefore, this part of the process will be limited to identifying what might be considered the two most important ideas that give each perspective its distinguishing character.

The same situation applies to the next (third) level of the diagram, which concerns particular schools of thought within each major view. Because they are based on seminal ideas, each perspective gives rise to many theories over time. Some of them are powerful enough in their own right so that they become entire schools of thought within a perspective, although all such schools still embody the core ideas central to the perspective from which they emerge. Once again, since our aim is not to do a history of the field, this aspect of our investigation will only mention what might be considered as being the two most important theoretical positions within a perspective. When possible, I will select one school that is ideologically conservative in order to represent the ideas of a perspective in their "pure form," so that we can appreciate just how different these intellectual cultures can be. The other school will be one that is "mainstream" and much more representative of the perspective in terms of mental health research and care today. A complex problem for historians of social science is, of course, what to do with overlap between perspectives and schools, and I will make some comment in this regard at the end of our investigation.

The fourth level of detail in our information map attempts to show how these approaches help us to understand real people in real situations. Presenting a case study of a clinical problem, and then examining how different perspectives might understand its etiology and treatment, is an established way of doing that (Barton, 1974). Therefore, I will use a clinical vignette concerning an individual who suffers from depression to illustrate how each perspective moves from theory to practice. Depression is chosen for several reasons; it is a common mental health problem to which most people can relate and which most clinicians have seen frequently enough so that it is useful to us as an example; it is complex enough to have multiple dimensions, which is to say both biological and psychosocial components; and it has been studied enough for there to be a rather solid body of findings concerning which treatments are most effective. These characteristics should allow us to examine how the perspectives operate in theory and practice.

Finally, the fifth and last level of the map is an evaluative one: It focuses on the relative strengths and weaknesses of each point of view. The vertical columns on the diagram serve to identify how each perspective flows through the various dimensions we are considering (basic ideas, major schools, example, and evaluation, respectively), thereby creating a comprehensive view of behavior.

Let us move through the various levels of the diagram both in terms of theory and practice so that we can understand the scientific continuum of change in order to see if it is possible for Zen to have a place in it or not. In addition to discussing the major ideas, primary schools, and strengths and weaknesses of each major view, we will also see them in action through a case study. Our subject is a 26-year-old man who walks into the office. He is of typical height and build, possesses normal intelligence and appearance, has reasonably good health, and is from a blue-collar background. His parents wanted him to go to college because they did not have the opportunity and they knew that getting a good education would be helpful to him. This background makes him fairly representative of Americans in general. In addition, there is some history of mental illness in his family, but there has been no clinically significant indication of such a problem for him until now.

After putting himself through undergraduate school and working for a time, he and his wife decide that he should go back to school and pursue a graduate degree for their future. They met during college, found they had a mutual interest in metaphysical or "spiritual" values, and married on that basis, promising to be faithful to each other "forever." Together as a couple for two years now, they do not yet have children. He works the evening shift, meaning that they are separated much of the time. Seven months into the process of going back to school, his mother, who happened to suffer from schizophrenia, dies unexpectedly after a sudden brief illness. He manages to get through the end of the academic year successfully, but has delayed mourning the loss until the end of that period. As soon as the semester ends, his wife tells him she wants a divorce, that she is involved with an older man who is very comfortable financially (which is something she always admired), and that she wants her husband to find another place to live as soon as possible so that she can get on with her life. At first she agrees to marriage counseling, but consistently fails to show up for the joint appointments. Instead, she goes off with her lover on an extended luxury trip while the husband struggles to make ends meet in a small attic apartment 300 miles away from home back at school.

The client is now feeling grief from the unresolved death, rejection from his wife, betrayal through her infidelity, and confusion as to how all this could be happening to him. In addition, he is unemployed, financially distressed, displaced, and just in the midst of his studies with the end being very far away. In a word, he is depressed. The fellow does, however, have some very good friends who care for him and who urge him to seek out help, which he does. Note that this kind of misfortune could fall on anyone: It has little to do with ethnicity, gender, or age. In fact, such a scenario may even be more likely to involve a woman, as they are probably subjected to this type of betrayal, abandonment, and financial hardship more often than men in our society, at least historically. In any case, such a situation could lead to mild, moderate, or, under certain conditions, even severe or suicidal depression, all of which are real possibilities under such circumstances, which makes the situation a good example for a clinical discussion. Let us call him John simply because we have all known someone with that name and see what each perspective is likely to offer him, including one that incorporates Zen.

THE BIOLOGICAL PERSPECTIVE

First, the biological approach to understanding human behavior is based on the principle of uniformitarianism, especially as it applies to evolution. Such a position assumes that nature (the physical world and all that is in it, including people) is governed by a set of fundamental physical, chemical, and biological laws. Above all, these laws are consistent, hence the phrase "uniform," and not capricious or vulnerable to manipulation by forces outside of the physical universe. When something occurs that is unexpected, for example, it only becomes a matter of trying to understand the phenomenon better, which is to say researching it further and in greater detail. Furthermore, because these laws are natural and consistent, they can be investigated through observation and experimentation, or though the naturalistic paradigm of using the scientific method. Natural selection is one such principle that pertains to evolution, which is a central characteristic of a biological view of behavior, and this process plays a major role in determining behavior as a basic law of life. Therefore, understanding the rules that govern how organisms operate, the particular behavior of a species, and how these things change over time is an important part of this approach.

Second, the biological perspective approaches understanding behavior on the basis of its physiology, especially that of the brain and its mechanisms. Thus, the biologically oriented theoretician, researcher, educator, or clinician will tend to focus on understanding how the brain works, especially at the neurological level, and particularly in terms of the biochemistry of synaptic transmission. Of course, the laws of uniformitarianism and evolution are still at work: For instance, the neurons of a simple worm work according to the same biochemical principles that ours do. The chief difference is, of course, in the number of neurons an organism possesses and how they are connected to each other, or their particular organizations, which means that the structures of the brain are important, too. Thus, the more complex the brain of a particular organism happens to be as we move up the evolutionary scale, the richer and more sophisticated its behavior will look. For example, the neurons and structures of primitive organisms produce basic behaviors like reflexes, as in a lizard. If an animal's brain is sufficiently complex to have a limbic system, then emotions may be present, as the case may be with a dog. Similarly, if the cerebral cortex is large and complex enough then consciousness also occurs. Of course, the building blocks of any brain are genes, which is precisely where the two principles of evolution and physiology come together, making this the "ultimate reality" of the biological perspective.

All biologically based theories of behavior are set upon these foundations and they all practice a clear preference for the naturalistic or hard scientific paradigm. But the most radical of these views goes one step further. In the case of sociobiology, which is "the systematic study of the biological basis of social behavior in all kinds of organisms, including humans" (Wilson, 1998, p. 150), for instance, biology *is* behavior, and it must be understood that way. According to this school, each species is concerned with only one thing—survival. To this end, behavior is primarily driven by and directed toward the future through reproduction, a process that is helped by natural selection or the survival of the "fittest," which is to say the most adaptive characteristic or behavior given a particular environment or change in it. The two forces of survival and adaptation give the species the opportunity to increase its number until it is maximized, which occurs when the organism reaches the point where the environment can support no more creatures of this particular type. In theory, at this point a natural balance occurs that can be maintained more or less indefinitely, as long as nothing major changes in the environment. If change does occur, then the processes of adaptation begin again, which might lead to new characteristics becoming more fit and then being selected by nature until new possibilities prove more valuable, and so on. Of course, there are no guarantees in nature, which means that failures to adjust can occur, particularly in the form of extinction.

An interesting thing happens, however, when we take this approach to the level of human behavior, because then culture becomes involved. In this case, "the adaptiveness of the epigenetic rules of human behavior is not the exclusive result of either biology or culture. It arises from subtle manifestations of both" (Wilson, 1998, p. 150). The interplay of biology and culture as a combined evolutionary force allows evolutionary psychology to explain higher levels of human behavior, even those as complex as morality, in a completely naturalistic fashion.

Morality and other such types of high level human behavior provide a good example of how it is possible to say that "all" behavior is biological, even that which may appear otherwise at first glance. For instance, many social institutions, such as putting the welfare of the group ahead of the individual, marriage, developing and maintaining the concept of right and wrong, and so forth, are seen as having evolved in ways that increase the chances of children having the resources and stability required to reach adulthood so that they can reproduce and the species or culture can continue. Since reproduction is the primary business of any species, when children grow up, it behooves them to maintain the same general behaviors, customs, morals, and social structures, as long as they are "fit" enough to bring forth yet another generation successfully. In other words, they develop and are passed on from generation to generation, as a social equivalent of reproduction. Should these and related phenomena no longer have such an adaptive quality, then modification can occur through accident or experimentation and new ones may emerge or the group may vanish, just like the theory of evolution predicts. It must be said that sociobiologists and evolutionary psychologists are only one part of the biological perspective on human behavior and they are a minority that constitutes the extreme form of this type of thinking. However, they are an influential force and they do illustrate the power of a perspective to understand behavior comprehensively.

The rapidly emerging dominant school of this perspective, however, called "biological psychiatry," is more temperate in its philosophical claims and it is an extremely powerful force in the world of mental health research and care. Biological psychiatry is "a distinct perspective claiming that psychopathology is a matter of biological malfunctions" (Fancher, 1995, p. 253) and offers at least two important contributions to the field in general. First, it defines mental illness as biological in nature, which means that it must be treated this way, too. Second, this name reflects a movement aimed at reestablishing psychiatry as a medical specialty, which distinguishes it from more psychosocial understandings of mental illness and those who approach it that way. Researchers, educators, and clinicians who work from this position, and they constitute the major force that drives modern psychiatry today, affirm the biological view concerning the importance of the brain, including its biochemical and genetic foundations, as well as the basic principles of evolution. Similarly, they advocate the hard, quantitative, natural science paradigm over any other. However, this school tends to suspend the ultimate implications of evolutionary thinking in terms of the philosophically larger questions, such as morality or the existence of God, and so forth, which separates them from the sociobiologists.

The key principle of biological psychiatry is homeostasis, or the idea that organisms seek out a state of balance between physiological systems and once it is achieved, strive to maintain this steady state. Behavior, then, is an attempt by an organism to reach and to maintain a balance between need and satisfaction. All the systems must work together to accomplish this fundamental biological goal, so disrupting one system causes imbalances elsewhere. For instance, homeostasis is disturbed when we are short of fluid levels in the body, resulting in a state of thirst, which, in turn, changes our behavior in the direction of seeking liquids. But after we have satisfied the need for water and restored homeostasis, it is disturbed once again when we need to eliminate wastes, thereby influencing behavior in yet another direction. Such a view of behavior is extraordinarily elegant: Normality occurs when biology functions as it should and abnormality results when it does not. The more serious the disturbance, such as in the case of physical or mental illness, the more severely our behavior is affected, too. Similarly, the more quickly homeostasis can be restored, the more rapidly behavior will take its normal course. Therefore, from this point of view, it makes good sense that we should concentrate our scientific and helping energies on understanding and using biological principles as the first priority.

Now let's look at how the biological perspective might typically go about understanding and helping John. First and foremost, of course, the individual presents various symptoms: His sleep is poor, his appetite is off, his energy is down, and most of all, his mood is melancholic. In order to understand these things, he must be examined, diagnosed, and, ultimately, treated. In this case, of course, it will be found that, like all illness, the condition is a result of a disruption in otherwise normal homeostatic functioning. In the diagnostic process, various organic possibilities will be considered, because depression can result from many kinds of illnesses, which makes diagnosis and the language of diagnosis a key aspect of the helping process. Most likely, it will be hypothesized that John's brain is in a state of chemical imbalance. The focus of the clinician's attention (or what is "really" wrong with him) is probably going to be understood as involving synaptic transmission. Various neurotransmitters and their specific mechanisms of transaction such as reuptake will be regarded as the likely culprits. In keeping with the general principles of biology functioning, it will be understood that disruptions in these lower order systems lead to difficulties in higher ones, which means that eventually behavior and even cognition can become affected, as is occurring with John.

Typically, John will see a general practitioner for his condition, because they are more readily available than are psychiatrists and because many people still feel there is a negative connotation in seeing therapists. If so, his doctor would probably complete an evaluation of him in 15 or 20 minutes, a process which is often characterized by a series of directed questions to the patient and to which he usually gives relatively brief answers. More time will be spent in this intake process if he happens to see a psychiatrist first or is sent to one. Once the diagnosis of depression is made, he will probably be relieved to find that there is nothing wrong with him psychologically. Rather, it is only that his brain suffers from a "chemical imbalance." Instead of having to take a look at his role in the divorce, for instance, treatment consists of reestablishing synaptic balances, which is done through the judicious use of medications capable of passing through the blood-brain barrier. A follow-up appointment is set up to check on his progress and a suggestion may be made to "get some counseling."

Augmented by his chemical tune-up, John's neurons begin to resume more normal functioning, the symptoms begin to disappear, medications are terminated, and in a few weeks John is "cured": he no longer meets the criteria for depression, signaling that the illness is over. John may wish to get that counseling they talked about, but it is pretty expensive, very time consuming, and he no longer suffers so terribly much. In short, John becomes better able to function again and society gets its productive member back with a minimum of disruption: clearly, treatment has been successful in the terms specified by this traditional culture of healing. It is very important to appreciate that there is good evidence for using this perspective for treating depression: it usually helps. After all, the chief strength of the biological perspective is that it is *factual*, or thoroughly grounded in the empirical, testable, and duplicable methods of hard science. In fact, the biological approach to mental illness is essential in dealing with more severe forms of mental illness. It is certainly a welcome advance over burning, confining, or warehousing people, all of which have been practiced by well-meaning "care givers" in the past.

Moreover, such a modern view fits very well with the Zeitgeist of our culture, particularly our respect for natural science and our positivistic view of the world. As Valenstein (1998, p. 1), says, American psychiatry is said to have changed from "blaming the mother to blaming the brain."

> The idea that mental disorders are physical diseases has been widely promoted and accepted for several reasons. It is known that people suffering from mental disorders and especially their families generally prefer a diagnosis of a "physical disease" because it does not convey the stigma and blame commonly associated with "psychological problems." Also, a "physical disease" often suggests a more optimistic prognosis and a briefer, less expensive course of treatment. (1998, p. 225)

In addition, major pharmaceutical companies play a key, sometimes hidden, role in advocating this perspective: They help train physicians through corporate sponsored continuing education programs; they fund much, if not the majority, of scientific research on severe mental illness; and these global powers are very active in terms of publishing findings or in making it difficult to publish them, depending on the degree of control the company exerts over a research or agency (Valenstein, 1998). Now, of course, they even advertise to the entire population on television. All of these things and more express and advance the biological perspective at the theoretical, research, and practical levels. Given the power of these forces, and the fact that they are part and parcel of major health care traditions of the West, it is no wonder that this particular culture of healing dominates mainstream mental health today (Fancher, 1995; Valenstein, 1998).

However, there are at least two serious limitations of such an approach to consider as well. The first one focuses on the science of the day. It turns out that although there is good evidence to indicate that biological psychiatry works, the same science tells us that there is no reason to believe that it works the way it is often presented as working, for example, in terms of neurotransmitters plugging into receptors like electrical sockets on walls. As one well-respected investigator who is largely sympathetic toward the biological perspective describes it:

> Understanding just why some drugs work and some do not is generally beyond the current capabilities of science. Even understanding how the ones that clearly

work manage to accomplish their tasks is beyond current knowledge. Most of the original hypotheses about neurotransmitter deficiencies or excesses have not stood up especially well to testing; even where we do understand the effects on synaptic transmission, no one understands why that should translate into changes at the level of thought, feeling, and action. In the sixth edition of the highly esteemed text on neuropharmacology, Cooper, Bloom, and Roth say that " . . . at the molecular level, an explanation of the action of a drug is often possible; at the cellular level, an explanation is sometimes possible; but at the behavioral level, our ignorance is abysmal." (Fancher, 1995, p. 262)

He goes on to say that over 60 neurotransmitters have been identified so far, but that only a half dozen or so have been investigated. In addition, there are other complicating factors to consider, such as another group of molecules called neuromodulators, the fact that a single neurotransmitter may plug into a dozen or more receptor sites each of which has different functions, that neurons themselves can change in sensitivity, and that the brain makes new connections and sculpts itself in new ways all the time.

Understanding the complexity of the biological picture is extremely important because it stands in stark contrast to how it is presented to the public, in undergraduate textbooks, via educational pamphlets in the physician's office (which, in the case of mental disorders, are often little more that glorified advertisements for drugs), and even in physician training provided by pharmaceutical companies (Valenstein, 1998). Indeed, I always find it striking that this literature, particularly that which is available to the lay public, often fails to point out (or simply minimizes) that, with the exception of bipolar disorder, cognitive and interpersonal therapy is at least as effective in treating most depressions as are medications. Similarly, most medication studies use placebos to give to control groups, but the placebos do not produce the same side effects the "real" medications do, which makes the research on the effectiveness of medication over therapy more questionable than people usually realize (Fisher & Greenberg, 1995; Valenstein, 1998).

The criticism here is that, although medications can and do often work, they do not do so for the reasons most people who advocate their use offer, which leads to the perpetuation of overly simplified ways of thinking about behavior and how to change it. In short, the fact of the matter is that we simply do not know what causes a "chemical imbalance" and how medications may affect them. Of course, there are several unfortunate consequences of maintaining a strong biological bias. For example, because biological research is the most expensive type, it consumes huge amounts of increasingly limited funds, some of which might be better spent on researching different approaches to helping and healing. Similarly, medications tend to become the first line of treatment when a health care system adopts a strong biological bias, when it might be wiser in the long run to hold them in reserve for situations where less invasive forms of treatment do not work.

Another major criticism of the biological point of view concerns how it diminishes the importance of the person and the role that individuals play in determining the quality or direction of their lives. The tendency to ignore the significance of the person in these ways is reductionistic, a characteristic which,

> Refers to explanations of a phenomenon based on the properties of the constituent elements that compose it. Thus a reductionistic explanation of water would be based on the properties of hydrogen and oxygen. Molar explanations, on the other hand, are based on the properties of the whole, with the assumption that the "whole is more than (or different from) the sum of its parts". . . . While reductionism often provides insight into underlying mechanisms that may prove helpful in understanding some properties of more molar phenomena, it is an error to assume that the "bottom-up" approach is the only way, or even always the best way, for science to proceed. In pursuing the biochemical approach to mental disorders, an enormous amount has been learned about neurochemistry and drug action, but it is questionable how much has been learned about mental illness. (Valenstein, 1998, pp. 137–138)

The weakness here is not that the biological view is wrong or unimportant. Rather, it is that by focusing primarily on the substrata of human suffering, this approach is likely to miss other important, perhaps even more important, dimensions of behavior. For example, there is the classic chicken-and-egg problem to consider. Research shows that some mental disorders do have biological underpinnings that can be observed through brain scanning technologies, such as with some cases of obsessive-compulsive disorder. It can even be observed through the same technology that medications affect these areas and return them to "normal," suggesting that biology is the key to the development and treatment of these conditions. The problem is that cognitive therapy produces the same results as medication and these effects can also be observed, using the same scanning technology, as occurring in the same areas of the brain (Durand & Barlow, 1997)! Therefore, the question is not one of which perspective is "right," but which one is the best to use in any given instance. In other words, is it better to flood the brain with powerful chemicals the long-term effects of which we do not know in order to offer the possibility of a reasonably rapid intervention? Or is it best to respect the integrity of the brain, help the individual deal with his or her problems through some other form of therapy, but in doing so risk taking a longer time? The sad fact of the matter is that, all too often, it is only the bias of the therapist that propels the individual down one path or the other!

Similarly, biology won't tell us why John is depressed, how he should handle the losses he has suffered, what to do with his anger and humiliation, how it is that he always seems to be the one left when his relationships end, and what he can do about his own interpersonal style to help relationships in the future. These are not merely incidental or even just philosophical questions: If we really want to treat the depression effectively, they must be addressed because if they are not, then relapse is likely to occur. Indeed, even if relapse does not occur, getting into another unsatisfying relationship is still likely because medications don't help us learn how to do things differently. The absence of disease may define health for the biological perspective, but a satisfying life involves much more than that. Reducing us to mere organisms, two-legged protean worms chasing other ones, if you will, fails to address the more meaningful aspects of being human.

Lest this presentation of the biological approach seems unduly harsh, I should point out that it is not intended that way. There can be no doubt about the facts that the biological approach has been extraordinarily helpful and that general practitioners and psychiatrists care greatly about their patients. Our goal, however, is to cover all the major perspectives in a way that gives equal weight to strengths and weaknesses so that we can understand the continuum of mental health care. It was necessary to spend more time on this one than we will on the others because it is first, which means setting up the discussion as well as engaging in it, and because this culture of healing dominates traditional mental health care today, which makes it the largest and perhaps most important part of the background for considering complementary and alternative views.

THE LEARNING THEORIES

The next perspective as we move from the left or "hard" side of the continuum toward the right or "softer" one is that of learning theory. The two most influential ideas of this approach to understanding human behavior are that all important behavior, for example, higher order behavior, is acquired, learned, or conditioned through natural, which is to say observable or measurable, principles of learning, and that the environment, particularly the cultural environment when it comes to human beings, is where most important learning occurs. It is not the case that learning theorists fail to appreciate the biology of the brain. Indeed, no learning could take place were it not for the capacities of this organ, especially in regard to memory. Rather, borrowing from the 18th century philosopher John Locke, the brain is seen as a *tabula rasa* or blank slate upon which the lessons of living are written over time. Once again we see that science cannot avoid philosophy altogether, and it is important to appreciate just how powerful this idea was and is in our Western understandings of behavior.

For one thing, this position played a fundamental role in the development of democracy. If, for instance, all babies are born like blank slates, then the concepts of "royal" blood or "divine right," two principles that supported European political structures for centuries, are seriously undercut. Similarly, 100 years later, we see the same principle alive in the Civil War: If all men are created equal, then slavery cannot stand up to reason. Today the same principle of basic equality also undermines dictatorships or sexism. In addition, if it is also true that even though we all start out the same but always end up different as individuals, then there must be reasons for that to occur, too. The principles governing this phenomenon can also be studied, understood, and applied to all kinds of things. In fact, the groundbreaking work of such figures as Pavlov in Russia and Watson in the United States did just that, and in doing so created the first genuinely scientific psychology. Indeed, there are some who say that it was learning theory that legitimized psychology as a "real" (i.e., naturalistic) science, especially since the major alternatives to understanding human behavior at the time were religion, philosophy, and, of course, psychoanalysis, none of which could be proven in ways that are compatible with the hard end of the scientific spectrum. Moreover, just like any good scientific theory, this research led to practical applications in several areas of human life, most notably the educational and clinical settings, and with measurable results.

There are so many schools within the learning perspective that it might be more accurate to call it the learning *theories* perspective. However, two of them stand out to most authorities. Like before, one is very radical, which is to say it takes these ideas to their extreme, and the other is more moderate and widely used today. The radical behaviorists, such as Watson and Skinner, did not see a need to consider such notions as the mind in understanding human behavior. Since their influence in American academic psychology was so great, such topics as consciousness were virtually expelled from psychology and other social sciences from the 1930s to the 1960s or so. For a long time, the basic premise of learning theory was that behavior results from orderly processes, which can be observed, studied, and manipulated scientifically. So pervasive were these ideas, that just like Freud's, the learning view of behavior became a part of our everyday language and identity. Every time we say to parents, for instance, "Don't reinforce his behavior," we are speaking this language; each time a teacher "rewards" a student, the behaviorists are at work.

But modern learning theory has gone way beyond both Skinner and behaviorism. Now what is generally referred to as social learning theory dominates the perspective and this approach to learning is much more sophisticated than its behavioristic predecessors because it emphasizes the forces of culture. Of course, all social learning theories still reflect the basic orientation of the perspective: learning and environment determine behavior. But whereas earlier learning theories like classical or operant conditioning emphasized the learning part of the equation more than the environment, social learning theory focuses more on the latter. To be sure, social learning theory continues to affirm the basic principles of learning discovered through classical conditioning, such as repetition, generalization, extinction, and so forth. Similarly, social learning theory also affirms the basic findings of operant conditioning, especially, for instance, the process of shaping behavior. However, the addition of such cognitively oriented learning processes as imitation, modeling, or observational learning expands the ability of learning theory to account for human behavior by leaps and bounds.

The example I like to use for understanding the power of social learning theory concerns my wife, Marsha, and how we negotiated the household chore of determining who was going to be primarily responsible for cooking. In the "old days" (circa 1950s) the decision probably would not have been much of an issue: Everybody "knew" that cooking was "women's work." But like many modern dual career relationships, we married on the basis of mutual interest, mutual attraction, and mutual support for our professional interests. Cooking did not fit into this picture for either one of us, but it soon becomes an issue after the honeymoon, unless one is fortunate enough to be able to eat out all the time. To make a long story short, I do not like cooking because of family history and adamantly refuse to do it unless I absolutely must, which means that future meals are likely to be inconsistent in terms of meal times and quality if they are left up to me. Marsha, who never practiced cooking like girls growing up in traditional families might, at least was not adverse to it, so she chose to assume this duty as one that is primarily hers. The story is not a sexist one, because I got cleanup, including the bathrooms, which she, if not most people, considers a very fair trade! The point is one of how we are to understand the fact that she turns out to be an extraordinary cook and finds great pleasure in it today, even though she was neither trained nor rewarded for learning such a behavior in the past? So far, all we can say is that either the sociobiologists are right and women are better at such things because the biology prepares them for nurturing related activities, or that something very different than biology or simple conditioning is at work.

It turns out that although Marsha never did cooking in her home, it was a very traditional place where life centered on the kitchen. Even though her parents pushed education and not traditional female gender typed behaviors, it is no surprise where she did most of her homework night after night: in the kitchen! Although not practicing it herself, the social learning theorist might say that she was surrounded by a culture or environment of cooking. No doubt her mother, who was very traditional in these ways, exposed her daughter to much of the techniques and culture of cooking, albeit indirectly. Apparently, when it came time to cook, the observations Marsha could not have avoided as a child served her well as an adult: From the learning perspective she covertly acquired much more about the processes and behaviors of cooking than she had been conditioned to know overtly, or had even been aware of knowing. Thus, learning and culture are inseparable for human beings, and very sophisticated mental processes like those involved with observational learning must be involved for higher order learning to occur. In fact, the modern day version of social learning theory, which is usually identified with Alfred Bandura (1997), is now called social cognitive learning theory (Rathus, 1999) in order to better include these processes in its view of behavior. Of course, learning theorists also apply the same concepts and principles to modifying behavior in the clinical setting.

In John's case, for instance, a traditionally oriented behavioral therapist might begin by asking him to describe what he does during the day, especially when he is feeling depressed. He might tell her that most of the week he gets by with showing up to work or classes on time, getting most of his duties done, though not with the enthusiasm he used to feel, and that he then goes home and watches TV until he falls asleep, which is often late at night. As a result, he wakes up tired and repeats the process. "Weekends," he says, "are the worst, because my wife and I used to go out on Friday, spend Saturday with friends having fun, and then just hang out together on Sunday. Now all I do on the weekend is sit and watch TV." He wonders if there is anything more to life and is starting to feel like there is very little to justify going on with it much longer.

Where the biologists approach behavior at the physical level, learning theorists start with the behavior itself, or with what a person does. Put most simply, life consists of a series of negative and positive reinforcements: We have pleasant experiences and unpleasant ones, good days and poor ones. As long as the good outweighs the bad, one's "reward ratio" (Frey & Carlock, 1989) is positive and life is reasonably satisfying, if not enjoyable. Whether through the behavioral notion of "learned helplessness" or ordinary misfortune, depression occurs when the pendulum falls to the other side for an extended period and creates a negative reward ratio. The lack of positive reinforcement causes depression, because it extinguishes the individual's attempt to obtain positive reinforcement, thereby setting up a vicious cycle of failure, avoidance, and, eventually, withdrawal, all of which decrease the chances of obtaining positive reward even further. John has clearly fallen victim to this negative behavioral cycle: The positive rewards he received from his mother are gone, as are those that came from his wife; he can no longer even count on the comforts of home because he is not living there; and the rewards that used to come from weekends filled with the anticipation of love, fun, and companionship have been completely destroyed and replaced with loneliness and other negative feelings.

Knowing that the situation is likely to only get worse, perhaps even to the point where brain chemistry changes, John's therapist devises a treatment plan that is designed to break this vicious behavioral cycle: He must reestablish a positive reward ratio and his current behaviors must be modified in order to do that. The key to the plan is, of course, to help him find new sources of positive reinforcement. Since the weekends are the most difficult period, she decides to concentrate her energies on that part of the cycle. Thus, she asks John to start asking people out for a date for Friday evening and to make plans to be out of the house most of the day on Saturday and Sunday. John resists the idea of asking anyone out because he is still "too hurt" to think about getting involved with anyone else. But he does understand the need to do something, so he agrees to make a list of possibilities for the other two days, such as going to the local museums, taking walks, calling up a friend, joining a new club, taking part in church activities, volunteering for some worthy group or cause, whatever he thinks he'd like to do. The therapist is also experienced enough to weigh the possibilities and assign "homework" that means actually trying some of them out for a while.

Much like the physician hoping that the right medication and dose will be found sooner rather than later in the process, the learning oriented therapist is relying on the possibility that John will eventually find activities rewarding enough to break the negative reward cycle or "learned helplessness" as many learning theorists prefer to call it. Hopefully, he will even find things that he looks forward to, things that bring him genuine excitement and real pleasure. John does seem to find some relief after a while, but not enough for the cloud of depression to disperse, so she asks him what is lacking. He responds that he feels lonely and "needs" someone. She then takes her techniques one step further and asks him to modify his Friday behavior by going on dates once more. This time he agrees to try that, only to report later that, "Nothing is happening, nobody wants to go out with me." She asks him to describe how he goes about getting a date in considerable detail, and finds that his approach is to wait until Thursday night, call up a friend or acquaintance, and say something such as, "Hi, you wouldn't want to go out with me tomorrow night, would you?" to which the answer, of course, would usually be quite understandably, "No."

Since John's approach is not likely to be an effective one, his therapist begins to modify it, using the same social learning principles mentioned earlier. She might suggest, for instance, that he is to make a date at least one week in advance, pick out an exciting place he thinks he and the person might enjoy that is within his means, and ask her out in a pleasant, enthusiastic fashion. Then, she requires him to role-play and rehearse with her how he goes about asking someone for a date. With practice, he starts to become more successful in asking people out and, although he still "can't find anyone," at the very least, John's problem with isolation on Friday evenings is addressed. Eventually, it is very likely that he will date someone with whom he can develop a relationship, thereby restoring the reward ratio on the positive side of the scale and alleviating much of the depression. When ready, he may also be asked to share how he has gone about the grieving process to evaluate whether additional work needs to be done in that area. Either way, the therapy ends with John being able to move beyond depression into a life that at least brings some pleasure once again, tipping the reward scale to the positive side and avoiding a further slide toward despair.

The evaluation of this perspective is very straightforward because it is similar to the one we did for the biological point of view: After all, they are both on the "hard" side of the scientific coin. Thus, on the positive side, this approach to helping is very factual in that its findings are reliable, valid, and may be applied to behavioral challenges with a good degree of confidence. In a word, learning theory works: It offers a practical approach to understanding and changing behavior. In addition, the value system in which this perspective is grounded is much more optimistic than its biological companion. For example, happiness is not necessarily a part of the biological culture of healing, but learning theory legitimizes the "pursuit of happiness" in a way that is very consistent with the American dream. After all, what could be more rational than using scientific techniques to modify behavior and alter the environment in a way that optimizes positive reinforcement and minimizes negative reinforcement, as long as one does not run afoul of society's basic rules concerning social behavior? It is the "smart" (i.e., logical) thing to do, according to this perspective, and it is consistent with many traditional values in our culture. Indeed, in many ways, learning theory is particularly American: It is perfectly consistent with our concern with the pursuit of life and personal happiness that is a part of so many of our institutions. It should be no surprise to see the same ideas embodied in the way we envision health and practice mental health care.

The downside, of course, is that learning theory, even social or social cognitive learning theory, is also largely reductionistic. This time, the reductionism occurs as a form of mechanistic thinking. Although the learning theorist may look at individual behavior, the look is a mechanical one that records actions, observes what they are contingent upon, determines what reinforces them, and uses the information to condition behavior in ways that adjust it in a socially acceptable fashion. Society itself, however, is seldom the question. Personal thoughts and feelings do not need to be addressed beyond the point of establishing and maintaining rapport, because they are epiphenomenal: Thoughts and feelings will spontaneously change once behavior does. Finally, there are no inherent values according to this perspective, only acquired ones, which can lead to a state of mere social relativism or even emptiness. This time our dehumanization does not take place in being seen as "large worms." Rather, it is as though we are simply very "smart rats" that can be conditioned into and out of all kinds of behaviors. Finally, the focus on adjustment and the lack of fundamental human values makes this approach to understanding and helping others potentially Orwellian in its application.

THE COGNITIVE APPROACH

In the broadest sense, the cognitive perspective "would appear to define psychology as the study of internal processes, conscious or not, which may be inferred by an outside observer on the basis of an organism's behavior" (Baars, 1986, p. 9). This perspective is uniquely situated in that it occupies the center of the continuum between the hard and soft general paradigms. Unlike their biological and behavioral brethren, however, cognitive psychology stresses the importance of mental processes, particularly those that are involved in determining how an organism perceives and organizes (understands) the world. Thus, this perspective focuses on two key phenomena: information and representation (Gardner, 1985). The former concerns how an organism gathers sensory data about the world based on its biology as a species, and the latter is concerned with how the organism uses such information to construct a working model of the world, the possibilities within it, and how to navigate them in a way that gets its needs met more times than not. Since human beings are aware of the world, self, and others, consciousness is a key aspect of our behavior and, therefore, an important part of the cognitive approach (Baars, 1986; Gardner, 1985).

How organisms represent the world depends upon a number of key factors and processes. On the one hand, information includes data about the world, especially the surrounding environment, as well as internal feedback, including that which is based on current bodily sensations and on past experience. Mental representation involves the organism's nervous system, especially the brain's ability to recognize patterns, which is based on "schema" or basic ways of representing information characteristic of a particular species or individual. The process is quite complex even in lower organisms which are limited to fairly rudimentary concerns, such as where to find food, how to avoid becoming food, and reproduction, but matters quickly become exponential as we move up the neurological ladder.

One school of the cognitive perspective, often referred to as the information processing approach (Gardner, 1985), emphasizes understanding the mechanics of these processes in as great detail as is possible. Consider, for example, a possible cognitive understanding of the experience of going to the airport to pick up a loved one returning from a long trip. One stands in the waiting area and looks at the people getting off the plane. The retina is stimulated in a way that excites various "feature detectors" in the brain that are good at recognizing circular patterns (such as eyes and heads), horizontal patterns (such as mouths), and triangular patterns (such as noses). These neural excitations, in turn, are detected by other "agencies" (Minsky, 1986) that "bind" the data together in terms of higher order schemas, eventually reaching beyond simple gestalts like lines and circles to the mental representation or schema for human faces. Now that individuals are being perceived, higher levels of memory become involved, which allows us to sort through the dozens of faces getting off the plane in terms of a particular decision-making strategy, for example, curly hair, pretty smile, a certain walk, and so forth. When the pattern that is detected matches the one that is stored in memory, other processes may come into play more strongly, like emotion, consciousness, and behavior. Suddenly, for instance, we find ourselves directing our bodies toward the other whom we have just spotted, and moving toward them with open arms and smiles which clearly express our feelings and thoughts about being reunited. As soon as we hug the other, new sensations occur, different information is transmitted, other patterns are identified, and perhaps we even begin to anticipate a lovely evening together.

This process of information and mental processing is a dynamic one that goes on during all of our waking experience, and perhaps as we sleep as well. Of course, much of this processing is not done consciously, but automati-

cally, like a computer, which is a favored analogy for the information processing approach to behavior, albeit a very simple one in comparison to the
wonder of the human brain. As we develop, the processes become more
complex and mature: They have a cumulative effect so that over time the
organism slowly constructs an adequate, which is to say reasonably accurate,
model or map of the world in which it lives. In the case of human beings,
of course, there are three kinds of maps to consider: One is a model of the
physical world and the various laws that govern it, such as gravity which is
a very important one for two-legged creatures; another is a map of the social
world, which includes an understanding of how people behave in relation to
one another and how behavior is regulated in a given culture; and the third
one is a "self-theory" or a mental representation of ourselves, which includes
a self-concept, or how we see ourselves, and our self-esteem, or how we feel
about what we see in ourselves (Epstein, 1980). Of course, all of these maps
and the relations between them develop over time, which means that new
schema come and go in a relatively orderly fashion as we move through the
life cycle, thereby making human behavior enormously complex.

The other school, which is generally known as cognitive therapy, is explicitly clinically oriented and gives particular emphasis to understanding how
people construct knowledge about the world, self, and others, rather than to
the biological processes involved in doing that. Depending upon how much
detail the cognitive therapist and client want to develop, they aim at developing
a reasonably accurate understanding of the client's cognitive maps, especially
where it does not correspond well to reality. In this process, they take special
care to identify what pre-reflective or "automatic" assumptions the client
makes about these things. Of particular interest is how causality is understood,
or who is responsible for what in life and when. Attention is also given to
how clients envision the future, especially as to whether it is realistic or not.
Assumptions clients make about others are also important. For instance, it
is important to know whether they perceive people as being basically good
willed, forbidding, or dangerous. Similarly, basic ideas concerning interpersonal communication may be examined. Last and perhaps the most important,
it is necessary to understand how clients understand themselves, particularly
in terms of whether or not the perceptions and self-evaluation are accurate.
In all three dimensions of life, the therapist typically looks for what are called
"irrational thoughts" (Ellis & Harper, 1977) or "cognitive distortions" (Burns,
1980), which is to say areas where these assumptions do not correspond to
observable reality accurately, especially when the discrepancy contributes to
unnecessary pain and suffering.

Each particular version of cognitive therapy has its own method for developing an understanding of how the client constructs reality, and each one

will have a list of typical cognitive distortions people make that create or exacerbate pain. These lists are used to help identify and label problems in thinking that interfere with seeing the world, self, and others, realistically. This cognitive "diagnosis," is shared with the client and various techniques are then employed to help the individual identify these problematic thinking patterns when they actually occur in life. This process is accompanied by teaching ways of breaking these unrealistic, which is to say unhealthy, perceptual and thinking patterns in order to construct more accurate, and presumably healthier, maps instead. Clients are asked to practice these activities until they become reasonably skillful at them. Notice that all the steps in this process are consistent with the cognitive perspective in general: People, like organisms, are designed to construct cognitive maps that help them navigate their particular worlds effectively. Good, that is, detailed and accurate, maps make this process easier and even pleasurable: they help us to prioritize goals, to minimize difficulty attaining them, and to avoid unnecessary obstacles. Poor, that is, distorted or inaccurate, mental representations not only make satisfying needs more difficult, but they also create more problems, often painful ones. A more rational course is to develop a better map, which usually means modifying old ones though "reframing" or other reconstructive techniques. Sometimes, if the person's map is very distorted, it may even be necessary to construct a new one, which is a process that requires considerable time and work.

This time we find our client meeting with a cognitively oriented therapist. After hearing John's complaints about loss and depression, she begins to explore with him the kinds of assumptions he makes about relationships, the durability of relationships, and what he thinks it means to lose a relationship. John tells her that he understands that sometimes life is unfair and people die prematurely like his mother, but that he "can handle that kind of thing as everyone's parents die someday." Then he goes on to say, "It's the marriage that's got me down, I'm such a loser, no one will ever love me again," as he looks down despairingly. After a careful review of other areas of his life which seem to be fairly healthy, that is, realistic and functional, such as friendships and work (in this case school), the therapist identifies the problem for John: Although infidelity and divorce are painful realities that happen to people all too often in life, he is suffering more than he needs to suffer in comparison to others who have gone through such things. She goes on to explain to him how a person's thoughts can alter their perceptions, which in turn, can influence their feelings and even show up in their behavior, such as setting himself up for continuing rejection and loneliness. In short, the therapist shows John how certain negative thinking patterns can cause unnecessary suffering, including self-defeating behavior and even depression. She also offers him an implicit hope that is very much a part of the cognitive perspective: if he breaks these patterns, then there may be different and more satisfying possibilities to consider.

Being a fairly rational individual about many things in his life, John realizes that there is no point in suffering more than he must, so he agrees to try his best. Over the next few weeks, he and his therapist identify the particular type of cognitive distortions he is prone to making habitually, and they begin to correct them by substituting more realistic thoughts each time an unrealistic one occurs. When he laments that he is a "loser," for instance, she points out to him that such a thought is irrational, because he has won a lot of things in his life and still has the chance to do that in the future. The thought is labeled as involving a particular type so that they can identify it more easily in the future. Perhaps it is an example of "name calling" (Burns, 1980), which is a very common type of distortion. After having taken this step, they then rephrase the thought more realistically. He ends up saying to her, "I'm a reasonably competent person: I've won in the past and, just because I lost this time, doesn't mean I don't have a chance in the future. After all, there are more than one fish in the sea."

Later on while at home, he starts to feel that life is hopeless again because he "knows" that he will never experience love once more. This time, he remembers to take out his pen and paper and examine this kind of a thought. Getting better at this new skill, he quickly realizes that another kind of error in thinking is causing him to suffer in order for his thought to be true, he would have to be able to tell the future, and that if he could do that, he should play the lottery more often! Once again, he seeks to make a rational substitution and remarks to himself something such as, "This relationship was better than any other I've had; who knows how much better the next one will be. After all, I'm only 26 years old and who knows what will happen by the time I am 40." He notices that he feels a little better about the future, not great by any stretch of the imagination, but things do seem less gloomy now, just as his therapist said it would. Though still hurt and lonely for now, he begins to think about other women who may be interesting to know. John is intelligent enough to notice that this technique can be applied to other kinds of problems in life and the chances of his depression returning after therapy diminish considerably.

The chief theoretical advantage of the cognitive approach is probably its integrative capability. In addition to making mental processes most important to human beings, such as consciousness, the center of the stage, this perspective allows the researcher or therapist to work with more of the person. Since maps and models can always be expanded or modified, the approach also enables its proponents to integrate ideas, research, and findings from other perspectives, especially those from biology and learning theory, in part because they all share a preference for the same hard or naturalistic paradigm. For example, a good map of behavior would include understanding the neurological structure of the organism, the characteristics of its particular environment (including family, society, and culture for human beings), and an individual's learning history, which is to say how the brain and environment interacted over time to produce individual response patterns, some of which are common to the species and some of which are more unique to the individual. Advances in any area, such as in neurobiology, understanding social processes, or new information concerning an individual's history or experience, do not threaten a cognitive view of behavior, because such developments can be used to improve the accuracy of the models and maps used to understand it.

The second major strength of a cognitive approach may be even more important in terms of health care. First, as Fancher (1995) puts it, cognitive therapy is very "practical." It identifies clear problems, offers a step-by-step approach to dealing with them, and is based on logical connections with reality, all of which correspond to many of our cultural preferences. Furthermore, there is a strong empirical case for a cognitive approach to helping behavior that makes it appealing. For example, cognitive therapy has been found to be just as effective for most depressions as the biological approach, and perhaps even more so since relapse rates seem to be lower with cognitive therapy (Clinician's Research Digest, 1999; Nathan & Gorman, 1998; Valenstein, 1998). Similarly, this approach is beginning to show itself as being reasonably effective for other important conditions, with or without biological therapies, such as some anxiety disorders. Finally, the clinical techniques of cognitive therapy are clear and logical enough for almost any therapist to follow, regardless of theoretical background. This characteristic makes the approach an almost ideal one for what is often referred to as manualized psychotherapy, which is favored by managed care. Indeed, with promising science and much academic support behind it, it is no wonder that this perspective is now part of traditional mental health care and is so popular among clinicians today.

Nevertheless, there are limits to cognitive psychology to consider, too. First, it is still reductionistic. It is true that seeing human beings as individually mobile packages of carbon-based hardware and reprogrammable software that is capable of transforming sensory inputs into behavioral outputs in ways that usually conform to socially perceived reality is a very elaborate view of human behavior. However, although this perspective takes us beyond protean tubes and past the capabilities of well-trained animals, we are still reduced, this time to "wet computers." In other words, the problem is that the most fundamentally human characteristics of a human being, such as creativity and free will, become algorithmic "search spaces" and probability-based internal decision making trees, respectively (Dreyfus & Dreyfus, 1986). Second, as with learning theory, adjustment is the goal of treatment and mental health. Once again, the cognitive perspective tends to see the problem as being within the individual, not within society, and that we are supposed to respond to a realistic vision of the world. Such a view runs into interesting theoretical and practical difficulties, however, when it encounters socially constructed realities that are unhealthy or destructive to begin with. For example, a society that encourages people to embrace superficial materialistic and hedonistic values as does our own, rather than deeper but more satisfying ones, may even be a case in point!

THE PSYCHODYNAMIC PERSPECTIVE

The psychodynamic perspective is the first one we encounter on the right side of the continuum and, as such, it is more subjective and less concrete than the others. This view has become so much a part of modern Western culture that I do not need to spend much time explaining its basic orientation. In the interest of saving time, then, let me simply remind us that there are at least two basic ideas which all the schools of thought in this perspective assume, share, and build upon even today. One of them is that of the unconscious. Although there is some debate as to how much of this idea was Freud's and how much of it came from German philosophy just prior to his time, he was the one who presented it as a "dynamic unconscious" (Hunt, 1993, p. 167), meaning that it is characterized by powerful subterranean conflicts that drive human behavior without the benefit of conscious direction. Moreover, he did so at a time when the larger culture was extraordinarily receptive to such a view due to various social and intellectual changes.

Historically, Freud's ideas concerning the unconscious and how it drives behavior became a powerful source of new thoughts and possibilities. As Wolitzky and Eagle would have it, "To a significant extent, the history of theoretical developments in psychoanalysis can be understood as a series of successive reactions to Freudian drive theory, with its emphasis on libidinal and aggressive wishes as the primary motive for behavior" (1997, p. 39). Although there is less general agreement on the next point, Freud's second major contribution involved showing how such drives were transformed by developmental processes, especially those associated with specific ages in a person's life. Once again, the idea of natural, unfolding stages can be traced further back in European philosophy, at least to Rousseau. But it was Freud who tied the two sets of ideas together in a way that explained both normal and abnormal behavior in a consistent fashion.

For a good while the psychoanalytic school was dominant in this perspective, in part, because Freud tolerated few deviations when he was alive. But eventually followers broke away and transformed his ideas into other schools, especially Jungian psychology, ego psychology, and object relations or self-psychology. Today there are relatively few pure psychoanalysts writing or practicing, but there is a large number of people who use modified versions of these ideas to do clinical work. We can collectively refer to them as being "neo-analytic." In this case, Freud's two foundational ideas remain the same, but they have been modified to include more contemporary understandings. For example, where Freud's view of psychological life sees it as involving primarily internal and psychosexual processes, more modern psychodynamic thinkers understand the mind and development as being much more interpersonal and psychosocial in nature. Where Freud envisioned only five stages of development, most of which stopped playing a crucial role by age six or so, Erikson (1985) saw eight (and later nine) occurring throughout the life cycle, with all of them being instrumental in shaping our lives. Similar changes have occurred concerning the way this perspective goes about changing behavior today. Where classical psychoanalysis involved a patient reclining on a couch several times a week, modern psychodynamically oriented therapists face their clients, typically only once a week. Similarly, where the analyst is usually silent and lets the past announce itself indirectly through free associations and dreams, today's psychodynamic psychotherapist is likely to ask questions about the client's history, to more readily invite the client to reflect on various interpretive possibilities, and to play a more active role in helping the person to "work through" the difficulties they find.

This time we see John with a psychodynamic psychotherapist at a local community mental health agency: Fortunately for him, they are willing to accept a lower fee so that he can work on his issues for a longer time than he could otherwise afford. The therapist begins by letting him talk about what he has been through in whatever way is possible for him at the moment, knowing that she may be setting the foundations for a long-term relationship. She offers a judicious combination of support and gentle questioning and he feels that she is accepting of his confusion, pain, and shame. Over time, they begin to explore how this recent loss resembles other losses, and John begins to realize that he is dealing with much more than his recent betrayal and abandonment. Not surprisingly to his therapist, there are certain similarities in the relationship John had with his mother with the one that he had with his wife. He remembers, for instance, when mother "betrayed" him when she began to develop her mental illness when he was a child. For the first time in many years, he recalls how it was to visit mom in the "state hospital," which he was told to never tell anyone about lest they "look down on the family," and then carrying this secret with him into adulthood. Soon, he begins to feel overwhelmed by the fact that the illness had changed her so much. For the first time in years, perhaps ever, John feels the emotional loss of his mother as she changed from the beautiful, intelligent, socially graceful person that a child sees in his or her parent into someone different who appeared confusing by contrast. "Where did she go?" he cries. And then John lets the feelings and questions he has kept bottled up for years flood their way out of his psyche in a torrent of tears. Finally, he also begins to understand how this tragic event affected his father who did his best to struggle with the situation, as well as his mother.

Over time, his therapist gently invites him to think about how this new loss in his life might be a hidden opportunity to deal with an old loss that he no longer has to "repress," because he is no longer as vulnerable as a child. As they talk about the relationship with his mother and with his wife, John begins to realize that he "picked" her for the "wrong" (i.e., neurotic) reasons. For example, where his mother was sensitive and weak, his wife was callous and strong; and where one was faithful to her husband, the other was not. It was as though the marital relationship was based on some form of reaction formation to the parental relationship. In making such insights, he also begins to appreciate that his chances of having a lasting relationship were fairly low until he worked through these issues; that he was doomed to repeat them otherwise. Over the period of a few months of therapy, he begins to accept the loss of the marriage because it makes sense now: Where confusion reigned, there emerges a sense of understanding; and where there was anger, he now feels sadness instead. Most of all, he sees himself as beginning to shed the relational baggage from the past that has limited his interpersonal development until today. Eventually, John begins to realize that his friends have always been a saving grace in his life, giving him some things he should have gotten elsewhere, so he turns to them in his time of grief. Freed of the past, he now notices how Mary always makes him feel good about himself. They always seem to laugh so much and have fun just going to museums. John realizes that he finds much more satisfaction in her sensitive approach to life than he did with the more hedonistic one of his former wife. He realizes that he is not ready for another relationship until he gets a better handle on what he does with them, but he also knows that there is no reason to sit around on the weekends now and thinks about asking her out for the next one.

Freud's contribution was so powerful that his thinking became embedded in the very fabric of the West. Even today, it is easy to find examples of this influence in popular culture, such as the frequent use of Freudian humor in television situation comedies with which most of us have grown up. However, the shine has worn off psychoanalysis, so it is important to focus on what the neo-analysts bring into the next century. Today, the chief strengths of this perspective actually seem to rise out of the limitations of the other perspectives. Instead of focusing on the observable realities of the body, behavior, or mind, for example, the psychodynamic therapist looks in a very different direction: toward the subject and his or her inner life and personal experience. In addition to attending to the subjective world of feelings, emotions, desires, this process of mutual exploration is done "with" the client instead of "to" them, which further differentiates the psychodynamic approach from the others we have seen so far. The process of helping this way is usually much more affective, more interpersonal, and more intimate, for instance, than the other approaches we covered tend to be. The idea is to identify conscious and unconscious conflicts, to understand how their histories may be alive today, and to help the individual wrestle with these slippery problems so that they can reduce the stress they create. Similarly, the psychodynamic perspective is often genuinely concerned with healing such things as the narcissistic wounds created by abandonment, abuse or trauma, and not just helping to solve problems of living (Levin, 1993).

Of course, the major weakness of even modern psychodynamic thinking is just as glaring as it has always been: It is highly subjective and difficult to validate, or as it is sometimes said, "psychodynamic theory explains everything and proves nothing." Indeed, except for a small body of work concerning the unconscious, there is very little empirical support for the major concepts of this approach, and even what evidence might be supportive in this regard can be accounted for just as well, or perhaps even better, by the cognitive notion of subconscious mental processes. Although interpersonal forms of therapy do have decent research support concerning their efficacy, there is no reason to believe that they are so for the reasons psychodynamic theory claims. Finally, the perspective is still reductionistic. Although we no longer resemble worms, rats, or even computers, we exist as some kind of a noble yet tragic beast: We struggle valiantly against our evolutionary animal past by trying to sublimate primitive instincts into meaningful alternatives.

As such, we are capable of creating great works of art or even great cultures—until the dark regions of our collective minds destroy what we've built, like a Greek play.

THE HUMANISTIC APPROACH

As mentioned in chapter 1, the humanistic perspective began as an alternative to the behavioral and psychodynamic views that dominated American social science and mental health care through the 1920s to 1960s or so (Misiak & Sexton, 1973). This "third force," as it became known, is different from all the others in several ways, but especially in terms of its radical insistence on free will as a fundamental and irreducible characteristic of what it is to be human. Such a stance, of course, is absolutely incompatible with the determinism that all the other perspectives have in common. Whether biological, learning, cognitive, or psychodynamic in orientation, the other four perspectives treat human behavior as though it is based entirely on natural laws that act to "produce" behavior in a deterministic fashion. According to these points of view, if we knew how these laws work and how they were active in a given individual's life, then we should be able to predict their behavior at any given point, at least in theory. However, the humanistic response to this type of thinking takes issue with determinism itself. The disagreement would not be based on a rejection of natural laws, because the world and all that is in it must be accountable to them. Rather, the objection is based on the position that the individual brings an additional principle into play when it comes to selecting behavioral outcomes which violates or transcends mere mechanical orderliness no matter how sophisticated it might be: free will.

Of course, humanistic psychology does not understand freedom in a simplistic fashion. We are not, for instance free to flap our arms fast enough to fly or free enough to go back into time and erase the past. Rather, our freedom is always *situated*, which is to say that it is set in a context that is defined by the realities that constitute our current circumstances, and what is possible within such constraints. Yet within this context, we are seen as being truly free to enact whichever possibility we decide upon, regardless of past behavior, thinking, or history. Although, for instance, the past cannot be changed, it is seen as a living history, which is to say that although its events cannot be altered, their meanings can be. It is this fact that allows one to transcend the past and act in new ways, providing one accepts the responsibility for taking an active role in the creation of the future. The humanistic position also acknowledges the fact that people seldom act authentically in regard to their potential freedom, and that instead, they usually choose to simply continue to do what their biological predisposition, learning history, habits of thought, or early childhood experience prompts them to do. However, this tendency to act as though we are determined does not negate freedom in any way, because human freedom involves uncertainty and responsibility, both of which we seek to avoid due to the anxiety they create. Therefore, it is a lack of courage that makes us appear to operate by natural laws of cause and effect: inauthenticity, not our lack of freedom, keeps us prisoner to these masters of behavior.

Another distinguishing central ideal of the humanistic approach involves the ancient Greek axiom of being "true to the self," which takes us way back to the idealism of Socrates and Plato. In other words, we all have an inner self that motivates us to transcend our current realities no matter what they may be, in order to reach higher (i.e., more complex, integrated, and sophisticated) levels of consciousness and behavior. Carl Rogers called this essential aspect of being human the "growth tendency" and sometimes characterized it in terms of his "homely analogy" of a potato left in a basement with only one small window for light (1977, p. 8). Yet one day he came down to the cellar and saw that in spite of overwhelming odds, the plant sprouted toward the light in an attempt to reach for the sky. Maslow conceived of this fundamental human drive in terms of an orderly process called self-actualization that included a hierarchy of relatively clear stages of human development, with each one being freer than the previous one. Both of them understood the development of the self as a key psychological process that never stops; it is something that is rooted in the human spirit that is shared by us all. Consequently, humanistic social science believes that it is possible to use the methods of science to study the "farthest reaches of human nature" (Maslow, 1971). Indeed, they would maintain that any approach that does not investigate this aspect of human behavior could never hope to be comprehensive in its knowledge or application, because this part of being human is the most distinguishing and important one.

As before, there are many theoretical variations of these and related ideas in this perspective. One crucial issue in this perspective seems to be just how far psychology should go in terms of the mind-spirit dilemma we examined in chapter 1. On the one hand, there are those who focus on understanding traditional psychological phenomena such as emotional states, individual behavior, social interactions, and so forth. They may even be willing to accept the fact that people experience things that they describe and understand as transcendent. However, such humanistic social scientists usually suspend the question of whether or not such things "really exist." Instead, the focus is on using scientific inquiry to understand the experience, how the experience is structured and what it means for the individual. Although Rogers and Maslow would likely be sympathetic to this position, phenomenological psychology is probably the most rigorous school of this kind of humanistic thought.

Phenomenological research, contrary to some opinion, is not "antiscientific" (Giorgi, 1971). Indeed, phenomenological social scientists investigate human behavior using the scientific method: This kind of research begins with data (in this case the data of human experience), requires a methodical or step-by-step analysis of that data, and involves clear documentation of those processes so that others can duplicate them and by doing so confirm or question the results. A key difference between phenomenological investigation and traditional social science does occur, however, in terms of their respective goals. As we have seen time and time again, traditional research seeks understanding by reducing a given human phenomenon to its components, which ultimately enables it to manipulate them in order to control behavior. However, the phenomenologist's goal is to let "that which shows itself be seen from itself in the very way in which it shows itself from itself" (Heidegger, 1927/1962, p. 58), which is almost the opposite process. Here the research is on how a given experience or phenomenon is structured and lived out experientially. Understanding takes place through identifying the components of an experience, but does not stop there like an experiment does. Instead, the phenomenologist must also describe how the various components of a situation interact with each other to result in meaningful experience for the individual and for other people who have similar experiences. This level of understanding is often referred to as the "general" or "fundamental" structure of a human situation, experience, or phenomenon (Giorgi, 1971; Mruk, 1994). In other words while experimentation is the best way to break something down into its parts, meaning can only be understood through a more complete form of description (Jackson, 1984).

On the other hand, the school of transpersonal psychology goes a step further than phenomenologists are typically willing to take and in so doing distinguishes itself in two important ways. First, whereas phenomenological social science is interested in any type of human experience or behavior, transpersonal social scientists and practitioners are primarily concerned with one class of them: Those that transcend the individual person.

The word *transpersonal* simply means "personal plus." That is, the transpersonal orientation explicitly and carefully includes all the facets of personal psychology and psychiatry, then *adds* those deeper or higher aspects of human experience that transcend the ordinary and the average—experiences that are, in other words, "transpersonal" or "more than personal," personal plus. Thus, in the attempt to more fully, accurately, and scientifically reflect the entire range of human experience, transpersonal psychiatry and psychology take as their starting point the entire spectrum of consciousness. (Wilber, 1996, p. xviii)

Next, by being open to the entire range of human experience, the transpersonal school also sees many aspects of behavior in different ways than do those who do not include a transpersonal dimension to behavior.

Transpersonal psychiatry, therefore, is psychiatry that seeks to foster development, correct developmental arrests, and heal trauma at all levels of development, including transpersonal levels. It extends the standard biopsychosocial model of psychiatry to a biopsychosocial-spiritual one in which the later stages of human development are concerned with development beyond, or transcendence of, the individual. . . . *Transpersonal experience*, in addressing all human experience beyond the ego level, includes spiritual experiences but also includes embodied human experience of higher levels. (Scotten, 1996, p. 4)

Traditional approaches do not give such transcendental matters the same degree of concern, let alone validity. For instance, it is possible to understand this class of experience from the other perspectives, but in so doing the meaning of the experience is always reduced to basic components, such as brain chemistry gone awry, socially prescribed trance states, perceptual oddities, unconscious longings for a Freudian "oceanic feeling," and so forth. Even the phenomenological school is only willing to go as far as saying that such phenomena have important personal meanings for the individual or social meanings for the group. Transpersonal social science, by contrast, is very much interested in such possibilities, especially at the highest levels. Unfortunately, however, this openness comes at a certain cost: it is the "softest of the soft" in terms of both data and conclusions.

Now, we find John talking with a humanistic therapist. Although she is not sure whether she is phenomenologically or transpersonally oriented in her own thinking about human behavior and how to change it, she always is "client-centered" in her approach. This means that more subtle scientific and philosophical questions are suspended in the service of being fully present to her client and learning about him, particularly how he experiences the world and life from his frame of reference as a unique individual. Always addressing him in a mode of compassion, but not necessarily always agreeing with him even in the sessions, they talk about his pain and how he understands what he is going through in the "here and now." Together, they both come to understand that what John is experiencing at the deepest, most intensely personal level is a loss of meaning. His basic view of reality, which seems to have been based on such ideas as fairness, hard work, getting ahead, and loyalty have been shattered, first by the way that life treated his mother (becoming chronically ill, dying early, and so forth) and then by his wife (her betrayal of him and the spiritual ideals they both professed). He now realizes that he doesn't understand very much at all about how life works, how to see others, or even how to live his own life: "It wasn't supposed to be this way," he laments, "I tried to do everything right, it's all so unfair." For a moment, client and therapist share this pain and at least John feels that he is no longer alone.

Slowly, practicing all the regular therapeutic principles of building rapport, timing, and confrontation, the therapist invites John to consider other possibilities, too. "Yes," she says, "life is unfair to people sometimes, what do you think that means when negative events happen to decent people?" Together, they begin to explore his understandings of the world, what it means to believe in happy endings and simple truths, and how he may not have been so innocent in the decline of the marital relationship, although he cannot be responsible for the actions of another. Now that the theme of responsibility has emerged in a nonthreatening way, client and therapist begin to look at his life as a series of choices, actions, and consequences leading to more choices and so on. John begins to see that, since he never really learned much about himself, he couldn't make very good decisions about with whom to get involved or whom to avoid. He now begins to understand that certain values, like fidelity, are important to him, which means that a more responsible way of selecting potential partners might be to look for such values in them before considering other, less important characteristics. He also comes to realize that he does not do well with responsibility and seeks to blame things on others, which probably makes him difficult to stay in a relationship with for most people.

Eventually, John realizes he has a choice to make: He can either do something about knowing himself better and about accepting more responsibility for his life—or not. He knows that the latter position seems to have led to a dead end, but does not know what the former will bring except that it offers new possibilities. He is cautious, but as a result of his being accepted so unconditionally by the therapist, he knows that he is not a "bad" person, a "reject" or "a loser," as he once felt. Their mutual journey has also shown him that there are other things in life that he values: For instance, his work gives him meaning. Thus, he decides to enhance it by doing some volunteer activities with people who need some help, some of whom are also women near his age. "It won't be easy," he says, "but I do feel more in touch with myself now and maybe that means I can make better choices in the future." Even though he is lonely, he knows that life is what we make of it, today and tomorrow.

Like the psychodynamic point of view, the chief strength of the humanistic perspective is that it focuses on the individual. But this time, there is absolutely nothing reductionistic about it. The humanistic psychologist recognizes the unique characteristics of any particular person, accepts them, and embraces the other's essential humanity, the humanity we all share and can cherish regardless of how different people may appear to us in other ways. Thus, the humanistic therapist engages the other in the mode of authentic encounter that creates a relationship based on meaning, not technique. Neither one is concerned with eradicating an illness, fixing a problem, creating a more rational view of the world, or mucking through the past. Instead, they focus on discovering value, perceiving possibilities, making better choices, and taking responsibility for the direction of one's life. From this point of view, we are never only large worms, smart rats, wet computers, or noble beasts: instead, we are human beings, first, foremost, and always.

Unfortunately, there are two major problems with this perspective, too. First, it suffers the same difficulties with empirical support as psychoanalysis does: It is very hard to prove much about these ideas, and the transpersonal possibilities might even be out of the realm of a scientific view by definition, making it the most extreme theoretical position on the continuum. Second, in taking that final step, the transpersonal position actually moves us back to the beginning in a certain important way. For once again, we encounter the paradox found in chapter 1. Even within the humanistic perspective, which lies at the farthest ends of the scientific continuum, the problem is curiously familiar: The school of phenomenological psychology embraces consciousness or "mind" as being essential to a real, complete, or holistic understanding of the person, but does not need to deal with "higher levels" of transcendence other than to acknowledge that people describe such experiences and sometimes find them meaningful. However, the transpersonal school is holistic in the fullest sense possible, which means that it might be able to consider more possibilities of perception, experience, and behavior. Yet the evidence for such reified phenomenon is always very questionable to the scientific method, even as it is used by most phenomenologists. Apparently it is true that, as was said at the beginning of this chapter, psychology cannot escape philosophy and the paradox is still with us even here.

ZEN AND THE TRADITIONAL PERSPECTIVES

Those of us who were trained only in the methods of the traditional psychotherapies often have a difficult time accepting Zen as a legitimate approach to helping and healing others, or at least may feel put off by it upon first encounter. There are many reasons for such a reaction, most of which I have experienced myself: Zen can seem too different, too foreign, too religious, too philosophical, or, most of all, too unscientific to merit serious research, academic, or clinical attention. One of the main reasons for conducting the investigation of the therapeutic continuum we just completed is to address these concerns. For as surprising as it may have seemed initially, we now see that there actually seems to be a legitimate theoretical context for Zen in traditional mental health care. Providing that we keep the idea of Zen as a middle path clearly in mind, it is compatible with the humanistic perspective in at least six important ways.

First, like the humanistic perspective, Zen's search for truth is more Socratic or Platonic than Aristotelian, more ideal than real, more mind than matter centered. In other words, both approaches are oriented more toward a search for higher personal "truth" than objective facts or socially constructed realities, which places them at the soft end of the continuum. Second, both disciplines are insight oriented and make use of the here and now instead of just the past. For example, where humanistic therapy helps individuals "get in touch with themselves" through exploring the richness of immediate experience, Zen encourages people to do that through meditation and personal reflection. Third, both orientations aim at personal liberation. On the one hand, for instance, humanistic therapy frees the person from being a prisoner to the past or to inauthentic decision-making by encouraging him or her to exercise their free will through taking responsibility for their decisions. On the other, Zen masters help to liberate their students from the suffering caused by attachment to seductive or deceptive illusions by accepting pain instead of avoiding it. Similarly, both pathways to freedom require the individual to grow by increasing personal awareness, facing inner fears, and transcending challenges whenever they emerge.

Fourth, both humanistic psychotherapy and the practice of Zen are intensely interpersonal processes. Where the former emphasized honest and open communication in a client-centered fashion, for instance, the latter often occurs between student and teacher, which can be described as being "learner-centered." In each case, attending to the other, listening to them empathically, and engaging upon honest dialogue or occasional instruction are all exchanged in a mode of nonattached caring. Fifth, personal growth is a teleological process in either framework, which is to say that it is directional, not random: Development tends to go somewhere over time. More specifically, there is an "upward" direction to this movement in that growth is seen as a never-ending process that steadily moves toward higher, more integrated levels of experience, understanding, and behavior. Sixth, these two approaches are concerned with some form of transcendence in that both the humanistic psychotherapist and the Zen master believe that it is always possible for persons to rise above themselves at any moment. This process is also seen as being absolutely essential to physical, psychological, social, and spiritual (however one defines that term) health.

In addition to this basic compatibility of frameworks, there are many more similarities between Zen and the humanistic perspective if we would compare it to the transpersonal school. In this case, for instance, we might look at the openness to different modes of consciousness that can be of interest to both. However, there is no need to go that far because we are simply trying to determine whether there is a place for Zen in traditional approaches to helping and healing, or not. For it is very clear that we have an answer to our question of whether or not there is a place for Zen in the traditional continuum of scientific approaches: It is "Yes," there is. Not only is the Middle Path compatible with several basic humanistic concepts, but it also does not have to be off the traditional therapeutic chart, so to speak, providing we do not stray too far from the balance this form of Zen offers.

To finish our case study, which actually turns out to be a real person Joan or I know, we now find that things have not gone well for some time now. Both John and his traditionally trained therapist feel that their work together is not progressing satisfactorily no matter what they try. John continues to be depressed about his losses, worries that he cannot afford the sessions much longer, thinks that he is a loser even in a therapeutic relationship, and even seems to be beginning to become visibly angry. In fact, his daily experience now includes feelings of worthlessness and obsessive ruminations. For example, he often remembers one of the last conversations he had with his wife, where he told her that he had thoughts about suicide and how she said, "Well, that's one solution!" His anger knots up his stomach and spills over into his relationships with others in the form of constant complaints about this, that, and other things, too. The therapist is becoming frustrated, and worried, as well.

She could move on to medications or, if she has been using them as an adjunct to treatment, to a higher dose. However, that might either interfere with John's academic performance or create a greater sense of hopelessness and low self-esteem, because he might interpret medication as signifying that he is "defective," just as his ex-wife often implied, so his therapist does not pursue this path. Further, his constant comparison between new relational possibilities and what he thinks he had before makes his attempt to modify dating behavior a continual disaster. Although he sees the logical faults in these ruminations, he seems to engage in the kind of "emotional reasoning"

(Burns, 1980) that renders cognitive therapy less effective, because his feelings keep starting up the negative cycles faster than he can break them. And whenever she interprets the loss of his wife in regard to his earlier losses, he seems to become even more depressed, so she is reluctant to allow him to regress further. In other words, John and his therapist reach one of the issues we talked about in chapter 1: a classical therapeutic impasse.

Now it is time to see what, if anything, Zen has to offer. Since Joan actually practices this approach, we can depart from the format I have used so far with John and ask her what she might do in such a situation.

Joan: If someone came in talking about losses and such, I would have the person talk with me, and I would really want to *hear* him. I see him as a person who is suffering. I could not tell him that "I am listening," but I think that in my sorrow for him, I would grasp the pain and the loss so that as I listen to him, something would come up. I don't know what it would be before it happens, but I trust that something would come up so that a connection would be there and then the person would know he was not alone, that his words are more than words; that his story is a story, but more than a story: It is his heart being cracked open, or being closed up as the case may really be, because he is closing himself off to the future by staying attached to the past and to his pain.

I would have a very deep connection with this person so that he would know that I am there with him, suffering with him, though not in a neurotic or unhealthy way. I would realize that he would have to go through what he would have to go through to be healed from this pain. He has reason to cry and I would help him find a way to not be afraid of being a human being with his sorrow, with his suffering. There is no one way to suffer, so I would honor him in his suffering in any form that it may take, because he is conveying something from his heart. I would honor not just his loss, but what took place prior to that loss, too, such as the relationship he had with his wife and mother. It is almost like painting a picture of the significance of this relationship for the person and the sorrow connected with the loss of not being able to go back and redo something. I would try to provide an environment that is totally filled with compassion, with love, with understanding.

It is hard for me to say what I would do without being there because I wouldn't know what I was going to do until I was there, but I would want to know about some things, such as what happened and the extent of the sorrow. I want to know about these things to give him the opportunity to open his heart up all the way, to crack it wide open, to let all of the sorrow come out, to not be afraid to experience all of the feelings in their richness and depth, so that he can learn about life from them. That is what I have learned to do: provide a circumstance where people who are overwhelmed by their feelings are not afraid to have them. Something happens in that moment, they are no longer afraid when that happens. I think a lot of the problem he is having is connected with fear, with a fear of being exposed to himself that comes with such questions as what has this loss meant to him, whether it means he is weak, whether he should cry, whether he deserved it, and so forth.

I would also want to know about the fear that is connected to the sorrow, so that it could be accepted. When a person really opens up their heart, they open up to the rest of their life. Maybe the fear is about losing a part of the self that is not even connected with the mom, or wife. But loss can be a catalyst that brings the fear to the surface. I have often thought about that in relation to trauma: It is a catalyst that can become a blessing, even though the loss is severe. It could be an opportunity for someone to open up to themselves and to all their pain. Being open to such suffering, in turn, can lead to cessation. It is not a technique that allows this to happen, but the truth. I hope when I talk with people, fearlessness is a part of the process; that we both open more to *life*. That is my hope, but not an expectation, that no matter what it is, whether it is loss, an addiction, whatever, that the person will see that through that suffering something wonderful has taken place, that life is more open because of it. Sometimes I have even said to people who have been severely hurt by others, "You should write them a 'Thank-You' note!" Of course, I only do that when they come to realize that the event can, is beginning to, or has changed their whole life for the better!

At first John feels put off by this suggestion, but it is *Joan* saying it, not some "therapist." For a moment or two, he wonders if there might be another way of looking at his pain and the recent events that caused it. In his connection with Joan, it occurs to him that feelings come and go, and that the going of feelings can be just as important as their coming, providing one does not interfere with that process. He sees that there is a "lesson" here and shares this understanding with Joan. Sensing that they have reached an important junction in their work, she begins to explore the themes of suffering, attachment, and acceptance with him more fully by simply asking him about them like she would anyone for whom she cares. She notices that by the end of the session he seems more relaxed than usual, not happy by any stretch of the imagination, but more at ease in his body and voice.

Although nothing dramatic seems to occur on the outside, both individuals are aware that something important has occurred. As they say good-bye that day, Joan finds herself looking forward to the next session, feeling more confident in her sense of who John is and what is going on in him. John begins to think about endings and beginnings and finds that in doing so he is able to let images of his ex-wife come into his mind and pass out with greater ease than before, not much to be sure, but at least he does not dwell on the pain they generate as much as usual. Experiencing on his own that this or that image or thought will "pass" if it is not fought against so hard gives him a new tool to cope with his suffering. He begins to look forward to sharing this insight at his next session, now seeing Joan as a fellow traveler as well as a mental health professional.

Of course, we will have to wait until chapter 4 to see how Joan actually brings Zen to her work through various clinical examples, but even here we can see some differences between Zen and the traditional approaches, even the humanistic one. Perhaps the most important one is that the Middle Path does not lock us into the paradox between idealism and realism that the others do. The question of whether Zen is to be used to help us transcend life's difficulties and grow in meaningful ways or whether it should be seen as a genuinely transpersonal pathway to transcend difficulty based on a metaphysical understanding of spirituality is meaningless here. As we will see with a story of the student asking the master whether there is a "real" self or not, the Middle Path allows us to accept either possibility without, as it were, worrying about it in theory or in practice.

But there is a more subtle issue to consider. Those who practice Zen as more than a complementary approach may become more committed to it over time, perhaps even to the extent that, like Joan, it becomes more of an alternative than complementary approach. For instance, the practice of meditation may start out simply as a way of helping to relieve stress or assisting in reflection. But, like regular physical exercise, prolonged practice seems to take the individual to quantitatively and qualitatively higher levels of ability and performance. Sometimes the process of meditation becomes increasingly more important and more central to an individual's life in a way so that it generates changes in values, attitudes, and life-style. Eventually, the individual may even become more Zen-like over time and adopt this orientation as his or her primary one, instead of just using it in a complementary fashion. We will return to these possibilities in chapter 5 when we try to integrate the two approaches and discuss how that can be done in traditional academic and training programs as well as clinically.

A WORD ABOUT THEORETICAL
AND INTERDISCIPLINARY OVERLAP

Most behavioral scientists and practitioners are familiar with the five perspectives in one way or another, and many will notice that I left out a discussion of at least two important technical points. One concerns the fact that some very important therapeutic modalities were not mentioned. Family therapy and narrative therapy are probably the two major ones, but there are others. The reason for this omission is twofold. First, the goal in presenting the major perspectives was to provide a context for Zen as a complementary therapy, not to offer a comprehensive review of the entire mental health spectrum. For those who are interested in greater details about the development of the major perspectives and how they relate to each other, I strongly recommend the works by Fancher (1995), Hunt (1993), and Wachtel and Messer (1997) that I have cited frequently. Second, certain important therapeutic approaches, including the two just mentioned, can be used by different perspectives in different ways. For instance, family therapy can be done from a social learning, cognitive, or psychodynamic perspective, depending on whether one emphasizes focusing on systems of interpersonal interaction, information processing and communication patterns, or unconscious conflicts, respectively (Wachtel & Messer, 1997). Similarly, both psychodynamic and cognitive therapists can use narrative techniques, such as is the case with Lacanian analysis or constructionist therapies. In other words, it is how a particular therapy or technique is used that counts, not its name, and identifying all of them are not central to our work.

Another kind of overlap that needs to be briefly addressed concerns the fact that there are a number of theoretical positions which "blend" perspectives together. Probably the most common example of this phenomenon is what is usually called "cognitive-behavioral therapy," where acquired patterns of behavior (learning theory) and acquired patterns of thinking (cognitive theory) are both addressed in order to understand or change behavior. But other combinations occur, too, such as the one we briefly encountered concerning Bandura's Social Learning Theory, which was originally very much a part of the learning perspective and is now called Social Cognitive Learning Theory, because of a new emphasis he places on cognitive processes. A similar issue can occur when a new school emerges in an old perspective. The so-called sociocultural position (Rathus, 1999) is a good example to illustrate this variation of the theme. Should this new point of view in social science be seen largely as an extension of learning theory that simply emphasizes the role of culture? Or is it a genuinely different new perspective on human behavior as several undergraduate textbooks present it? Clearly, one could argue a reasonable case for either position in regard to all three cases just described. However, it is necessary to remember that, although these are fascinating questions to those of us who are concerned with theory, they are not particularly relevant for our purposes: For we are concerned with how Zen stands in relation to the traditional mental health care picture in general, which means dealing with the perspectives and not all their particular variants or combinations. After all, they are just smaller manifestations of the larger views.

Before moving on to asking Joan questions about applying Zen in the clinical setting, a final issue inevitably occurs as we move from theory to practice. In exploring the major theoretical perspectives that dominate traditional mental health care, we sometimes referred to them as cultures of helping or healing. As such, each traditional approach gives rise to various mental health professions and relatively distinct disciplines within them, each of which offers a way of understanding, diagnosing, and treating mental disorders and other problems of living. Like societies, each approach has its own core set of values as to what constitutes the "good" life, or a particular version of mental health as well as illness. Like cultures, each one also possesses a particular technical language that divides people into in-groups and out-groups depending on whether they have been trained in it or not. Similarly, each of them sanctions or licenses some behaviors in the form of acceptable practices and offers this "product" to the larger academic, social, and professional marketplace, which includes patients, students, administrators, and funding sources, too.

To continue Fancher's metaphor, we can also see that, like cultures, becoming a member of a mental health profession or particular discipline within one involves processes of socialization: We enter our particular perspective or professional group with the naïveté of a novice; we learn what our elders pass on to us as worthy; we practice sacred rituals until we do them automatically; we undergo various rites of passage certifying us as citizens of this or that particular community; and finally, we proselytize our values and views to anyone who wishes to consider them, especially those who are in our offices or classrooms. These individuals, in turn, are sometimes socialized into the culture as new citizens and the cycle begins once again.

Sometimes the lengthy process of professional socialization begins in very elaborate, well structured, and heavily supported programs, such as medical school. At other times the path is much less formal, as in the case of a substance abuse counselor who has "been there" and dealt with the issue of addiction through personal experience before helping others. But each culture of healing has its own "high priests" (e.g., leading biologists or Big Books), sacred values (e.g., homeostasis or abstinence), exclusive initiation processes (e.g., medical school or personal recovery) and privileged practices (e.g., medications or 12-steps). Although we may not become completely socialized, all of us go through the process and most of us begin our work as representing, if not defending, one culture of healing or another. Finally, each society of like-minded researchers, educators, and clinicians continues to expand until it meets resistance from competing groups, at which point conflict invariably occurs.

In researching this chapter, I was disappointed to find that, as a field, we have a very good sense of our theoretical preferences and technical orientations, but that we generally fail to address the more competitive interdisciplinary issues outside of trade newspapers, closed meeting doors, or, upon occasion, court rooms. There simply does not seem to be much open discussion about the conflicts between the traditional cultures of healing in professional journals or in clinical training texts. Yet, such conflict occurs in spite of the well-known facts that most research on the topic of the effectiveness of the various mental health professionals clearly indicates that the particular discipline of a given clinician does not seem to matter greatly in terms of client satisfaction (Consumer Reports, 1995), or that the major traditional approaches to therapy often appear to be relatively equal in terms of their general effectiveness for most types of disorders, as I mentioned with depression in chapter 1. Indeed, even the more biologically based conditions fare better in their treatment when medications are combined with other kinds of support.

Fortunately, except for the "true believers" of a given culture of healing, most of us who practice probably end up being much more eclectic in our orientation than we were at the beginning of our careers. Time and experience soon show us that, in our work, whatever we were taught in school was inadequate to the tasks that face us in the "real world." The simple facts of the matter are that human life is simply too complex for one perspective or discipline to grasp and that our work often requires us to find ways of getting along with others who hold views different from our own so that we may be more helpful to our clients. As we shall see, just as we found that there is room for Zen at the theoretical context of our field, we may also find that the 10 concepts and principles may be helpful in terms of the interdisciplinary aspects of our work. If so, then we might want to rethink some of our academic, clinical training, and supervision practices, which is an important topic both Joan and I will address together in the last chapter of this book.

CHAPTER **4**

Practical Applications: Zen in the Clinical Setting

So far, we have examined the contemporary movement toward complementary and alternative psychotherapies, considered Zen and its major concepts as an example of a nontraditional approach, and explored the ways in which Zen stands in relation to traditional approaches. Now it is time to consider the use of Zen in our work as helpers and healers. In keeping with our format of alternating voices, Joan speaks as the primary author of this chapter. Chris will ask her questions that a traditionally trained or oriented psychotherapist might inquire of Zen's basic teachings and how to apply them to clinical work. We used two criteria in selecting these questions. First, we tried to identify issues that might need to be addressed for practitioners of traditional methods before they could even begin to consider whether or not Zen is something that would be beneficial to their work. Second, we attempted to address practical questions that those who are interested in expanding their clinical horizons in this direction might need to know about in order to begin to incorporate Zen techniques in their work. These questions tend to focus on how Zen may be helpful with certain clinical populations, how Zen may help the therapist minimize various occupational hazards such as burnout, and how Zen may help when facing other practical problems, such as dealing with colleagues, supervisors, and administrative policies.

QUESTION 1: MEDITATION REVISITED

C: Joan, can you talk to us about why meditation is so important in Zen and how it can help with therapy? At one time in my early adulthood, I explored

Transcendental Meditation as well as a few alternative philosophies. In general, I found that although meditation was physically relaxing, it didn't seem to take me anywhere in terms of improving my perceptual, cognitive, or empathic abilities. Part of the problem seemed to be that I was just doing it because I was told that it was going to be helpful, but I really didn't understand why or what to expect from meditation, so I gave it up.

J: Chris, let me begin with an ancient story about the Buddha. Epstein (1998, p. 56) tells a story about a man called Angulimala that I think describes the real meaning of meditation. Let me paraphrase it for you. This individual was a rugged bandit that all the countrymen feared. He had a habit of cutting off the fingers of the people he murdered and wearing them as a garland around his neck. The Buddha's devotees pleaded with him not to go to the area where this man might be. But the Buddha disregarded the pleas of his students and set out to walk in the direction of this notorious person. According to the story, Angulimala saw him from a distance and pursued him. However, the bandit was unable to catch up to the Buddha because of the extraordinary power he possessed. Angulimala became so frustrated at not being able to catch the Buddha he shouted out to him, "Stop!"

The Buddha continued to walk and called back, "I have stopped, Angulimala, you stop too." This response confused Angulimala because the Buddha was still walking, not stopping as he had said. "When I have stopped, you say I have not stopped. Yet when you say you have stopped, it looks to me as though you have not. I am puzzled by your words. How is it that you have stopped and I have not?" At this point the Buddha turned the full intensity of his divine attention directly into Angulimala's eyes and captured his full attention. Then, the Buddha explained that he had indeed stopped, stopped creating suffering for himself, while it was clear that Angulimala was not only inflicting the worst kinds of suffering on his victims, but also on himself. As the Buddha continued to share his wisdom, Angulimala became one his most devoted followers, which is expressed by Shakyamuni Buddha in the phrase, *"Suffering I teach—and the way out of suffering"* (Farrer-Hall, 2000, p. 14).

The point of this story for our purposes is that the Buddha was teaching his newly found pupil that by "stopping" our mind through meditation, we have the opportunity to become familiar with it and how it works. Through the process of stilling the mind in this way, we become more able to have insights into our emotions, thoughts, and behaviors, as well as how they are connected to each other. In meditation, which is the process of quieting the mind, we become more aware of its repetitive nature, which is to say that we come to develop an awareness of the habits of thought and perception that keep us trapped in our suffering. The marvelous movie *Groundhog Day* (Ramis, 1993) depicts this kind of being trapped by ourselves in another way. For those who are unfamiliar with the story, the protagonist was doomed to repeat his life again and again and again, until he got it right, until he liberated himself from the habits of mind that trapped him in his own hell. Not only did he become happier when he found out how he imprisoned himself, but he also became involved in helping others be happy. Or, as Jack Kornfield said in his tape *Meditations of the Heart,*

> So the work that we do on ourselves is the work that we do for someone else; it's the same work. Now the art of meditation is to turn your difficulties into the path. It is not that your difficulties are obstacles to get over so that then you can be spiritual. Forget it, you know when things are groovy it's fine to be spiritual. Yes, very easy, peaceful and very fine, it's in the difficulties that the heart becomes liberated and awakened; it is in those very places. (1994)

Something seems to happen when a person practices meditation regularly: We find that meditation is liberating because it involves a realization of truth. "The only way we can find peace in our own hearts, find the pathway that leads to liberation, is by changing ourselves, not by changing the world" (Farrer-Halls, 2000, p. 110). In addition to creating insights, then, meditation also helps us change ourselves by freeing ourselves from our attachments, and therefore, from suffering. Thus, meditation is important because it both helps us learn and helps us walk the Eightfold Path to freedom. Of course, it is important to remember that the path of Zen takes a lifetime: Meditation is not a "quick fix." Like anything else that is worthwhile, it is a slow process and takes time to learn to do well. However, that should not be a deterrent because the same is true with many other things in life, such as becoming a good musician, an athlete, or a therapist.

Earlier I shared a clinical story about a man who quieted his mind by sitting outside with his chickens. Hearing the clucking of the chickens and listening to the sounds of these two-legged animals calmed his mind and relieved the anxiety he was experiencing at that time. In my mind's eye I can visualize Tom doing what may be called a "walking meditation" with the chickens. I can see him following them slowly, with his head bowed slightly, and his palms gently pressed together, concentrating on the next step he is about to take on the ground before him and nothing more. On second thought, maybe he wasn't following the chickens at all—maybe they were following him! The details about the walking don't matter, as long as the walking was good. The same holds true for the way I have been taught to understand meditation, though I know that other approaches to Zen place much more emphasis on correct form, degrees of mastery, and so forth. However, it may be more important to select an approach that works for you than it is for you to follow a particular approach.

Another story that makes this point involves a woman with whom I was working who had great anxiety talking about her mother. She even had trouble sitting still in her chair when this topic came up. One time, I noticed I could barely detect her breathing. I usually don't suggest to a client the possible usefulness of meditation unless they ask, but I do talk about the value of quieting the mind from time to time. I thought it might help Rebecca talk about her mother if we sat quietly in the room, closed our eyes, placed our hands in our laps, and did some breathing together. I suggested that she concentrate on the feelings of the air coming in and going out of her nostrils, to be aware of the physical sensations the process of breathing creates. She was a bit reluctant to do this with me at first, but agreed to try once she knew she could stop at any time. We sat together using this simple breathing technique for about ten minutes when she began to cry. She cried quietly at first, but then began sobbing. I felt her despair as I listened to her pain. Rebecca's body was bent over in so much anguish that her head touched her knees. I allowed her to continue until she stopped on her own.

Then, we sat for a while and digested the moment in a gentle way. When Rebecca began to talk about her mother again her demeanor was different. She sat quietly, talked softly, and expressed in a heartfelt manner how much she missed her mother and longed to have a relationship with her. After that session, whenever Rebecca felt tense and agitated, we would stop for a moment to create and to use this "quiet time," so that she could become conscious of her thoughts, which allowed her to talk more clearly about what was troubling her. As the Dalai Lama says it,

> Similarly, when you are able to stop your mind from chasing sensory objects and thinking about the past and future and so on, and when you can free your mind from being totally "blanked out" as well, then you will begin to see underneath this turbulence of the thought processes. There is an underlying stillness, an underlying clarity of the mind. You should try to observe or experience this. (Dalai Lama & Cutler, 1998, p. 313)

Unfortunately, sometimes therapists and others labor under the impression that they must meditate like clockwork and in a certain prescribed way. Epstein describes a patient who had very little time for meditation and addressed the issue this way: "I explained to her that meditation need not be done exclusively in a silent environment or in a cross-legged position, that the Buddha had taught mediation in four postures; sitting, lying down, walking, and standing. The idea was to develop awareness of bodily experience or, at first, to develop awareness of how little awareness there was of bodily experience" (1998, p. 107). The point is that one is free to meditate in a style that works for them as an individual. But there are other benefits to meditation as well. For example, in addition to helping the therapist be more fully present to the client by clearing the mind, meditation also helps the therapist deal with such things as countertransference. Although complex, becoming free of this form of attachment is just as much a part of meditation and the Eightfold Path as any other, which means that the therapist can learn from it, too. Of course, these benefits do not even include the physiological and stress-reduction benefits of meditation that are so well documented today.

QUESTION 2: USING ZEN AND PRACTICING A TRADITIONAL RELIGIOUS FAITH

C: Given the climate of the day, Joan, what can you say about incorporating Zen into their work for those who are Roman Catholic, Jewish, Christian, Muslim, or Agnostic? Naturally, I am not talking about integrating Zen with any fundamentalist approach to religion, because the Middle Path warns against the dangers of extreme positions at the outset. Rather, is there any way I can still practice one of these faiths as most people who believe in them do, and still use these teachings in my work?

J: There are two points to keep in mind about Zen and religion in regard to this question, Chris. First, although Zen can be adopted and understood as a religion or as a philosophy, our approach to the teachings is based on the Middle Path, which means "to avoid two extremes of self-indulgence and self-mortification or, in more contemporary terms, of idealization and denial" (Epstein, 1995, p. 91). The second is that there are many points of compatibility between the teachings of the Buddha and major world religions. For example, there are many books written about the similarities of the Buddha's teachings and Christ's teachings. The highly respected Vietnamese Zen master Nhat Hanh (1998) has written two of them.

Another example concerns how Buddhism and Judaism can be combined. In the book, *That's Funny, You Don't Look Buddhist*, Sylvia Boorstein, who is a psychotherapist that teaches mindfulness and who leads workshops all across the country, explains how the teachings deepened her Judaism through meditation practice.

> I am a prayerful, devout Jew because I am a Buddhist. As the meditation practice that I learned from Buddhist teachers made me less fearful and allowed me to fall

in love with life, I discovered that the prayer language of "thank-you" that I knew from my childhood returned, spontaneously and to my great delight. (1997, p. 5)

Similarly, one of my first Zen "teachers," Shunryu Suzuki, makes it clear that zazen (sitting meditation), "has nothing to do with some particular religious belief. And for you, there is no need to hesitate to practice our way, because it has nothing to do with Christianity or Shintoism or Hinduism. Our practice is for everyone" (Suzuki, 1970, p. 76). He feels there is no need to be concerned with whatever religion you believe in and there is no need to compare Buddhism with any religion. All that he is interested in is to practice with a pure mind. Finally, there are those in Zen such as Neem Karoli Baba, the beloved guru of Ram Dass Maharaji, who honors the purity of spirit, no matter what the tradition or lineage. Baba draws us back from our concerns about individual differences, back beyond the forms, with his oft-reiterated remark, "Sub Ek (All one)" (Das, 1997, p. 345)!

> All religions are the same; they all lead to God. God is everybody. . . . The same blood flows through us all, the arms, the legs, the heart, all are the same. See no difference, see all the same. (Dass, 1979, p. 354)

The World Community sponsors the John Main Seminar, which is held at Middlesex University, London, for Christian meditation in memory of John Main, the Irish Benedictine monk who taught meditation. In 1994 the Dalai Lama was asked to participate. "The famous religious historian Paul Tillich said that from the meeting of Christianity and Buddhism would come a spiritual revolution. Perhaps he was right" (Bstan-dzin-rgya-mtsho, 1996, p. 175). The Dalai Lama has also helped to distinguish the difference between spirituality and religion in other work. "I believe that it is essential to appreciate our potential as human beings and recognize the importance of inner transformation. This should be achieved through what could be called a process of mental development. Sometimes, I call this having a spiritual dimension in our life" (Dalai Lama & Cutler, 1998, p. 294). In short, Zen and meditation do not necessarily conflict with any particular religion. Conflict only occurs if one approaches religion, philosophy, or even Zen as a fundamentalist. Western Zen and the Middle Path have no interest in such things.

QUESTION 3: HOW TO PRACTICE MEDITATION

C: OK, Joan, let's get practical. I can see the value of quieting the mind. How might I go about that as a beginner, a beginning meditator that is? Let me state this more emphatically. How do I get started? To me, meditation seems to be such an effort. I cannot tell you the number of times I've said to myself, "Today is the day that I will begin to meditate regularly!" But it never seems to happen. Is this problem unusual? How do I deal with it? For example, do I need a book, teacher, master, guru, or should I just start on my own?

J: Just as in becoming a therapist, Chris, it is best to learn under the tutelage of a teacher. In the case of Zen, the teacher should be one who can be like a mirror for their students. This learning process is like having a beloved professor that you trust and admire, not for his intellect alone, but for his or her compassion and respect for you as well. Being in the presence of such a teacher usually brings with it a welcome, sometimes healing, sense of complete acceptance. Such teachers are people who are in sync with themselves because they are not trying to win your favor, nor are they interested in how you might behave to be in favor. For example, Ram Dass (1987) speaks of his guru, Neem Karoli Baba, with nothing but love and acceptance. He goes on to describe a time when he believes his guru is reading his mind. Of course, Ram Dass is stunned when he realizes what is happening, and embarrassed, too. Who wouldn't be! Whether mind reading is possible or not, his point is that no matter what one happens to think or feel at a particular time, he or she knows that the teacher accepts them, completely.

Another learning path is to attend retreats or workshops as often as possible for teachings, meditation, and to refresh yourself. If possible, connect with a teacher you can call regularly to guide you with your practice. It is helpful to have friends (*sangha*) to meditate with and with whom to discuss the meditative experiences. Some people find it helpful to read books and listen to tapes. I do. Fortunately, there are many excellent ones available that are produced by distinguished teachers who are well known, respected, and loved. This way of learning is a blessing for people who are not able to attend a workshop, retreat, or have the opportunity to have a personal teacher. In any case, the most important factors are wanting to practice and then doing it. To paraphrase a very overworked but absolutely appropriate quote, this particular journey of a lifetime begins with a single step. "Even when you practice zazen alone, without a teacher, I think you will find some way to tell whether your practice is adequate or not" (Suzuki, 1970, p. 72).

Most of us who walk the Middle Path have struggled with meditation, so the following words from Suzuki have always been comforting and reassuring to me.

> If you think the aim of Zen practice is to train you to become one of the best horses, you will have a big problem. This is not the right understanding. If you

, right way it does not matter whether you are the best horse or
nen you consider the mercy of Buddha, how do you think Buddha
.he four kinds of horses? He will have more sympathy for the worst
.he best one. (1970, p. 38)

He the. es on to describe the four types of horses: excellent, good, poor,
and bad ones. Even if you are a "bad horse," the regular practice of meditation
can be of help. Indeed, if what Suzuki says is true, perhaps meditation will
make the greatest degree of difference in this particular case, because one
can realize the greatest growth from this position! More often than not, I
feel like I am the "bad horse." Suzuki's words have comforted me and that
allows me to have more patience with myself when it comes to the practice
of meditation.

I prefer a quiet place to meditate. Posture is very important, too, and one
can either sit cross-legged in the lotus position or half-lotus position upon a
meditation cushion (*zafu*) or on a substantial pillow. However, you may
prefer to sit comfortably on a firm, but not hard, chair, as long as you do
not lean against the back. Always try to keep your spine straight but relaxed,
as if you were balancing a book on your head. Resolve not to move unless
absolutely necessary. Then, put your hands on your thighs near your knees
or, if you wish, barely touch your thumb with your index finger to make a
circle. Hold your head so that it is looking slightly downward and focus your
gaze on a spot on the floor about three feet in front of your body. Many
people place a candle, flower, or some other item in that spot upon which
they can comfortably focus. Some people close their eyes, but it is not
necessary. Now, turn your attention to your breathing. As you breath out,
count "one." Then breathe in and count "two." Breathe out again and count
"three." Breathe in again, count "four." Continue this process until you reach
the count of "ten." Huston Smith, a distinguished scholar, teacher, and author,
speaks about a time he was doing a workshop on meditation.

After the first session I asked for questions. The first question was, "How do you
get to number two?" Well, that drew a laugh of course, because everybody got to
number two, but it is amazing how quickly our minds deviate. What one sees as
never before is how restless the mind is. (1995)

The point is that every time you have a thought that comes into your head,
no matter what it may be, just start over again.

As a beginner, I would suggest meditating this way for 10 or 15 minutes
at a time. Of course, watching the clock is distracting, so I have found that
setting a timer to go off in another room is helpful. Try to practice meditating

this way every day or as often as you can find the time. It is not unusual for people to lose interest at first, but don't worry: It is OK to be a "bad horse." Of course, it is important to mention that I do not wish to oversimplify the role of meditation in Zen: There are many levels of meditation and each one of them is important to freeing ourselves from suffering. Some of them take years to learn and some of them require a high degree of commitment, so it is important to keep in mind that when we are talking about meditation, we are actually talking about a process, not merely a technique. A slogan Michael Toms (2001b) used while interviewing the beloved monk Tulku Thondup seems to sum up the situation nicely: "Slowly, slowly, get there fast."

QUESTION 4: THE EGO, SELF, AND ZEN

C: One of the most confusing things about Zen to me, Joan, has always been how differently it seems to address key concepts that are central to the psychology of the West. For example, in the psychodynamic perspective, the ego is seen as the healthy, rational, mature part of the person. It is the very thing that we try to strengthen for a person when we work from this view or even from a cognitive perspective, where rationality and making rational decisions is valued. The same problem seems to occur concerning the way the concept of the self is used in Western versus Eastern thought. For example, a humanistically oriented practitioner tends to see the self as the primary source of personal knowledge and development. In this sense the key to therapy as well as personal growth is to "know thy self." Indeed, transpersonal psychology will even talk about how the self is the most important dimension of our lives in that it is the part of us that is not only inherently good, but transcendent as well. Yet, in the East, it seems that the self is often seen much like the ego, which is to say that it is something that must be transcended, rather than something which is transcendent.

I will never forget the time that I discussed this issue with a colleague of mine who came to this country from China and who happens to be a Buddhist. He had read a draft of this chapter and asked me to explain the concept of identity that is central to much of Western psychology because it seems so elusive to him. At one point, I told him I was having a difficult time reconciling a psychology that focused on the self with one that focused on getting rid of it. He replied, "That's easy, because there is nothing to get rid of—*there is no self!*" This dilemma also appears in my own field, which is the psychology of self-esteem. For instance, David Burns, whose work on depression has received international recognition for decades, now seems to run into the same phenomenon when he deals with self-esteem. On one hand, he sees increasing self-esteem in terms of going up a ladder.

> I like to think about the process of gaining self-esteem as climbing up a ladder. If you feel worthless and inferior, you may start out on the ground because you have very little self-esteem. On the first rung of the ladder you develop conditional self-esteem. . . . Once you have conditional self-esteem, you can climb up to the next rung on the ladder. On this step you develop unconditional self-esteem. You realize that self-esteem is a gift that you and all human beings receive at birth. (1993, pp. 186–188)

On the other hand, he concludes this very thought by saying that there is no such thing as self-esteem, which creates the same dilemma.

> On the next step, you can adopt the even more radical position that there is no such thing as self-esteem, just as there is no such thing as a worthwhile person or a worthless person. . . . This solution to the problem of self-esteem is in the Buddhist tradition because self-esteem is rejected as a useless illusion. . . . The death of your pride and your ego can lead to new life and to a more profound vision. When you discover that you are nothing, you have nothing to lose, and you inherit the world. (1993, pp. 186–188)

At times, Joan, it feels like Zen would ask me to give up half of my clinical training! It challenges basic psychological constructs such as the ego, identity, the self, and even individuality, all of which many traditional practitioners, social scientists, and teachers hold very dear.

J: Yes, Chris, this particular difference between Zen and traditional psychotherapy seems to be a chronic source of confusion and misunderstanding—for practitioners from either perspective! There is, indeed, a great difference of opinion about the ego or self between Eastern psychology and Western psychology. What I really want to say to you about this problem is that for me, it is a big deal, but it is not a big deal. It seems like a big deal until you get beyond it, then it is no big deal at all, because things are so clear. Perhaps it will help to realize that understanding the nature of the ego is the very foundation of Buddhism, just as it is for much of Western psychology, but that is done in a very different way.

The Buddhist monk, Lama Soygal Rinpoche talked about the ego the first time I heard him so many years ago. It made sense to me as a person, not necessarily as a practicing mental health professional. Michael Toms asked him where basic fear and the feeling of being threatened come from. The response to the question was,

> I think the fear fundamentally comes from ego. In some ways that ego actually survives on fear. It is insecurity which is the nourishment of ego. From the very beginning, as we have been distracted from our original nature, from the moment that the sense arrived or ego developed, it was actually within the realm of a sense of loss that it created its world and in doing so it created a feeling, perception, intellect, concept of its own kind in order to kind of protect itself. (1984)

In other words, Chris, the ego arises as a developmental necessity. We need it to survive and to reach adulthood. But that comes at a great cost, the cost of ignorance. The ego's concern with perceiving and dealing with reality in terms of self-preservation, which is necessary for our survival at first, eventually creates a world full of attachments and distortions in which we become trapped.

> So, now from that sense of ignorance, develops a kind of ego's version of hope and fear, which are the two areas that it begins to work with. For instance, hope for gain, fear of loss, hope for happiness, fear of suffering, hope for fame, fear of obscurity, and hope for a kind of compliment and reassurance from people and fear of blame, and as such, for instance, when it doesn't work out this way, then anger, desire, jealousy things come, which are also expressions of insecurity. (1984)

One way to look at the complementarity between psychological and Zen approaches to the ego and self might be to see them as two sides of a picture. On the Western side, for example, we see a psychology that typically moves from childhood, through adolescence, to adulthood and then tends to stop there. Much of this kind of psychology focuses on the emergence of the ego (childhood) and the role it plays in forming an individual identity (adolescence) and how that sense of self changes over time (adulthood). On the Eastern side, we might say that we find a psychology that does the reverse: It starts with the ego as it occurs in adulthood, and then attempts to remove insecurities and self-illusions that inevitably accompany its development.

In Zen, then, although the ego is necessary for survival, its development is accompanied by what are metaphorically termed the five "heaps" or Skandhas. The first one is *avidya*, which means Ignorance and is akin to the psychodynamic mechanism of projection. As long as our perceptions are colored by our ego or identity, we will see what we have learned to see rather than what is there. In this sense we are ignorant because we are not aware of how our ego or self blinds us to the "truth" of the here and now. The second heap is *vedana*, a very strong reaction, that obstructs our vision or our consciousness by giving too much weight to our feelings and emotions. Although it is natural to have reactions to circumstances and events, the ego has a tendency to treat them as facts. Thus, instead of simply experiencing events as they unfold, we become trapped by the feelings they create.

The third Skandha, *samjna*, is perception-impulse which is much more energetic. This heap concerns the fact that we often mistake our conscious and unconscious perception for reality and then act on them accordingly. Once such a transformation occurs, we begin to treat a particular point of view as though it is reality itself and defend it as such, sometimes passionately. We might call the fourth Skandha *sanskara*, which is more of a cognitive or conceptual trap than an emotional or perceptual one. This illusion results from making assumptions and failing to realize that we have done so. When this happens, we treat our beliefs, opinions, and judgments as though they are truth itself and then proceed to act accordingly, which is to say ignorantly. Lama Surya Das says that the fourth Skandha is about intentions,

> Why do you do what you do? This Skandha includes all volitional activities. As the Buddha pointed out, your intentions create your karma. Your will and intentions direct your mind, which controls the way you think, speak, and act. Your intentions establish the priorities in your life. Your past intentions condition or perpetuate your present intentions, habits, and propensities. This is where karma is created. (Das, 1997, p. 81)

The fifth heap, *vidyana*, concerns consciousness itself. By creating a sense of individual identity through the process of constructing a self, the ego sets up an artificial division between subject and object referred to as a "duality."

This function of the ego is necessary in order for us to establish the foundations for an identity and that is an important part of becoming a person. But these developmental processes come at a certain cost or create a certain by-product that involves the distortions of reality that are called illusions in Zen. For Zen, the truth of the matter is that we are all connected, not separate, and the failure to see this basic condition results in suffering. The two are not necessarily antagonistic in Zen. On the contrary, the ego is an essential part of our humanity: It helps us become who we are and, as we take apart that illusion through meditation, the ego becomes the "royal road" to liberation, to being free from illusions and the sufferings they create.

In his book *Going to Pieces Without Falling Apart*, Mark Epstein questions Ken Wilbur about why there is a need for an ego. He replied. "You have to be *some*body before you can be nobody. . . . The ego must be formed before it can be dismantled; the self must be consolidated before it can be transcended" (1998, p. 34). Zen is designed to help us to dissipate the illusions created by the ego, or to deconstruct our self-identity rather than smash it, so that our perceptions become more accurate, less distorted, and more open to the truth.

"Thus, meditation is not a means of forgetting the ego; it is a method of using the ego to observe and tame its own manifestations" (Epstein, 1995, p. 94). However, it is important to note that although Zen aims to deconstruct a socially constructed self as we see it in psychoanalysis or cognitive psychology, there are some similarities between egolessness and certain aspects of a transpersonal self as presented by the humanistic perspective. For example, the kinds of perceptions often described in peak experiences are probably similar to Zen modes of sensation and perception, so we do not have to talk about eliminating the use of the concept of self altogether, just its illusions.

QUESTION 5: PRACTICAL USES OF ZEN

C: Joan, I will have to think about that for some time to come, because I still struggle with the "hard" versus "soft" approaches to understanding human behavior. Although I do find some comfort in what you say, and may even glimpse some possibilities of reconciliation, I suspect that the desire for empirical knowledge still makes such a resolution to the problem difficult to embrace. However, using Zen to complement our work rather than as an alternative framework for it means that we do not have to take this issue much farther in order to reach our main purposes. Therefore, let's talk more about the practical uses of Zen. For example, how can including Zen principles into my work help me with difficult clinical situations or clients? How does Zen help you, for instance, respond to an angry client, deal with clients who are severely mentally ill, face the possibility of suicide with a patient, work with a depressed or grieving client, help someone who has an addictive disorder or has a tendency to use manipulation as a way to communicate their wants and needs?

Zen and the Angry Client

Chris, you have asked me about "difficult patients." For whatever reason, I do not profess to know what it might be; I have to say that I have never actually experienced a "difficult" patient in the sense that you ask me. Of course, like anyone in this field, I have often been with patients who were fearful, resistant, and even angry in their response to any kind of treatment. For example, I recall working on a general adult psychiatric unit in a large city, when a young woman was admitted on an involuntary basis that might be an example of what you are asking. This patient was not cooperative because she was very frightened: she did not want to be there. When the nurses were going to begin searching her, which was standard procedure on the unit, she became even more apprehensive and resistant. Without being offered even the slightest opportunity to compose herself, one of the nurses said, "If you do not remove your clothing yourself, we are going to do it." A struggle ensued. The woman became more frantic. As the nurses undressed her, this young woman began to struggle physically with them. It was the consensus of the nurses she was to be medicated in order to calm her and get her under control, so the nurses simply overpowered her by sheer number. Unfortunately, this kind of response to anger or fear is all too common in our field. In terms of the perspective we saw in the Eightfold Path, however, it is built on a complete misunderstanding.

From a Zen point of view, the underlying cause of anger is usually fear and the proper response to this kind of suffering is *maitre*, which is a Sanskrit term for "loving-kindness." It is very tempting to overreact in such a situation because things can get out of hand very quickly. However, the use of force, even if it is only the force of words, looks, or gestures, can only make most situations worse. Instead, it is important to remember to "walk in another's shoes." Loving-kindness means approaching someone as a fellow human being, a person with whom you wish to make a connection. Loving-kindness is like greeting a stranger as though they were family. From this perspective, the woman's resistance was actually an attempt to hold on to her identity, not "acting out." Rather than saying, "Take your clothes off," and following it with a threat, the hospitable thing to do would be to welcome the person, listen to them, and try to offer hospitality; after all, we are talking about the word hospital!

Another example of loving-kindness occurred when I was asked to see a young woman on an emergency basis. She had been arrested after striking a police officer. This officer was very professional: He knew that she had been a client at the Center some time ago and brought her there instead of to jail. This visibly agitated and angry but intelligent and attractive woman was dressed somewhat provocatively in a sundress. I was struck by her physical activity: She couldn't sit still. She kept crossing her legs back and forth rapidly and talking so loudly that someone came to my door, inquiring if I needed help. Jean had a traumatic background, which included being gang-raped, along with other forms of sexual abuse. She also had a very active history of heavy drug and alcohol use. At the time, she was involved with a man who seemed to care for her, wanting to protect her by letting her live with him. She also had no relationship with her family. In addition, she said that she was in therapy two years ago and did not like the idea of having to see someone ever again. I felt the sorrow and frustration in her voice and in her body, so I sat near her and listened to her barrage of words which came as fast as the movement of her body. I liked her directness and sensed some courage, as well as a strong desire to survive, along with a deep form of depression that seemed to touch her spirit.

I was glad she decided to set up an appointment for the following week, but it was not easy for Jean to come for sessions. Typically, she would check behind the chairs as if she had to check out the room and make sure she and I were alone, that no one was listening to our exchanges. I didn't sense she was suspicious however, because to me her behavior seemed sort of a drama she wanted or needed to play. There was no reason for me to be concerned with her behavior, so after a few sessions I teased her when she checked behind the chairs. It was not unusual for me to laugh with her at some of the comments she made about the police; she was bright and witty. My laughter or teasing did not imply I was insensitive to her insecurities and suspiciousness, just that loving-kindness can also be light-hearted. After a few more sessions she stopped this ritual of checking behind the chairs.

I liked something about this person right from the beginning. Over time, we seemed to connect as people, not as patient and therapist, but as two women talking together; no one was the boss. It took a while for Jean to relax enough to tell me what had been happening and the suspicion and disgust she had towards the police and mental health systems. Her experience of therapy in the past seemed to teach her that she was going to be judged before she had time to tell her story, that she would be seen only by her actions and not who she was as a person. Yet, underneath her chronic anger and cursing, she seemed to want to be happy. In other words, Jean is no different than any one of us. She gradually found out through talking over time that she had the potential to live with less fear and anguish. She needed some help to do that, of course, and I provided a space where she could learn to see her inner light. She loved gardening, so I used to tease her that she was like a tomato seed and the farmer. Only in this case, she was playing both roles. As a farmer, she was caring for a seed; as a seed, she was a thing of promise or potential. She got it and realized that although I could help her open the door, she had to go through it alone.

Occasionally Jean and her male friend would come together. At times we talked about her collective emotional wounds. The focus of our work became the fact that they both had a need for respect and honesty as well as the fact that they both seemed to have difficulty in letting go of the past. It seemed that with a third person present, they were able to transcend their individual fears of abandonment and speak about feelings that had been hidden for a long time. They were two wounded people looking directly into the eyes of rage, fear, and addiction together because they did not want to spoil a relationship that was developing into something meaningful for both of them. It was a connection we all gained from because it was a relationship based on loving-kindness. The careful reader may also see that the police officer practices loving-kindness in his work as well, where it helped both Jean and society in general.

The point I am trying to make about including loving-kindness in our work is twofold. First, the Zen attitude of loving-kindness allows the person to feel at home—it permits the person to focus on their suffering with an eye toward liberation. Second, we often forget how powerful our role or position can be for someone who is frightened, confused, or in pain. If we are not cognizant of their experience, our behavior can make a tough situation worse. In some ways, then, loving-kindness can make a therapist's job better, or worse, depending on whether it is used or not.

Zen and Severe Mental Illness

Chris, I know you are curious about how someone who practices from a Zen perspective might approach a person who has been diagnosed as suffering from schizophrenia or Borderline Personality Disorder as examples of severe mental illness. I want you to know that I appreciate how important this question might seem for a traditionally oriented therapist, but I can only say that I don't do anything special with either diagnosis. In a certain sense, such a question misses the point of the teachings of the Buddha because one's stance toward others is always the same when working from this perspective no matter what a particular diagnosis might be: it is one of connection based on compassion.

When I am practicing the Eightfold Path, I am not focused on myself. During these times the client is the most important person to me, not their diagnosis or even how bizarre or anxious their symptoms or behaviors are. Instead, I first try to give my full attention to the person that I am with and, second, I try to do no harm. As subjective as that is, that has been my mainstay in this work.

> The strongest influence of the Buddhist tradition on my own thinking has been the emphasis on the central role of compassion in the attainment of knowledge. According to the Buddhist view, there can be no wisdom without compassion, which means for me that science is of no value unless it is accompanied by social concern. (Capra, 1988, p. 37)

For our work as therapists, this means that no matter how well trained we might be, and regardless of what medical breakthrough we are using in our treatment, being connected to our clients in a mode of compassion and understanding is the foundation of our work.

The Dalai Lama has not received training in how to *treat* a person who may exhibit some unusual behavior in the "Western" clinical sense of the word. However, there is a story about his reaction to a man who was manifesting unusual behavior that is worth noting here. The Lama was at a reception with a doctor who had coauthored a book with His Holiness, when he observed a man whose appearance was notable; he was tall, thin, disheveled, and exhibited signs of anxiety and depression. He also had slight repetitive involuntary movements of the musculature around his mouth that may have been a side effect of a psychotropic medication. A crowd had gathered to see the Dalai Lama and the young man was pushed to the edge of the clearing so the Dalai Lama took the time to speak with him.

> The man was startled at first and began to speak very rapidly to the Dalai Lama, who spoke a few words in return. I couldn't hear what they were saying, but I saw that as the man spoke, he started to become visibly more agitated. The man was saying something, but instead of responding, the Dalai Lama spontaneously took the man's hand between his, patted it gently, and for several moments simply stood there silently nodding. As he held the man's hand firmly, looking into his eyes, it seemed as if he were unaware of the mass of people around him. The look of pain and agitation suddenly seemed to drain from the man's face and tears ran down his cheeks. Although the smile that surfaced and slowly spread across his features was thin, a look of comfort and gladness appeared in the man's eyes. (Dalai Lama & Cutler, 1998, p. 310)

In order to understand, one must first "listen," not only with our ears, but with our eyes and heart as well. When we go beyond the words, we encompass the whole person. In order to do this well, we need clean ears and a clean mind free of perceptions and projections. Such a state of openness occurs more readily when we remember how important it is to try to walk the Eightfold Path, because that approach is concerned with helping to be present to the here and now realities of life. The fewer distractions that intrude upon the exchange, the better. Epstein describes another reason to cultivate this form of awareness and presence:

> A provocative British psychoanalyst, W. R. Bion, famously declared that a therapist must be free from memory and desire if he is to be of any use to his patients. To think about the end of a session, to wonder what time it is, even to hope for a cure, is to add an agenda that becomes an interference, because it is sensed as a demand.

People are exquisitely sensitive to each other, especially in a stripped-down relationship like a therapeutic one. (2001, p. 56)

Distractions, worrying about if the client is severely troubled, being concerned with how others might view me or my work, or trying to "make" the client do something, is like using a soiled bandage to cover a wound; it can complicate or even spoil the healing process. In the case of psychotherapy, of course, it is an unclear or unfocused mind on the part of the therapist that is like a dirty dressing, so the point that I am trying to make is that I really don't do anything different for "severely" mentally ill persons than I do for anyone else I see. Having said this much, I can now discuss some particular people I have known and how Zen seemed to help me with them.

Zen and the Suicidal Client

For four years I had been a therapist to a woman who had not been able to deal with some fairly severe emotional and physical traumas that began when she was a child. Starting at a very young age, Merle's mother would lock her in a hallway closet when she was angry with her. In addition to speaking to Merle hatefully, it was not unusual for her to be punished physically for the slightest thing, such as spilling milk on the table or if her brother had done something wrong. Merle had a phobia about spiders, probably because they were often in places where she had been confined. Her younger brother, who was also abused, committed suicide when he was 18 years old. This event had been very difficult for Merle to accept because she felt guilty about his death: Merle believed that she was responsible for his suicide because she had not protected him enough.

Being afraid to leave the house seemed to be another manifestation of Merle's emotional trouble. She was so fearful that even going on her porch was extraordinarily difficult for her to do. At such times, she became convinced that something was going to happen to her, that she was going to die or that someone was going to kill her if she left her home. This kind of paralysis created problems at home with Merle's family because she had little contact with the outer world, whereas her husband and son had fairly active social lives. No matter how they would encourage her, support her, or beg her, Merle could not leave the house. She was aware of how she was affecting her family. Therefore, Merle agreed to try psychotherapy, though with great trepidation. She was able to keep most of her appointments with me because of her family's support.

I was taken by her appearance immediately. She was quite pale, fragile looking, and would often wear sunglasses while in session. It was very clear that Merle was not well and initially, Merle would not look at me during our time together. It was clear that we had to reestablish a relationship each time we talked. Rather than simply dismissing her behavior as some form of resistance and instead of trying this or that technique, I turned to the Eightfold Path. Right Understanding helped me to see the need to be patient, which in this situation meant simply waiting until Merle wished to engage in some form of dialog. At the end of the session, we talked. After that, it was not unusual to hear her express gratitude that I did not "give up on her." Right Understanding allowed me to respect the fact that it was very difficult for her to let her feelings come to the surface because it was like reliving some horror of the events she had gone through. To push her would have been cruel. The Eightfold Path allowed me to let her lead the way and I followed close behind.

Due to her husband's work schedule, Merle was usually my last appointment on the days she was to come to therapy. Prior to one particular session Merle's attitude and mood toward life had gone from serious self-doubt to extreme self-doubt and anger, which resulted in a great deal of tension at home. When I greeted her in the lobby she made it clear that her husband was not to be involved with her session. It was obvious Merle was angry. She began the session describing the situation at home as being unbearable and that she felt very stuck because she had no place to go. According to Merle, her husband told her he did not love her anymore and threatened to leave her. "Everyone thinks Stuart is a saint, but they don't have to live with him. They all want me dead!" I was very glad I didn't have to concern myself about time that day. Instead, I knew that I could stay with her until some resolution could take place, a resolution that would be in her best interest. She spewed out anger for over two hours, while crying, accusing me of not being sensitive to her needs, talking about how uncaring her husband and son were to her, carrying on about the futility of living, articulating her mistrust of me, and sharing her growing desire to end her life.

Then, something unusual happened; Merle asked to see the psychiatrist because she wanted medication. This was the first time she had ever asked to see the doctor. When I told Merle that if she wanted to receive a prescription for medication, she would have to go to the local medical emergency room for an evaluation, her anger then transferred from me to the system. She could not understand why a doctor was not available even though by that time it was about 7:00 in the evening. Yet, I was struck not so much by her threatening suicide as I was by the fact that she was actually asking to see a doctor, which is to say speaking up for herself instead of giving in to her pain. I remember sitting across from her, looking at her very intensely, listening to her words, seeing the fury in her eyes, yet not wanting to interrupt her.

For whatever reason, and I think it was related to the fact that Merle was free to be herself in my presence, some kind of psychological spell was broken. A deep and authentic connection seemed to occur between us. I believe she knew that I would stay with her, no matter what, and that I would give her time to go through what she needed to go through without condemnation or impatience. Neither of us tried to avoid what was happening. I did not try to talk her out of her misery. I stayed with her and listened. I could almost taste her anguish. I understood her in a way that suggested that I stood beneath her in order to support her from bottom to top. I was not silent, but my instincts to try to talk her "out of this mood" would have been absolutely "nuts." I had faith in the idea that in order for her to come closer to healing, she had to have a wide pasture in which to dig up things in order to ruminate about them and then understand them more fully. "Faith gives birth to diligence and this diligence continues to strengthen our faith. Animated with diligent energy, we become truly alive. Our eyes shine, and our steps are solid" (Hanh, 1998, p. 173).

Then, with Merle watching, and with her consent, I phoned the medical emergency room to speak to the nurse-in-charge. I told her about Merle's need to see a doctor. When Merle agreed to go to the hospital, we went together. We told Stuart, who had been waiting in the lobby, what had taken place and about the need to go to the hospital. As we parted, Merle and I embraced. She thanked me for staying with her and I supported her decision to get further help. I told her I would be contacting the hospital staff to inquire what happened after the physician evaluated her. The medical emergency room physician decided that Merle should be admitted to the psychiatric unit for a limited time. She disagreed and was then hospitalized on an involuntary basis. Later, I was told that Merle raised quite a fuss about that. "I didn't want to be in the hospital; I was scared." However, she felt the nursing staff was very kind to her and she liked the psychiatrist who was assigned to her. Merle told me that what she had feared did not come to pass: She had left her home and lived! Most of all, she found people who were compassionate. She even acknowledged that the doctor's decision to have her admitted was in her best interest.

When we had our first session after the hospitalization, we reflected about the evening and what it meant to her. Merle told me that it seemed to her that the angrier she got the calmer I became. I was pleased that she was able to make this observation. For the first time, Merle did not have to avoid strong feelings. Merle is not entirely out of the woods, however the events of that evening opened up her world to such a degree she is feeling less fear. Merle's husband has told me how different she is since her hospitalization, especially that she is rarely as angry or as fearful. Now she is functioning at home, cleaning, cooking full meals, sleeping better, and welcoming a few people into their home. The relationship between Merle and her son Paul has also changed for the better; an example of this is the fact that the destructive squabbling has stopped.

It is not unusual for a therapist to become anxious when faced with a suicidal client. There are many reasons for such a reaction and they are easily understandable. For example, there is always the threat of a potential lawsuit to consider if something goes wrong. A sense of a lack of control over the future that is characteristic of this situation is troublesome to some. Feelings of frustration, insecurity, or a sense of incompetence can be experienced. However, I must say that what usually happens for me when I am interacting with someone who is suicidal is neither the future nor my own issues; it is the now. Right View, or keeping my attention on that which is in front of me, makes it difficult to be distracted by a lack of control, by the uncertainty of the future, or by the fear of failure. These issues, while understandable, fall away in the face of maintaining the Right View and that fosters Right Action, although there is no guarantee things will work out each time. I am not saying that I can teach you how to react with someone who is suicidal, but I feel comfortable in saying the Eightfold Path helps me to remember what it is like to be human, that I would not want to abandon someone emotionally any more then I would want someone to abandon me if I was facing intense fear. Living the Eightfold Path seems to lead to a connection with the client, and what more could we ask for realistically at such times?

Zen and Depression

A number of years ago I was called to the office of an internist. A patient of his, who was a social worker by profession, had come to the office crying and visibly upset because her three-month-old baby girl had died from SIDS early that fall. The death was devastating to this woman. Unfortunately, Elizabeth felt she could not express herself freely with her husband and their families, but there was an unusual twist to her story. That day, which was just a few months after the baby's death, she had told her husband she wanted to go to the cemetery, dig up her baby, and hold her because of the cold. In actuality, she had no intention of doing this but just saying it frightened her husband and they exchanged cross words. Elizabeth had the impression she was to get over the death and "go on."

It seemed a relief when I told Elizabeth that I understood, was not worried about what she was feeling, and did not find it bizarre or crazy. We did very little other then exchange a few words about what had happened that day while she sobbed. I too had tears in my eyes as I listened to her speak of the almost insurmountable pain. "I was told I would have more babies and that made me feel worse," she said. "This was my baby and she died! They don't understand how I feel!" After that first meeting we met for several months once a week in the doctor's office. This young woman did not go through the grief process in the way it is usually described. For example, she did not express denial or anger. Instead, she dealt directly with what could be called the heart of the death. What she expressed was always clear, direct, and profoundly sad. Instead of the gravesite, she found a place in therapy to express the grief she felt, the longing she had to hold her baby, and the freedom to voice her thoughts no matter how bizarre they might seem without having to worry about what her husband or family might think of them.

When her words were heard with the heart, they simply reflected a young mother who needed to feel she was not being blocked from grieving. In such an atmosphere, she could be with her feelings, instincts, and memories of holding her baby, even very lucid ones such as the smell of her baby, without seeming bizarre. She could even fulfill the need to repeat these things until there was a sense of total recognition and understanding of her grief. Elizabeth needed to know she didn't have to be told to "go on with her life" because she already was going on with it. The important thing to remember was that ignoring her feelings would prolong her grief. When she was ready, Elizabeth asked her husband to join our sessions, but only after she made the decision that she was ready to be open about her anger and hurt toward him. She wanted to give him an opportunity, in this safe setting, to express what he had been going through, especially the fear for his wife, his grief about the baby, and his worries about the future of their marriage.

From a Zen point of view, grieving for the loss of a loved one or a personal tragedy is not something that one "comes to closure on." For example, Howard Cutler tells a story about the Dalai Lama that makes this point most poignantly. An older monk asked the Dalai Lama to teach him a high-level esoteric practice.

> I remarked in a casual way that this would be a difficult practice and perhaps would be better undertaken by someone who was younger, that traditionally it was a

practice that should be started in one's mid-teens. I later found out that the monk had killed himself in order to be reborn in a younger body to more effectively undertake the practice. (Dalai Lama & Cutler, 1998, p. 161)

Afterward, Cutler asked the Dalai Lama how he dealt with this tragedy, especially the feelings of guilt it might generate. The Dalai Lama said,

> "I didn't get rid of it, it's still there." He stopped again before adding, "But even though that feeling of regret is still there, it isn't associated with a feeling of heaviness or quality of pulling me back. It would not be helpful to anyone if I let that feeling of regret weigh me down, be simply a source of discouragement and depression with no purpose, or interfere with going on with my life to the best of my ability." (Dalai Lama & Cutler, 1998, p. 161)

The point here is twofold. First, the Dalai Lama feels the pain of this tragic event. Instead of denying it, he embraces it as the truth, as something that cannot be erased. Second, he realizes that he has to go on living a meaningful life in spite of the tragedy of the event—as does Elizabeth. She wanted to go on living, too, but in a way that honored her first-born. Over a period of several years Elizabeth has given birth to three healthy babies. She has even begun a group for parents who have grieved the loss of a child. Instead of being overwhelmed by her loss, embracing it allowed her and her husband to help others.

Zen and Addictive Disorders

One of the nicest compliments I have ever received from a patient came from a man in his late 50s who had a long history of alcoholism. This gentle and shy man was a farmer of German descent. In addition to having a working farm, he was employed by an organization that was aware of his addiction and wanted him to seek treatment because he was a valued employee; its Employee Assistance Program (EAP) representative referred Joe to me. I was given some history about him and was informed Joe had grave reservations about talking with anyone: His coworkers described him as a likeable man who was pretty much a loner. Unfortunately, Joe's job was in jeopardy because he was found drinking at work on more than one occasion. In spite of warnings, he continued to drink during breaks on the job. Joe decided to talk with someone because he was on probation; if he was found drinking one more time he would be fired.

At the beginning, it was clear that he felt uncomfortable and ill at ease. Therefore, to me it made no sense to do much of anything but to provide time for Joe to get to know me, something akin to two dogs sniffing each other to see if it was safe. Joe is a muscular 6'3″ and wears a strong, weathered complexion. I am just a little over 5'2″ tall and yet it was as if I had all the "power" to hurt this human being. To be other than sensitive to his fear and apprehension made no sense, so the first session was spent talking with him gently about what had happened and why we were connecting together. If I wanted him to return and to be open for help, then it was essential to put him at ease. I hoped the occasional silences that took place did not intimidate him, that he would know or feel that I was friendly and wanted to help him feel he had nothing to fear. It wasn't easy for Joe and I was glad he returned for the next session.

The early sessions consisted of talking about the farm and his childhood, which included a father who had a severe drinking problem. Life at home was based on uncertainty and trauma. His mother worked hard on the family farm and was verbally abused by her husband. We also talked about the loyalty of his wife, about his three grown children, as well as his work. He signed a Release of Information so I might be able to talk with his wife Emmie, who seemed to be caring and worried. She expressed frustration and despair. It was gratifying to know how much he was loved in spite of his irrational behavior when drunk. I talked little about Joe's addiction to alcohol; it seemed to me if I did he might not come back because he was so guilt-ridden. Surprisingly he never skipped a session; it might be safe to say something worthwhile was happening to him. I suspect a relationship not based on judgment and guilt might have helped put him at ease. Therapy provided an opportunity for Joe to talk about his difficult childhood, his father's lack of care and love, and how badly he felt repeating the same behavior his father had with his own children and grandchildren; the lack of being available for his sons had been weighing heavily on his mind. He was grateful for the love his wife had for him and felt he was not worthy of her loyalty.

During a Christmas dinner Joe drank unusually heavily and voluntarily admitted himself to a treatment program for alcoholism. The holidays had always been painful for him because memories were especially powerful for him at this time of year. Perhaps the time we spent together permitted him to take a gamble on trusting others for help and that it was worthwhile to risk taking the next step. At any rate, I will never forget the compliment he gave to me as his wife conveyed it to me. She said, "Joe felt he could talk with you about the price of corn," which, in the plainspoken language of Midwestern farmers, meant that he could talk about almost anything with me honestly. I trusted my intuitiveness to avoid doing "in-depth" therapy.

Yet to Joe it was, because he reached inside of himself and he learned he could finally trust himself and through that could take the risk of reaching out to his family. He had gone beyond the pain that had stunted his personal growth to becoming a "being" he could love.

Zen and Being with a Dying Patient

I was getting ready to go home on a typical Friday that was busy with discharging patients and making sure everything was covered for the weekend. Just as I was leaving my office, I received a call from a nurse requesting that I come to the medical floor and talk to a patient who was "giving them trouble." I would have liked to have waited until Monday, but felt I needed to respond, because two days can stretch out to be much longer if the staff is not in concert with the patient. The nurses reported to me that he was not cooperative, would not take his medication, and that he was "noncompliant," which meant things like not following the doctor's orders about bed rest and so forth. However, it was not clear what they wanted me to do other then address his behavior and to find out why he was being obstreperous. When I asked for clarification, the explanation I received was not helpful. Over the years there have been times I have not been able to discern how much of such problems actually stem from the attitude or behaviors of my fellow nurses, and suspect that finding out would make a very interesting study!

I felt sadness emanating from his being as I walked into the room and my heart opened to him as I sat down beside his bed. I saw before me a pale elderly man with sparse white hair, a thin craggy face, and a slim body under the covers of the bed. I felt that loneliness and sorrow were creating his suffering. Having met him, I felt it would have been embarrassing to actually pursue the complaints of the nursing staff. I suspect it would have made no sense to him either, though he might have chuckled if I did that. Instinctively, and I use this word a lot because that is how it both occurs and feels to me, I decided to have as enjoyable a time as one could have in this particular setting. Robert told me of his life work, the adventures he had as a young man, the people he cared for, his dreams, the pride he felt in his work while on the railroad, and so forth. Touching his arm, smoothing his brow with a cool cloth, we sat together for at least an hour. I listened as he talked. For a brief time, his suffering seemed to cease. To discuss anything other than what we did would have been a mistake, because it would not have been Right Thought, Right Speech, or Right Action for me. Only Robert was the focal point of my interest; it was not the nurses' issues that were important and they were not even mentioned. I want to emphasize that I was not sitting there saying to myself "Be mindful, be aware" or anything like that. Being present "in the now" is what is essential. Life happens, so be attending to it, there is no need to think about "what am I going to say, what am I going to do."

When I reported to the nurses the pleasant time I had with Robert, I was met with some humor and a bit of dismay concerning how different my time with Robert seemed from theirs. Then I realized just how "unclear" the complaints about Robert were. Sometimes when a patient doesn't react in a way that will allow the nurse to do her job and get "it" over with, there is little room for either negotiation or understanding. I suspect if Robert had been listened to and asked about how he felt regarding his hospitalization, if he had just been seen as a fellow human being, not just as the patient in room 1234 in bed 2, then I believe that I would not have been asked to speak with him about his "noncompliance." He responded as himself, not as a "good patient" who has turned his life almost completely over to strangers.

There are articles written about "difficult" patients and what to do, how to respond, and so forth. I am usually critical of them because they seem to offer "canned" answers, not ones that involve focusing on seeing, hearing, listening to the uniqueness of the patient. There was a great song in the 60s called *Where Have All the Flowers Gone* that comes to my mind in this regard. Where has all the sensitivity gone and why does it have to be taught in our health care system when it should be the most natural response that we have to those who suffer? Is there fear when talking about the need for charity from the heart? I believe that is what every person like Robert yearns for. As Suzuki (1970, p. 111) says, "The best way is to understand yourself, and then you will understand everything. So when you try hard to make your own way, you will help others, and you will be helped by others." That makes so much common sense to me here. When we know ourselves it seems as if we automatically respond from our hearts instead of our heads. In this case, there is nothing to learn from an article and nothing to be gained through a canned answer. Another way of saying the same thing comes from the Zen master Dogen.

> To know yourself or study yourself is to forget yourself, and if you forget yourself then you become enlightened by all things. Knowing yourself or studying yourself just means that it's *your* experience of joy, it's *your* experience of pain, *your* experience of relief and ventilation, and *your* experience of sorrow. That's all we have and that's all we need to in order to have a living experience of the dharma—to realize that the dharma and our lives are the same thing. (Chodron, 1991, pp. 83–84)

When I returned to work on Monday I went to the medical unit to visit Robert again. The nursing staff told me he that he had died on Saturday. I then understood that he had given me a blessing by sharing his time and life story. Robert was a teacher for me because he helped show me the power of connection. Even though we had just met, I experienced a response of love from one being to another. The time with him was a period of grace; there were no pressures, no expectations, just a quiet time of being present to an old man. In that moment, the hospital dropped away. It was as if we had escaped and together we were roaming the desert where he worked putting down railroad ties. His blessing is still with me today.

Zen and Psychosis (Schizophrenia)

Like most mental health professionals who work in acute care settings, I have been with many patients who were in psychotic states, such as those associated with schizophrenia. All of us know that such situations have the potential to be complicated, unpredictable, and tense for one reason for another. Zen has taught me that how much we know about ourselves has a good deal to do with the outcome of such an exchange. The easiest way to make this point is to consider the contrast, what happens when a therapist becomes either fearful due to the unpredictability of the situation or anxious for the client's well-being.

When a therapist errs, it is usually not because of a deliberate act, but a lack of self-awareness. I am convinced clients can pick up the "vibes" (or whatever one wishes to call these nonverbal indicators) when the therapist feels uneasy, is caught in their own "stuff," fears the patient's actions, is insecure or has insecurity about one's own therapeutic ability, has the need to control one's environment, is generally uncertain as to what to do next, and so forth. Under these conditions, the chances are high that the exchange will not be satisfying to either person. The Zen response, of course, would be Right View (which includes Right Understanding and Right Thought), which is to say to realize that the therapist is present for the clients' benefit, not the reverse. Seeing that the client is not there to serve the therapist by being "compliant" and "subservient" and so forth is actually liberating to someone who remains mindful at such times.

This kind of attention is useful in two ways. First, it decreases the possibility of the client reacting to the therapist's own needs, such as countertransference, and thereby helps to avoid many unfortunate complications. Mindfulness keeps us focused on the here and now, which is important because the fact of the matter is that we do not know what will happen. Under such conditions, we are much better served by paying attention to that which is before us rather than that which might happen. Right Understanding allows us to see time as an ally, not an enemy. With time on our side, it is more likely that we will see opportunities for Right Action when they present themselves. This kind of openness to the moment can make all the difference between having a person who is psychotic become destructive, and turning a psychotic experience into an opportunity for learning and freedom.

For example, I remember a young woman who was diagnosed with an acute schizophrenic episode that was admitted to our psychiatric unit. One of the more striking manifestations of Molly's illness was an intense fear of snakes. One day on the unit, she began screaming. The staff was alarmed and called me immediately. I went to her room. She was huddled under her bed, crying, scared, and trying to hide from all the snakes. I knew that I couldn't convince her that there were no snakes through words. However, I also knew that I did not want her to be alone in her fear, which prompted me to join her by crawling under the bed with her. I spoke only the truth: that I knew she was scared and I did not want her to be scared alone. Eventually, she grasped my hand and held on to it until she stopped crying. After a time, she calmed down and accepted my suggestion of getting out from under the bed. We sat on her bed together until her fears dissipated. This willingness to simply be with her instead of trying to do anything to her seemed to be a turning point in our relationship.

Later on in our work together, I learned that Molly loved the harmonica. Even though it was against hospital rules, I bought her one as a gift. She was delighted! I was aware that we connected with each other as human beings, not just as a patient and a nurse. Near the end of her treatment, her father took both of us out to dinner at a fancy restaurant in order to practice social skills for her upcoming discharge. She was very nervous, but got through the event reasonably well. Watching her try out her wings was gratifying. Years later, Molly wrote me to say that she had entered nursing as a career. "I want to thank you for all you did for me and the only way I know of returning it is by trying to do the same for others." The last thing I heard from Molly was that the psychiatrist suggested that because she seemed to have an unusually good ability to relate with psychiatric patients, she might consider psychiatric nursing as her specialization. What a tribute to her efforts and her heart!

Once again, however, I must say that it is important to realize that Zen is not magic. We all know that things often happen unexpectedly, that people can get out of control, that psychosis may lead to dangerous situations for the client and staff. All that I am saying is that these possibilities decrease as one's mindfulness increases, even if it is only a matter of the therapist knowing when to back off! Most of the time, an act of loving-kindness makes life easier on the client and therapist.

Zen and Manipulative Patients

Chris, you asked me about how I respond to patients who might be classified in mental health as "manipulative." There is no doubt I have been manipulated throughout the years, but my immediate response to this kind of behavior in people is that the patient is doing the best they can; that they have been conditioned to interact in these ways because of the lack of clarity and kindness in their lives. It is no big deal. But I have seen staff maneuver and manipulate people by threatening them with medication, not writing a pass to leave the unit, or by telling a patient that if they don't settle down they will be going to the "quiet room." To me, whether manipulation occurs or not seems to depend on who is the most frightened or unsure about how to address a particular situation. From a Zen point of view, I believe that people can only do what they can do. If this basic rule about human behavior is accepted, then it is incumbent upon the teacher to guide the student, because the master is supposed to be capable of more than the learner.

Right View, for example, means that instead of taking offense with manipulative behavior, the therapist would simply see it as "grist for the mill," which from a Buddhist perspective means understanding that the patient is doing what they are doing because they are suffering or fearful and unable to be any other way at the time. Seeing the manipulative behavior from this point of view does not make it less complicated, but it does offer two advantages. First, Right View helps the therapist to avoid falling into his or her own traps or countertransference. Here, Right View means that the therapist not only is not bothered as much by the manipulation regardless of the form it takes, but that he or she is also less likely to respond in a way that can seem defensive or controlling. Second, there is no "juice" (need, energy, driving force, impetus, and so forth) to help start an argument, continue a struggle, or fight about control. In other words, the calm of the therapist helps calm the situation.

Now that does not mean that Right View or any other Zen principle will make everything perfect every time. Right View simply helps the therapist to avoid the common mistakes of making things worse or more complicated and gives the client more of an opportunity to try another way of being. By contrast, the "Wrong View," which most often involves taking a hard-nosed stance with someone, attempting to manipulate a situation, or someone who is reacting defensively, makes no sense to me. To confront a patient is simply not in my vocabulary: To me, the word confront conjures up an image of conflict, defiance or opposition. Instead, I simply use the phrase "to talk with a client" because that is what goes on between two people when they are having a verbal exchange.

Consider how this approach is embodied in working with Eleanor, a 29-year-old woman who had never been married. She is very intelligent and attractive, but also has a drinking problem that started when she was in high school. According to Eleanor, her parent's marriage was unhappy. Her father was a successful businessman who spent little time at home and was an alcoholic and her mother was a Special Education teacher who had a violent temper that led to some physical abuse. There were fewer confrontations at home as Eleanor started to stay away beginning when she was in junior high school. However, in order to do that she had to lie about what she was doing, and where she was going, which was often inappropriate for her age. The distance between Eleanor and her parents grew wider over time and created a huge gap between them by the time she graduated from high school. Unfortunately, both sets of grandparents died when Eleanor was young, which meant there was no extended family upon which she could rely for support.

Eleanor was able to get through high school, attend a university, and earn a degree in Computer Science. While in school, she went to the counseling center at the advice of her faculty advisor, because she used alcohol to excess and suffered feelings of guilt after she had an abortion. This was her first attempt at counseling, which happened to be of the brief solution oriented type, but it did not seem helpful to her. She was also advised to go to AA meetings and get a sponsor. However, she made it quite clear she had no interest in AA because she felt it was "for losers." She was then referred to a Problem Pregnancy Program for the abortion issue, but once again did not feel understood or helped. In short, all the clinically "right things" had been done, but Eleanor thought that the counselor didn't know the score and that it had been a waste of time to see her. Of course, it was not unusual for her to find fault with authority figures.

Eleanor entered therapy with me this time because of a breakup with a man with whom she became pregnant. They had been dating for several months until she became pregnant. She felt she loved him but did not feel that he loved her because he wanted her to get an abortion. Eleanor agonized over what to do and, due to considerable ambivalence on her part, waited until the last possible moment before going to the clinic. Her boyfriend accompanied her to the doctor's office and took her home after the procedure. She had not seen him since that time and was so devastated by the events that she decided to talk with someone once again. This time, however, it was her choice.

From the onset it was quite apparent that Eleanor was still ambivalent about counseling. However, she did not have any close friends, did not want to tell her parents, and still felt the need to confide in someone. Given her ambivalence, her family background, and her history of problems with authority figures, it was inevitable that she would eventually become very angry with me. For example, she "tested" me concerning appointments and appointment times by becoming angry if I was a moment late getting her from the waiting room. She would then threaten to leave and would become verbally irate about my lack of caring. Sometimes she would call from the parking lot telling me she was there and expect me to meet her at the door instead of going to the waiting room.

Eleanor often verbally attacked people that she didn't know, giving some-one the "finger" if they got in her way while driving, or shouting an obscenity if she became annoyed over the least little thing. She had little control over her responses and held other people responsible for her behavior, as we see often with several so-called "personality" disorders, including the one that diagnosticians would give her. Discussions about this behavior often ended with, "Yeah, I know but I can't seem to stop it." Not surprisingly, talking and spending time with Eleanor was like riding out a storm until the wind calmed down. The threat of suicide would come up at various times, especially when she talked about how no one understood the suffering she had gone through. To make matters worse, her drinking seemed to result in rapid cycling between fear and anger, which played havoc with Eleanor trying to keep friends. As long as her acquaintances were showing her attention she was amiable and cheerful, but whenever she was rebuffed, she turned on people, drank, and threatened suicide, which she attempted several times.

Connecting with her in a way that did not make her fearful or angry seemed to be an important thing for me to do. I wanted her to sense my acceptance of her struggle and to understand that I had no expectations except to spend time with her. I did not want to create an environment where she needed to feel afraid of me, to manipulate my loyalty, or to test it. This goal was a difficult one because she could say something that was unclear, puzzling, accusatory, or hostile at any time: She was a clinical "work of art," metaphorically speaking. In addition, it was not unusual for her to tell me she felt worse at the end of the session than at its beginning, perhaps because I did not feed into her modus operandi. Fortunately, the Eightfold Path helped me to deal with Eleanor because it showed me how to embrace her as a teacher in my development as a therapist. This way of seeing her helped me like and respect her very much, which helped both of us in our work. I respected her because I had the impression she wanted something better for herself and she was willing to be courageous enough to face her fear of closeness, eventually. My mindfulness centered on not wanting to complicate her life anymore than it already was. Of course, there were times she had to run out of steam before we could get to her pain, and at those points I simply sat, listened, and tried to be present. Eleanor was used to getting responses to her ranting and raving that would allow her to avoid her issues, but Zen helped me avoid that trap.

Riding out the storms with Eleanor and not being afraid of her tirades gradually helped us to examine the fear that was under her rage. Finally, we reached the point where I could gently ask her if she was afraid of her own feelings when they occurred and if she could learn to face them instead of reacting to them so strongly. She agreed to try and no therapist could ask for more. In one session, for instance, she sat with her head in her hands crying, talking about the abuse she received from her parents and how unloved, lonely, and scared she was growing up. She felt she did not know how to communicate with people and used the only ways she knew to get the attention that she "thirsted" for so desperately. At this moment the symbolic connection between her rage and drinking became obvious even to her. She had made an important breakthrough.

Lest Zen seem all work and no pleasure, it is important to realize that humor is a part of it because it frees us, even if only temporarily, from suffering. Humor is important, then, because it gives us space. Thus, the moment when Eleanor and I could laugh about how furious she became when I was not at the door to meet her became another turning point for us. Now we were also able to connect with humor, not just compassion and suffering. At that point it became clear to Eleanor that I had no desire to manipulate her, threaten her, or in some other way control her. The atmosphere we created became characterized by compassion and trust instead of fear and avoidance. I knew her yelling at me had nothing to do with me, that it was related to the incredible sadness and pain she felt inside that needed to come to the surface. Her path involved becoming aware of what was provoking her and understanding that *she* needed to learn how to listen to herself. Over time, she learned to trust me and that allowed her to open up to herself. In that space, she found something that she had lost early in childhood. In modern psychiatric terms, she found a place from which she could begin to build the identity she never had. Now her fragmented sense of self could begin to come together in a way that made her less fearful, angry, and dependent on others.

I suspect that the hardest part of the work Eleanor did for herself was realizing that, ultimately, she was responsible for her life. It is akin to what the Little Prince said when he went back to meet the fox in de Saint-Exupéry's timeless story:

> "Goodbye," he said. "Goodbye," said the fox. "And now here is my secret, a very simple secret: It is only with the heart that one sees rightly; what is essential is invisible to the eye." "What is essential is invisible to the eye," the little prince repeated, so that he would be sure to remember. "It is the time you have wasted for your rose that makes your rose so important." "It is the time I have wasted for my rose—" said the little prince, so that he would be sure to remember. "Men have forgotten this truth," said the fox. "But you must not forget it. You become responsible, forever, for what you have tamed. You are responsible for your rose. . . . " "I am responsible for my rose," the little prince repeated, so that he would be sure to remember." (de Saint-Exupéry, 1943, p. 87)

For me, the "rose" is a symbol for a person's life and their responsibility for it. Eleanor's numbness and fear of exposure seemed to be healed by a combination of acceptance, listening, time, and trust, as is often the case in therapy. But most of all, her willingness to take the risk of becoming aware of herself in spite of the pain of doing so was the key. The Dharma (teachings of the Buddha) encourages people to become aware of themselves, and she did that by listening to herself without her usual fear or anger. "To study ourselves is to forget ourselves" (Suzuki, 1970, p. 79), which is to say that the more we know ourselves, the less we have to pay attention to our ego. Yet, one also needs "a teacher so that you can become independent" (1970, p. 77). In a certain sense, then, the work of a therapist is similar to that of a teacher and an archeologist: Sometimes we nourish the inner spirit and at other times we help uncover it.

QUESTION 6: ZEN AND WORK PLACE ISSUES

C: OK, Joan, I can see how Zen might help me deal with various clinical issues we are all likely to encounter. Now, I wonder if Zen can help me with nonclinical work-related issues. One of them might be how to respond to problematic colleagues or coworkers, especially those who think they "know it all."

Zen and Staff Conflicts

J: A number of years ago I was responsible for two psychiatric units: an adult general and an intensive care program. My predecessor was a person with a Ph.D. in clinical psychology and the hospital hired me to take this person's place when the position became vacant. The administrator of the hospital was a man who had worked with me for years as a therapist when I was the coordinator of the Emergency Service. He was well acquainted with my work and what I believe to be helpful in a clinical setting for both patients and staff. However, it was also quite clear that the rest of the staff, especially most of the therapists on the unit, were not impressed with my credentials, probably because my only degree at the time was in nursing and they did not have an appreciation for an interdisciplinary approach.

For a time, whenever I had a staff meeting with the clinicians, it was evident by their nonverbals and lack of participation that I was not welcomed. There was one woman who could not even stand the sight of me. She would sit with a large portion of her back turned toward me so that it was impossible to have direct eye contact. In my heart, I could understand their consternation because of three important issues: My philosophy was entirely different from that of my predecessor, they were very fond of this person, and not only was I a newcomer, but I did not have a degree they respected for the kind of work they did. What I did have, however, was experience and a sense of conviction about what I believed to be helpful in terms of caring for patients as well as about the crucial role staff played on units. After a time, I spoke privately with the woman to give her the opportunity to verbalize what she was thinking directly to me. It was the beginning of building a trusting relationship with this therapist. The Zen slogan, "Slowly, slowly get there fast" (Toms, 2001b) fit like a glove and served me well here. I made sure everyone had an opportunity to voice his or her opinions and I listened. It was not an easy transition for the staff and I understood their feelings. The acceptance of Zen seemed to allow me to have patience enough to give them the time they needed to make an adjustment without me taking it personally.

Through acceptance, patience, perseverance, and a lot of open discussions, the entire staff, including the nurses and the therapists, became a team. Previously the units had been managed rigidly by a list of rules set in stone. The result was that the staff had little input, so I encouraged them to get involved with the patients in order to grasp the significance of their roles in healing. Caring and creativity would be the philosophy and the backbone of the program. Slowly, the staff took the risk of becoming aware of their influence on the people in their care. They began to exercise their heart and their own intuitiveness. The result of this change was that the staff came to see patients as people who were in various kinds of emotional pain instead of as a mere diagnosis. When patients were admitted to the units they were no longer seen as interfering with the routine: Instead, they were welcomed as a person who was hurting. The clinical language on the unit changed from dismay at someone's disruptive behavior to positive interest and attention.

It was wonderful to observe the creative hearts and minds of the staff. Fear or anger was replaced with compassion, kindness and fun. There was a wonderful connection between the clinicians, nurses, auxiliary staff, and the psychiatrists. Team meetings provided many examples of this interdisciplinary sense of community. For example, the clinicians decided to invite patients to our staff meetings when it was agreed that such a meeting might benefit a particular person. Staff and patients become partners in care, with each one offering their own suggestions concerning what seemed to be helpful, what did not, and what the next step might be. The concept of interdisciplinary and cooperative openness became pervasive on the units. Although such an atmosphere is extremely labor-intensive and must be done with care, the extra degree of awareness and hard work that it required all seemed worthwhile to everyone involved.

Zen and Insensitive Therapists

One time I worked with a therapist who would not close his door when a patient was in his office and it was right across the hall from mine. One day in the lobby, I saw a patient of his extend his hand to shake that of the therapist. He did not reciprocate. The look on the patient's face showed how he felt and the wonderful smile that was there slowly faded into oblivion. I felt a great sense of dismay for the client and a sense of sadness for my colleague. The fact that he could not reach out to a person who was extending himself in an act of warmth or friendliness seemed tragic. The old adage "you can only give what you have" seemed to sum up what happened here.

The thing that bothers me most about therapists is when they seem to forget humanity, especially that of their clients. All too many times, I have seen and heard my colleagues laugh about clients, make insensitive remarks about them, judge some people, manipulate others, and disregard patients as human beings in a large number of ways. I am not sure what is behind this behavior but I do know that from a Zen perspective, it usually arises from ignorance and insecurities. Not surprisingly, I have had to fire staff for such things. It is always very painful for me to do that. Fortunately, they have not been people whom I hired. Instead, they were people who had already been working in an area when I took it over. I realize that in such circumstances, staff had very little idea of my expectations or my philosophy. Therefore, I spent some time talking with them about these issues. When I saw behavior that I did not approve of, I discussed it with the person and gave them some time to change. Firing people always seems painful to me, even when they do file a grievance, but the patient comes first. These experiences taught me the importance of developing a good hiring process, which I will talk about in chapter 5.

Zen and Supervisors or Administrators

In the 1970s a recently hired medical director for a program in which I worked called me into his office late one day. I was expecting this meeting because I knew he had talked with several of my colleagues about their job performance. Many of them said that the meetings were quite unpleasant and even cried in them. He found fault with their programs as well as their overall performance. I was prepared for this encounter, so when he called me in I was ready. Most of the time he talked. His "discussion" consisted largely of general ridicule concerning my philosophy, questions about my clinical judgment, castigations concerning the program I was managing, and more. The bottom line was that he felt I was not doing an adequate job and asked me to explain why I thought I was qualified for the position. I did not feel a need to defend myself because I can only do what I can do. I explained my philosophy as best as I could and at the end of the time we spent together I laughed at something he said. Although I don't remember the particular comment, I do remember that we somehow connected and he said, "You fared better than your cohorts." Taking the time to know the people who work with me and learning how the patients react to our caring served me well here because I knew that what I was doing helped. No form of attack on me, our work, or the program was going to change that, so I had nothing to fear in losing a job. It was all very simple.

Reflecting back at that time, I realize now that no one told me how to direct the program, that a good part of it was based on my experiences, on instincts and intuitiveness, and on the Golden Rule. As the Buddha said,

> Do not be satisfied with hearsay or with tradition or with legendary lore or with what has come down in scriptures or with conjecture or with logical inference or with weighing evidence or with liking for a view after pondering over it or with someone else's ability or with the thought "The monk is our teacher." When you

know in yourselves: "These things are wholesome, blameless, commended by the wise, and being adopted and put into effect they lead to welfare and happiness," then you should practice and abide in them. (Batchelor, 1997, p. xiii)

I listened to the medical director's comments, of course, but I knew there was no logic or truth connected with his words. Therefore, his expressions of anger and hostility flew past me without a hit. Indeed, a few days later the administrative director told me that he had received comments from David Ragan of the National Institute of Mental Health saying that, "The emergency service is exemplary and the inpatient, partial hospitalization, and volunteer programs are outstanding" (Freedman, Kaplan, & Shaddock, 1975, p. 2,318).

Zen and Paperwork

I have said many times that connecting with people is a key aspect of Buddhism. But most of us do not realize that we let others know in very indirect ways if we are interested in making a connection with them, too. For example, the posters we have on our office walls or in the hallways of an institution say something about how we regard others. The forms we give people to fill out and ways we introduce them to our organizational rules and procedures also tells something about our willingness to connect with others, or not. Unfortunately, the "not" is often the case.

For example, when I was responsible for the psychiatric intensive care unit (PICU) I just mentioned, I felt a great sense of consternation when I first read the existing unit rules. I knew right then that I would have to change the wording. Although reproducing the entire form is too lengthy for our purposes, let me show examples of the original language. Then I will contrast it with just a few of the revisions I made so that the difference becomes clear.

PICU UNIT RULES (STANDARD VERSION)

Because the Psychiatric Intensive Care Unit provides intensive care under controlled conditions, certain restrictions do exist in order to provide a safe environment. You are expected to follow the PICU 24-hour structure, rules, and scheduled activities. Adherence to this program will reflect your progress, and ability to be transferred.

1. The following items will not be allowed in PICU: wire, glass, metal objects, aerosol containers, sharp objects, belts, cords, ribbons,

matches or lighters, boots or high-heeled shoes of any type, panty hose or any type of nylons, shoe laces or other items specified by the staff.

2. Proper attire including undergarments, footwear, and sleepwear is required. No see-through or clothing endorsing alcohol or drugs will be allowed. Shirts must be buttoned. You may not be out of your room unless completely clothed. Unless otherwise indicated patients must wear soft-soled shoes or slippers. The safety standards dictate that all patients must wear shoes or socks when out of their rooms. If you leave the unit you must wear shoes.

3. Patients are to be dressed and have their rooms cleaned every morning by 8:30 A.M. Patients must wear street clothing during the day unless bedridden.

4. Visitation by immediate family only is recommended. No one under the age of 16 may visit. Visiting is restricted to the area by the nurse's station and the day room. No visitor is allowed in the patient room.

5. Self-destructive behavior will not be allowed, such as ear-piercing and/or body tattooing or anything else that is considered self-destructive.

6. Patients may be searched if suspected of possessing contraband material.

7. Patients may not borrow, lend, sell, give, or trade any of their belongings with other patients or staff.

8. Smoking will be allowed only in the uncarpeted day room and the telephones in the hallway. All patients' cigarettes will be kept at the nurses station and will be dispensed one at a time by the nursing staff on the half hour and on the hour.

PICU UNIT RULES (REVISED VERSION)

Welcome to our unit in the hospital. We want to make the time you spend with us a time of healing. Please know we are here to provide you with care and comfort. The following guidelines are written to help make your stay with us less confusing. Feel free to come to us with your concerns and questions.

1. To ensure comfort, please wear casual clothing. Personal toilet articles should be in plastic containers. There may be items the nursing staff will request to remain at the nurses' station; the reasons will be explained by the staff.

2. Please discuss with the nursing staff when a person younger than 16 years may be a visitor.

3. Fire regulations state smoking is permitted only in the dayroom and by the telephones.

As usual, I find simplicity to be more helpful than complexity. In this case, it is possible for three sentences to take the place of eight, which is sure to be helpful when people are confused or have a difficult time concentrating in the first place. As you can see, I believe it is essential to be hospitable to a person who is being admitted to a hospital. This approach requires us to be available, to be sensitive to the person who finds themselves coming into a "strange country" where social customs and expectations are unfamiliar. Questions may not make sense. Some of them may be intrusive. Restrictions are common. Medical orders may sound frightening. Leaving a loved one or being alone can be difficult, and so forth. The forms should be designed to facilitate people communicating and connecting with one another as human beings. The point is that although each treatment center or program is going to have written rules, they are words, too. Therefore, they should be used with an ear toward "Right Speech." Staff should always be mindful, charitable, and above all compassionate, and this applies to the forms in our work as well.

QUESTION 7: ZEN FOR THE THERAPIST (AVOIDING BURNOUT)

C: Finally, Joan, I wonder what Zen can do to help me as a therapist? This question actually has two parts. One is how can Zen help me deal with the stresses and strains of the kind of work we do, especially in terms of preventing what is usually called burnout? The other is how can Zen help me grow as a therapist and person?

J: Well, Chris, this may be a difficult question to answer because even after nearly five decades in the field, I have never experienced burnout, although I have experienced plenty of frustration at times. The work keeps "juicing" me, which is a Zen way of saying that it keeps energizing me. Wavy Gravy, who was a "social activist, a one-time presidential candidate, a circus impresario, a quintessential clown, and an ice cream flavor" (Leiper, 1999, p. 6), received a reward for altruism in 1999. At the time, he made a remark concerning the difficult kind of work that he had been doing most of his lifetime that is relevant here. When he was asked what inspired his commitment to service, Wavy Gravy said, "It gets me high. Service is a drug I can't find in the pharmaceutical cabinet. I do it for the buzz. It's strictly greed—greed for good vibes" (p. 7). When I read this I thought, "That's it, that is why I do what I do; he said what I feel." Ever since being in therapy with Sully I have had a great longing to give to others what he gave to me: acceptance, unconditional love, and compassion. From the moment I walked onto the psychiatric unit so many years ago, I felt at home. I have dreamed about doing things to help people as early as eight years old, when I wanted to manage an orphanage. In my mind's eye, I can still see the limestone building in Sandusky, Ohio, that housed "the orphans." For whatever reason, my heart longed to have these kids happy, just as I want my patients to be in an atmosphere where they are not afraid to face their fears.

As a practitioner of Zen, I believe that all people deserve to be happy, but since managed care has come to the fore I have struggled with the fact that there are people who come to us with serious emotional problems. There are all kinds of things to feel frustrated, even angry, about in our work today. For example, instead of focusing on developing a sense of connection with others as the primary goal in therapy, medication seems to be used as the treatment of choice, even in centers that used to focus on psychotherapy. It is like a bad science fiction novel: We now live in a country that has a serious drug problem, and yet it advocates treating life's problems with drugs instead of helping people learn how to find solutions and to live in healthier ways! It may be just as Koerner suggests: "Pharmaceutical companies have come up with a new strategy to market their drugs: First go out and find a new mental illness, then push the pills to cure it" (2002, p. 58). Because of my nursing background, I am very concerned about the side effects of these medications, which include potential liver damage, weight increase, a lack of energy, disruptive sleep patterns, elevated blood pressure, decreased libido, and, of course, the enormous financial drain on families. And this does not even mention the unknown long-term effects that may occur by pouring these powerful mind altering drugs into the developing brains of children, which is a trend that seems to be increasing by the day!

However, the picture is even darker than that: Cutting back on services for all ages, increasing the use of powerful medication, and ever expanding health care paperwork seems to have pushed concern for the individual client to the last spot on our contemporary services list! In addition, various other negative social and economic factors seem to have worked together to create a situation where money that had been designated to help poor people is no longer available. Our nation is going to end up spending money, but the decisions won't be made by those who are closely "connected" with the people who need help the most. There will be some money spent on prevention, but most of it will be spent on trying to protect society from itself in the form of supporting gated communities, prisons, and whatever else to keep people isolated from each other.

Like many therapists, I found myself being eaten up by these unfortunate conditions. It finally reached the point that it was beginning to interfere with my work because I was becoming preoccupied with the anger these forces seemed to generate in me. Coming to terms with all of this has been difficult. My anger was closing me up, which cannot be good for me or for my clients. While meditating on this growing sense of rage and frustration, I realized that keeping my heart closed to the pain would either lead to becoming a part of a system that turned away from people who are in the midst of suffering or to burning out and quitting altogether. In either case, staying caught in my own ego concerns would make me a victim of my own suffering. I knew that I had to open up my heart in order to let the anger go.

It was a very trying realization for me, but by centering on the Four Noble Truths, along with the concept of impermanence we discussed in chapter 2, I was able to get past my anger and the negativity that it often generates. Over time, facing the truth, increasing my awareness, and continuing to meditate helped: These are not just intellectual exercises. I realized I was very angry and fearful because I had no control over the situation: I could not understand how "they" could not see that there would be serious repercussions of such practices in our homes, our schools, our social services, and even our prisons. It is as though our society suffers from some form of "mass denial." Others who are more Biblically oriented might invoke the phrase, "They know not what they do" to characterize the folly of this situation. Buddhists, of course, would turn to the notion of karma to understand the vicious cycle we may have set in motion. It has been very difficult to face this demon. But now when I speak with people who have been hurt by our system, I feel a sense of kinship. My own "stuff" helped me become closer to people, to all people, even my family. Zen Buddhism is not a practice for my work alone; it is a practice for my life.

Thanks to the teachings of the Buddha, I am no longer as fearful about the uncertainty of life, including the changes in our field. The Four Noble Truths and the Eightfold Path speak the truth and show a *way* to be fearless in the face of it. These principles help me to wake up to myself and to others, to open my senses to what is actually present, and to experience the freedom of an open heart. In this way, Buddhism is never just theory or a belief; instead it is a practice, a way of being. Seeing uncertainty as a part of suffering helps me to face the unknown more honestly. Being more open to the future instead of feeling overwhelmed by its possibilities seems to lighten the load both for me and for those with whom I work. Fortunately, Zen's attitude toward the process of learning is helpful here because it is couched in an atmosphere of love and patience. To expect perfection is out of the question, but we can find meaning in our work every day, even under current conditions. The value of always having a beginner mind is that there is always plenty of room to "wake up" as Zen masters like to say, and to learn. I find the more I know myself, the more I'm able to give to others, and that through this process, I am a happier person. That may sound selfish but it is the truth and it helps me to survive in this field.

Another teaching that helps me here as well as in my personal growth, is learning how to look directly at fear, which is to say learning how to stop myself from being overwhelmed by fear or by the temptation to avoid it. Fear, which is often connected to anger, still has the capacity to undo me, but, through practice, it certainly doesn't have the power that it once did to discombobulate me. The Zen teachings concerning embracing one's fear, which means using it as a teacher, doesn't make being afraid any easier because I still feel the sensations of being scared. But, if I am open and fearless enough, I also know that what I am struggling with is probably related to some form of "clinging" or attachment. I realize that this statement may sound rather like "pie in the sky," so I am reluctant to talk about it in this way. However, it is the truth and I do not want to avoid it because of how it may sound to someone else. If we believe that it is possible to benefit more from going through the fire than avoiding it, fear becomes less dreadful. That may not be much, but it seems to be enough to make a difference.

Although I have never experienced the phenomenon of burnout, it doesn't mean I am not in sympathy with other clinicians. So let me share something about how I face the frustration, anger, and fear that I believe is usually at the bottom of this feeling. The story involves a mountain, a horse, and an event that shows how it is possible to avoid stress by surrendering to what "is" without giving up what one believes in. It begins with joining my daughter, two young granddaughters, ages 9 and 11, and my daughter's aunt on a trail riding journey in Arizona. This guided ride up into the mountain lasted two hours and all the others were experienced riders. Obviously, I was not really aware of what I was getting into when I agreed to go! For a short while I felt perfectly at ease on the horse and enjoyed the beauty of the terrain. I was the last person in line and my horse was not in a hurry, as he had a reputation of being slow. Gradually we began to climb and at first it seemed fun, even exhilarating.

Then, I began to realize that what goes up must come down—and it sure looked like a long way to go! As if that weren't bad enough, I then became aware that we were on the edge of a cliff and that the trail was narrowing. Now, I don't like looking down in general because I can get anxious around heights, so I found myself saying to myself, "I am going to end up a bucket of bones at the bottom of this place" more than once. The palms of my hands were getting sweaty. Because Coco, my horse, and I were last, I was in a perfect position to see the horse in front of me stumble on rocks and stones again and again. Soon I began to feel genuinely apprehensive. To make matters worse, we were beginning to travel up grades that seemed impossible. The guide told us what to do in order to help our horses, which was to lean back in the saddle and hold on to the saddle horn with both hands. But it sure didn't help me, because leaning back seemed to make the angle of our ascent even worse, as though we were going to tip over backwards.

I remember watching Bobby, our guide, go up one hill then on to another and feeling helpless: I felt trapped in the saddle, like a person on a roller coaster without rails. I followed Bobby's directions about how to sit on our horses and was very scared when I realized that there was nothing I could do except pay attention to what was happening *right now*. All I could say was "Oh, my gosh!" However, paying attention to reality instead of to my fears seemed to turn the tide. I began to focus on the task at hand, emotionally, physically, and as strange as it may seem, even spiritually. Not only was there no place I could escape to, but I was sitting on fear as well as leather. I realized that I had only two choices: to get off and walk back which would be very difficult for someone who was in her 70s, or to become one with Coco.

I was told to "let the horse go" and knew that doing so would be in his best interest as well as mine. So I began to focus on "being with" Coco and began talking with him. I remember encouraging Coco and patting his neck as we rode. Of course, I do not know whether my words and actions meant anything to him or not. However, the tone of my voice or not fighting him so hard may have been helpful. I do know that by letting go of my struggle for control, I was able to give myself over to the horse and to our situation. In doing so, I also became liberated from my fear and anxiety because now we were a team working together. I literally felt a new kind of freedom come over me and experienced a desire to shout for joy! The realization that control of the situation was out of my hands, that it was up to Coco to get us back safely, transformed everything. It showed me, for instance, the folly of trying to fight against the horse that was carrying me toward the future. The way was now clear and I felt free, which enabled me to experience the joy of the journey. I lost my desire to make him do anything. When I spoke to Bobby about how doubtful I felt at times, he smiled and said, "Coco wanted to get back safely as much as you did," which suggested to me that there was some wisdom in trusting to the present.

What I learned from Coco was this: Sometimes I have to put my trust in something other than myself because there are times in life when I don't have the power to do anything about a situation or event except to make it worse. This realization was very profound for me at the time because it showed me a way to come to terms with the difficulties and stresses created by the lack of control. It was a great lesson that is relevant here, because burnout often occurs when professionals are afraid—afraid that they are losing control of their work, of their circumstances, of their career, or of their ability to have a positive impact on others. Zen helps me to avoid burnout because it teaches me to ride the stress rather than try to control it. Dealing with the fear that often lies at the bottom of burning out and the stress it creates is a matter of practicing *Right View* and *Right Understanding*. It is not easy to get to this level, but we have a lifetime to do it.

In *The Song of God: The Bhagavad-Gita* (1972) the protagonist named Arjuna was talking with his teacher, Krishna. Arjuna was in a serious dilemma: He was to do something that he agonized over. Therapists also face terrible dilemmas concerning the nature of their work and how to go about it every day. Deciding whether one should focus on the client or on doing one's paperwork in a timely fashion, staying with someone until they get better or working within the time limits set by insurance companies, and deciding between helping someone discover their own path to freedom versus having to practice "manualized" approaches, are but three examples of what we face today. What Krishna said to his student also seems to apply to mental health work today. "Set thy heart upon thy work, but never on its reward. Work not for a reward; but never cease to do thy work" (Mascaro, 1962, p. 52). Many times therapists seem to become caught up on the horns of these dilemmas until they either give up or burn out. Either alternative involves turning away from helping others, so a middle path is needed, such as the one found in Zen.

Rather than risk the feeling of chronic anger at the system, frustration with the work I love, or fear of the lack of control, the Zen attitude of acceptance seems the best route for me to follow. I am not happy with the current trends because I see too much suffering that is not being healed, so acceptance should not be confused with withdrawal from the world and its problems or with a state of passivity. Unfortunately, many people tend to see Zen as implying this kind of passivity, but not Western Zen. Passivity is just not in my vocabulary as a person and I do not think I would be accused of advocating a passive stance toward social problems or injustice. Quite the opposite: Staying in the saddle instead of trying to control, cling to, complain about, or jump off the horse seems to take me to a place where I can continue to do my work, which is where I know I *can* make a difference. Roshi Bernard Tegsugen Glassman, who has done much for homeless people, seems to have dealt with the same kind of dilemma in his book, *Instructions to the Cook*. After a long time of facing the overwhelming task of trying to relieve this kind of large-scale human suffering with even less money to help, he comes to a certain point.

> And so I found myself renewing my vow. Maybe it would take forever to feed and house all the hungry ghosts in all the worlds. But however long it took, I thought, I would do my best to keep on cooking and serving the most delicious and joyous feast I could. (1996, p. 169)

Ultimately, I find myself remembering that people, especially clients, have voices. The fact that they need to be heard and that I want to hear them, helps me to keep doing just that.

There is one more thing that helps me avoid the experience of burnout that is just as important as learning about fear and control from my anger. It has to do with the fact that the work of a therapist is privileged: It brings us into close proximity to people who are growing, who are waking up to their own inner awareness in whatever way they can. There are two reasons that this aspect of our work motivates me to stay in it, even in the conditions we face today and in spite of the fact that I am well beyond the point at which most people retire. First is the honor that comes with being able to listen to someone's stories, to be an audience for their inner voice. I never tire of this part of our work; no therapist does. Even though our work is sometimes difficult and is becoming more so with each new regulation, I see it as a two-way process. Second, the Buddha teaches that through being present to the suffering of another in the mode of compassion, we have the opportunity to learn about ourselves as well as to help another. In some very real ways, then, doing therapy is a part of my Zen practice. For example, while Ram Dass was in India, he asked his teacher Neem Karoli Baba, "How do I get free?" The master said, "Feed people." Ram Dass expected a different kind of answer, so he asked, "How do I get enlightened?" Then Baba said, "Serve people" (Dass, 1987, p. 67). Now I understand that all the while I have been working with people who have been traumatized in one way or another, I have been in the process of opening up my heart to myself, too. It makes me wonder who gives more to whom?

In sum, Chris, Zen has taught me a few things about handling stress. One is to keep my heart open to people and to myself, even open to situations that I think are terrible. In this sense, Zen reminds me that it is possible to ride the horse near the edge of the cliff, instead of trying to deny or control reality. Although doing so is not easy, Zen teaches me to live things as they "are" because I can see, hear, and understand better that way. It teaches me that going through a problem or difficulty is usually less stressful in the long run than worrying about them or trying to avoid them. I have also learned that instead of trying to control it, accepting reality as it is seems to relieve some of the burden it can create. Similarly, I have found that the more I become aware of myself and my reactions to events through the practice of Zen, the easier it is for me to respond to daily hassles and frustrations in a way that is both realistic and healthy. Finally, though easier said than done, understanding the principle of *impermanence*, that "this too will pass," seems to offer a last saving grace that helps me to deal with the stress of our work. Impermanence is freeing for me because it stands as a hope-filled *truth* that comes in to play just when things get to their worst, namely, that things *will* change, providing I have the patience to let that happen. In short, the teachings of the Buddha have taught me to appreciate life. No matter how tough things seem to become, there is a lesson to learn. Difficulties are a part of our path, which is a never-ending process of waking up to ourselves and to others, but so is compassion.

When facing fear, or even when I am unsure of myself for one reason or another, I often turn to Charlotte Joko Beck, a wonderful Zen author and teacher who has taught at the Zen Center of San Diego for many years. Like most ancient traditions, Zen uses parables and stories to make crucial points, which is a practice that continues today. All of her stories are inspiring to me, but one of my favorites is *The Parable of Mushin* (1989), so let me attempt to describe how it applies here. Mushin is a man who desires to reach enlightenment so much that his inability to accept anything else almost prevents him from finding it. Mushin suffers many losses because of his personality, which could be being too "macho" in some cases, or being too "headstrong" or "compulsive," and so forth in others. In any case, at some point, Mushin buys a book called *How to Catch the Train of Enlightenment*. After reading it, he decides to pack up a few belongings and goes to the train station. He waits and waits and waits. The train finally comes, but it does not stop for him. The same thing happens over and over and over again. Pretty soon Mushin realizes that he is not alone, that many people want the same thing and they come to the train station to wait, too.

Soon, Mushin notices that some of the others have children with them and that bothers him because the kids don't have anything to do while their parents wait. Even though he is primarily interested in the train, Mushin finds himself becoming increasingly concerned for the children. However, being human, things are not that simple. Although he begins to give more and more of his time and energy to the welfare of the children, Mushin feels angry about the unfairness of the situation. After all, building shelters, setting up schools, and creating a supportive community for the children takes time and energy away from trying to get on the train. Eventually, he even experiences resentment and bitterness, perhaps much as many therapists do when faced with the constant needs of their clients in a world that doesn't seem to support providing the services they require. At one point, Mushin even becomes envious of those who are still pursuing the train of enlightenment because they seem to have it easier than him.

In the story, which should be read in its entirety for its beauty as well as for all of its lessons, Mushin continues to do his work. But his frustration and fearfulness increase his suffering to an unbearable level. Finally, he gives up and just sits, perhaps like the Buddha. As I understand the story, it is only when Mushin lets go of his feelings and preoccupation that he is free to realize his goal. For it is at this time that the train comes for him, bringing with it understanding, the understanding that there is no secret to discover, only the wholeness of life to appreciate, which is present all the time if we can but see it. Like Mushin, therapists who do not burn out may learn to attend to what is in front of them in spite of all the difficulties; doing the work that there is for us to do can take us to unexpected places. At least it seems to do that for me.

CHAPTER 5

Integrating Zen and Psychotherapy: Connections and Limits

The tempo of our dialog between Zen and traditional therapies began in a very metered fashion so that the participants could examine the fundamental issues or characteristics of their respective positions. For example, representing the voice of tradition, Chris introduced the goals, definitions, and parameters of our investigation. Next, Joan, speaking for the psychotherapeutic potential of Zen, did the same with its fundamental principles and their implications for psychotherapy. After these foundations were carefully established, it was possible to increase the tempo by moving to a question-and-answer format, with Chris asking Joan to address specific clinical issues from a Zen perspective. Now it is time to move into our final dialog, which we hope takes on the form of a very lively discussion.

This part of the dialog between traditional and nontraditional psychotherapy takes us through such questions as: Where does Zen stand in relation to the medical or "evidence-based" treatment models that are so prevalent today? How can Zen find a place in the expanding world of managed care that is frustrating so many clinicians and clients? Is there a way to incorporate Zen into clinical education or clinical supervision without losing our valuable scientific foundations? Last, and perhaps the most important for our purposes, we need to know whether Zen can be complementary to scientific psychotherapy or if it must stand as an alternative to it and what the answer may mean one way or another.

ZEN, THE MEDICAL MODEL,
AND EVIDENCE-BASED TREATMENT

C: Let us hear what you have to say, Joan, about how you, as a student of Zen, feel about such things as the medical model for understanding and dealing with mental illness and the evidence-based model for treating it. As we saw in chapters 1 and 3, these two related approaches currently dominate or are coming to dominate the mental health scene. In essence, this model involves a three-step paradigm that begins with the collection of information about symptoms, continues with a diagnosis, and ends in treatment. Ideally, the clinician gathers information about symptoms as objectively as possible, uses that data to arrive at an understanding of the problem, which usually involves a DSM diagnosis, and ends by turning to research-based information concerning treatment efficacy in order to select the approach that has been identified as being the most effective for someone suffering from the identified condition.

J: It is very simple from a Zen perspective, Chris. For me, the number one thing to keep in mind in regard to that model is that you simply disregard the diagnosis. Now I know that is a powerful statement, so let me qualify it. Of course, I realize that in the medical, insurance, and administrative worlds, diagnosis is essential. My point is that after this step is out of the way, it is important to forget about it because that approach, especially the labeling aspect of a diagnosis but the entire mind-set as well, can intrude on the connection between the client and the therapist. The danger is that one could end up seeing the diagnosis and not the person, which is a phenomenon I have seen countless times over so many decades of practice, particularly as a nurse in medically oriented psychiatric settings. An especially disturbing aspect of this model is that it is very, very easy to misuse a diagnosis because it makes it easy for the professional to focus on the diagnosis and not the person who is in need of treatment. Furthermore, it is not unheard of to have clinicians differ on the diagnosis, which complicates an already complicated situation. Clinicians, even good ones, may make assumptions based on a diagnosis about what a person is like, where therapy is going to go, and if they are looking forward to the work or not, *even before they meet the person or take the time to know them as an individual!* In fact, at one time when I was responsible for an inpatient unit, I would not even tell the staff the admitting diagnosis of a patient so that they would not have a preconceived idea of the person in order for them to develop their own relationship. All too often, a diagnosis is more than a word: It can paint a picture and that image, which the clinician carries into the office, can be totally off-center, not to mention that it always fails to convey something about the characteristics of the person that are healthy, unique, and creative, all of which are very important, too.

C: I remember a client I once had who seems to reflect what you are saying. She was a young woman, only 17, who had just suffered her first schizophrenic episode and was in our inpatient setting. After two weeks, she went home for her first weekend pass. That very night, she tried to kill herself and almost succeeded. Later, I asked her why she did that because she seemed to be doing so well up until that time. She replied, "Well, on the way out I passed by the nursing station and there was a big meeting going on. The door was open and I heard my name mentioned, so I stopped to listen. I heard my doctor say that I am a schizophrenic. We all know what that means, so I figured that my life was over anyway, I might as well just get it over with now." Joan, most of us learn about the power of labels and the danger of labeling from our sociology classes, but I think you mean those things and more. It is the more that I am interested in, especially how Zen approaches the problem.

J: Again, for Zen, it is a paradox. On one hand, the teachings are direct and simple. On the other hand they are difficult to live in a health care system that seems to stress intellectual knowledge instead of using our hearts, especially compassion toward others. It is very important to be open anew with each person you are helping. There is no need to complicate things with theory. For example, in many team meetings that I have been at, someone, and they are not being unkind, will say something like, "Well, she's a borderline," and all of a sudden there is a grimace on somebody's face. The grimace shows that the therapist has a certain attitude toward people based on that label and he or she may carry it internally into the session *without having even met the person.* The clinician is already assuming that the patient *is* whatever image they have of "the borderline," and they have more or less convinced themselves that they know how this patient is going to respond according to the diagnosis. This kind of assumption clearly robs the patient, the clinician, and their relationship of an opportunity to make an honest or clean connection. Such a closing off of possibilities and what might happen is very poor practice from a Zen perspective; very poor, because openness is a necessity. This kind of thinking is what we might call "wrong thinking." It certainly is not Right Thinking. Like I said, if a diagnosis is necessary, include it as you need to then forget it as quickly as possible. See what is there, not what you think is there. A few years ago a friend gave me a gift that contained a number of Zen sayings on them. One of them applies here: *The true person sees what the eyes see and does not add to it.*

C: How does Zen help us avoid these mind-sets?

J: You must remember the principle of *mindfulness*, Chris, which in this case means seeing the patient afresh. In order to do that, it would be helpful to disregard everything that you think you know about the person. For example forget about whatever you have read on an assessment sheet or a diagnostic report, so that you can be connected with the person in front of you and listen to that person and start a fresh beginning. In this way, being mindful helps to make sure that you are not clouded with preconceived ideas about what to expect, what to do, and whatever else that might come through your thoughts. Zen helps keep your perception clear, like a clear slate or clear pond. This metaphor is a favorite in Zen because a still pool of water creates an environment that is conducive to creating accurate reflections of reality, where, by contrast, one that is clouded or rippling does not. Such clarity allows one to be receptive to what is really present, not what the perceiver thinks is or should be present, which is often distorted. In so doing, one sees the client as an individual, as they *really* are. That means, for instance, that the client's history becomes important to the therapist because it is part of who they are, not just a report on a chart. Such openness is not a particularly easy thing to accomplish.

C: I think that is wonderfully "clear," Joan. Not just the example, but it seems to me that Zen makes "being clear" so much easier to grasp than what I learned from my training in humanistic psychology about achieving a certain kind of reflective presence. "Being present" seemed like a good therapeutic idea to me, but the traditional literature on what was actually meant by that word and how to go about achieving it always seemed rather vague to me, both then and now. Zen seems more articulate in this regard, probably because it has had several centuries to identify, articulate, and refine what being clear means and how to get there.

J: Well, there are some correspondences between Zen and the humanistic perspective as you noted in chapter 3, Chris, but there is a danger in using these kinds of labels, too. By using any kind of label, you encapsulate yourself. From a Zen perspective that is puzzling because it closes off part of reality by limiting you to preconceived notions about it based on ideas that are characteristic of one particular point of view. This is a reason why sometimes Zen masters seem so elusive about explaining what they do, how it is done, and why it should be. Sometimes I may sound this way to you, although it is not a deliberate thing I am trying to do.

C: Yes, indeed, Joan. I am glad you said that because, like many people, I have found Zen to be too elusive at times. Now at least I am beginning to understand why and that seems to help. Would you do away with the label of "therapist," too?

J: I am not so sure that I would, but anything that is attached to labels, including degrees and titles, is a potential limitation because it limits possibilities. Why would you want to do that to yourself as a clinician? You may miss important things about the person that way. I think with Zen, perception is clearer because it is more open due to the fact that, in part, Zen is a way of living, thinking, and understanding. Zen does not have a bunch of "shoulds" like so many other approaches. It does offer guidelines to help one keep on "the way," but Zen is more like an opening up than a closing off. This openness requires us to understand ourselves first because through it, we learn how to identify, trust, and use our "intuitiveness" as a tuning fork for others. When one does that, seeing, sensing, touching, and listening are on another dimension.

Remember that person I described who was angry and out of control? After one episode, she said to me "The madder I got, the calmer you were," which is to say that by understanding yourself first, something happens for the other, too. I don't pretend to understand what that is all about, but I can trust it. Must we label it? I don't think so because labeling, once again, is like something being squeezed into a box that is far too small for it. When we label ourselves we get the same results. Even when you label yourself a social scientist, Chris, you are limiting yourself. We all do it, but it is helpful to become aware of how we do that to ourselves and what it means for our perception and how it limits our possibilities of continued growth.

C: Of course, I see your point and cannot disagree with the importance of being open or that a diagnosis can interfere with our work, even though I am committed to the scientific approach. So let me ask you this instead, what do you "do" in regard to a client's symptoms? What do you see when you see them?

J: That is an interesting question because symptoms don't mean much to me either. I know that they mean something on a chart and I am not denying that whatsoever. But when it comes to being with somebody and connecting with them, the symptoms, no matter which ones they are, to me are simply what the person is *doing or saying* right here and now. I talked with a woman who was hallucinating yesterday and I still have to say that it doesn't mean anything especially different to me. By that I mean the symptoms don't alter what I am going to be doing. It is like I am walking *with* them. Although language always disguises as much as it reveals, a client's comments let me know something about what they are thinking, where the trouble is, and how they are suffering. That is all I need to know about them.

C: Let me clarify the question further. The biological perspective would tend to use symptoms to make a diagnosis, but the psychodynamic perspective might try to understand their symbolic meanings. A cognitive-behavioral psychotherapist would understand a symptom as something that is irrational and that needs to be understood as such, but the humanistic perspective would attempt to understand what they mean for the person suffering them. How would the symptoms look to someone seeing them from a Zen perspective?

J: Of course, I can only speak for myself. First of all, I would be aware of myself, aware of whether or not I was apprehensive, for example. I would also be aware of what I would like the person to know in order to lessen their pain or to help themselves. But mainly, I would be accepting of them, the situation, and the particular manifestation of their pain, because that tends to put both them and me more at ease.

C: Now how would your "acceptance" differ from that associated with the other perspectives?

J: You are asking me a question that is very difficult because I don't know what acceptance would be for a person practicing from any other perspective. All I know for sure is that I would be aware of my thoughts and whether or not they are making things more complicated than they already are for the client. My main concern would be to do no harm, to not make trouble, to not add to the suffering. I am very serious about that—and this commitment would guide my behavior. For instance, not wanting to do harm I would be conscious of the words and the tone of my voice. *Right Speech* guides my behavior in the *Right* direction, and so forth, according to the Eightfold Path I am trying to walk. This is why I say that Zen is a way of living, not thinking. It is not an intellectual thought process; it comes from the heart.

C: Let's pursue that some more, Joan, Right Thinking in this situation would be what?

J: That's easy! First of all, do no harm, be present and be aware that the environment must convey to patients that they will be cared for with kindness.

C: So you would keep that in mind.

J: Yes, always, it is the *Right* thing to do in both the Zen and the clinical sense.

C: Once again, I see Zen offering something that other perspectives do not seem to do well, at least to me, which is a clear articulation of what to do in terms of "being with" the other, especially when the situation is complicated by strong feelings, difficult decisions, or overwhelming problems. The principles of Zen, in this case those of the Eightfold Path, seem to offer concrete guidelines, not just ideas. I feel like I should write them down on a list and carry them with me, because they seem so clear and useful.

J: When somebody does no harm, something happens to the therapist as well as to the patient. In other words, it is a two-way street. I have seen so many instances over the years, Chris, where the therapist, the tech, the doctor, or the nurse, becomes "unglued" with a patient, or even with a fellow staff. When one is in the *Right* frame of mind, which is to say when one is mindful, anxiety seems to lessen. Perhaps because I am calmer, the patient is not as afraid of me and does not feel threatened by me. The same thing applies to difficult situations with one's colleagues or bosses, too! At least I don't add fuel to the fire: Zen helps me to do no harm.

C: Once again, I can see Zen in action here in terms of its "rightness." In this case, it seems that walking the Eightfold Path may help one to "hold back" just when "holding back" is exactly the "right" thing to do. Many times, for instance, I experience an urge to "rush in" in order to "make things better" for a person or to "prevent" something from getting out of control. Holding back may be the "right" kind of response if I was uncertain of what to do because anything else could add to suffering in the form of increasing anxiety, defensiveness, anger or whatever. Anything of that nature, by contrast, would be "wrong" thinking, speaking, acting and so forth. Maybe we should articulate the "Wrong Path" just so we can see what not acting in the "right" way would look like! I think I can also see where I would benefit from such things as Right Speech while in clinical staff meetings or when in academic committee meetings where an awful lot of "wrong speech" can certainly occur. Again, Zen seems like it offers a very practical and relatively clear guide for helping if not living. This aspect of Zen might be described as its "feminine" quality because it keeps us open to possibilities, though the word "receptive" may be a more descriptive term.

J: Yes, I like the word feminine very much here, Chris. The same point could be made about the young man I described earlier who was in a rage. I had a choice there, too. I could have tried to control the situation, which would have been the wrong thing to do because it would be like throwing up a red flag to an angry bull. Instead, I had an intuitive belief that, although I was certainly tense and very concerned, doing no harm would give events a better opportunity to unfold in a beneficial direction. Gratefully, I have found this usually does, but I don't take it for granted. I keep in mind "Do no harm."

C: Psychodynamic and humanistic therapists might do the same thing, but describe how and why in different ways, such as in order to let the clients "ventilate" or "get in touch" with their anger in order to "work through" or "encounter" the underlying conflict that gives rise to the problem.

J: Well, that is fine, too. I have no desire to compete with other points of view for theoretical dominance. I have found I connect with patients by doing what I do and I trust therapists will, too.

C: OK, Joan, we've talked about how Zen might handle symptoms and diagnosis, now what about the business of "treatment of choice"? A new twist on this approach is to call it "evidence-based treatment." This version of the three-step process mentioned above is based on the same rationale but stresses the third part more than the medical model: Only treatments with good empirical support are to be selected and, not so coincidentally, only they will be reimbursed by those who pay for treatment such as insurance providers.

J: That's a good question, but one that is in some way "nuts," which is my way of saying it is beside the point from the Zen perspective, and maybe even misleading. Here is where being connected with the client is so much more important from a Zen point of view than is knowing the diagnosis. Without that connection, everything can go "bonkers" at any time, even if there is good "evidence" for what was tried! The connection never fails, whereas symptoms can be misread, diagnoses can be wrong, and a "proven" treatment may not work for a given person in a given situation at a given time. *The real treatment of choice is being connected!* The moment I set eyes on somebody, Chris, connection is the most important thing. Without that, what follows may be quite hollow and artificial. I am convinced a client *intuitively* knows if a therapist is authentic and is present. I have emphasized over the years to staff how sensitive patients are to the environment and the attitude of staff to patients in general. *Patients sense incongruities and they are usually right.*

C: Oh, so it is not a matter of ignoring the literature concerning what works best for which conditions. It is more a matter that being connected is the treatment of choice in general, *in principle* as it were, even when using an evidence-based treatment of choice.

J: Yes! As far as I am concerned, though I also realize this point of view can be debated.

C: Well, what do you do, then, with the scientific literature concerning treatment of choice?

J: Do you really want to know what I do with it?

C: Yes, of course.

J: Well, I will try to be kind. The best way to say it is that I have read many articles on treating this and treating that, but they seem to take the heart out of the treatment picture time and time again.

C: OK, Joan, but I may have to take some issue with you here as a social scientist. So far, I can appreciate everything that you have said about symptoms and the labeling power of the diagnosis process. But I spent a considerable portion of my career studying symptoms-diagnosis-treatment and the treatment literature. There has been both a revolution in the field as I mentioned earlier in terms of a diagnostic system and an evolution in the field, especially in regard to some 30 years of research on "what works" that is still ongoing and that will be for the foreseeable future. These things cannot be ignored because in addition to finally being able to "prove" that psychotherapy "works" (Howard, Kopta, Krause, & Orlinsky, 1986; Seligman, 1995), knowledge is now being gained about which specific treatments work best for what specific disorders, although we have a long way to go here.

In other words, there is no denying that there is an important body of research knowledge on treatment and that it cannot be ignored by a conscientious clinician. I would even go so far as to say that treatment of choice also stands as an ethical issue. For example, not using documented treatments of choice means, among other things, not giving the client the care that they deserve as human beings, let alone for which they, or their tax or insurance dollars, pay. In many ways, then, treatment of choice is the heart and soul of what we do, so I would at least ask you this much: Are you disagreeing with the importance of what we are calling "the treatment of choice"? Are you saying that the concept is meaningless, which is to say that we should throw out some 100 years of work?

J: Chris, I am saying that I have never considered treatment of choice as an issue. Never, ever in my whole career, though I am concerned about negative forms of treatment or treatment that hurts, as I mentioned in chapter 2. I might add regarding treatment of choice, that is all well and good, but hopefully, the choice includes healing and relationships in the equation.

C: As a social scientist interested in complementarity, I struggle with such a position, Joan. What would you say to the claim that all the Zen in the world has little chance of helping someone with a significant degree of schizophrenia if they don't also have medications available?

J: OK, I see what you are saying and I don't disagree with it. If someone is psychotic, for example, I am very grateful for medications. I really am, but I have also seen medications abused by the medical profession. An example of this happened to a woman I had been seeing, who was told by the psychiatrist she would be on medication for the rest of her life. I was angry with the psychiatrist and addressed the issue at a later time. I told this woman I did not agree with the doctor, she was doing good work and chances were there would be a time she would no longer need medication. Another example, a woman told me her Prozac had been increased to 60 mg per day, even though she did not feel the medication would take away her underlying causes and feelings of depression. I do believe medication is dispensed on almost a random basis—if this doesn't "work" then the doctor tries something else and the client can be taking anywhere from one to four different medications at the same time. What this does to the functioning of the client and the body is questionable. Pharmaceutical houses seem to make a fortune at the expense of innocent people, including children as young as 3 years old.

If you were talking about a treatment of choice for severe mental illness, then I would definitely say medication is necessary. I have been around a lot of people who were psychotic or in remission and I am very much aware of the pain they suffer at those times of an acute episode. I want to make it clear that I do think there is often a need for medication. It is just that whether medication is indicated or not, there is still a more basic need, a need for connection, for compassion, sensitivity and gentleness, and that makes it more fundamental, and hence the actual "treatment of choice," at least from a Zen perspective. A sensitive relationship can help convince a frightened psychotic patient it is safe to take the medication that is being offered.

C: Although they do not talk about it in terms of being "connected," there are studies that indicate that the relationship is an important part, even in medical treatment. For example, some studies indicate that treatment compliance with medications occurs at a higher level if the patient trusts the physician, and others show that physicians are sued less often by patients they have a good relationship with than those with whom they have not "connected" (Moore, Adler, & Robertson, 2000). Would this be a fair statement, then? For you, as a Zen practitioner, the use of traditional therapies, such as those that use empirically based treatments of choice, would be a complement to your approach; whereas for me as a traditional therapist, the use of Zen would be a complement for my approach?

J: That makes sense.

C: So, an interesting reversal can occur with Zen, not just a mere dismissal of empirically based treatments. It looks to me like it is possible to achieve some degree of cooperation, if not integration, between Zen and these traditional models, providing the Zen involves the Middle Path rather than the extreme religious and philosophical forms.

J: Yes, it is important to realize that the Middle Path is not dogmatic.

ZEN AND THE WORLD OF MANAGED CARE

C: One of the things that I respect about you so much, Joan, is that your work does not occur in an ivory tower. You are "in the trenches," dealing with the stress of clients who have serious mental health problems and with the pressures of contending with managed care. I am interested in a firsthand look at how the teachings of the Buddha help you to endure such conditions year after year, even when you could have retired from it all a decade ago at an age when most people do that anyway.

J: I am grateful, very grateful to be doing what I am doing. Learning about the Buddha's teachings so many years ago through The Four Noble Truths and the Eightfold Path, have been more than helpful to me over the years personally and professionally. I continue to enjoy serving people as much now as I did as a student nurse.

C: How so?

J: Well, for example, I started in this field when everything was new, when we were encouraged, and sometimes even funded, to try new things, such as the emergency service model I developed back in the 1970s. Now in my work, I am being told what to do as well as how to do it! Insurance companies, government requirements, "manualized" care are intruding into my work more and more each week, it seems, and I have had to come to terms with that. The hinderances that this system creates have made me realize the preciousness of continuing to care for people.

C: Models and systems that you do not endorse are now dictating to you. How do you come to terms with that?

J: Although it is not fun, I am learning and living how the field has changed over the years. For example, the focus no longer seems to be primarily on helping people. Now paperwork seems to be the focus. For instance, recently

I was told to complete a 10-page assessment document for each client. This kind of paperwork is bad enough, but it is made worse by the fact that the forms do not even paint a clear picture of the patient or client: It only portrays what they "have" and not who they are which is much more important. It is shocking, Chris. I see the pronounced use of medication as the treatment of choice, or group therapy, which is also cheaper to use. When I review charts, which I often do as a nurse, I see the need for people to be in individual therapy where time is not an issue. It's not happening. I hear that people I had been seeing are calling to make appointments but, because of the new regulations, what the client is asking for is now available on a very limited basis. It makes no sense; I am convinced there will be a negative fall-out in the future.

C: How does Zen help in this regard?

J: First, I acknowledge my anger, and how I could either hold on to the anger by denying it, or, go on allowing myself to express it and becoming angrier, or, to get beyond the anger by acceptance of what "is." I could not afford to dry up like a raisin or have it destroy a part of me. This is very important for me as a person first, then as a clinician. The anger is just me, pure me. I do not like the disregard for human life; it is especially troublesome to me as a human being. Ignoring people in pain is terrible because these are not people who are the so-called "worried well," malingerers, or those who just use the system to get other benefits. These are people who are suffering. They are people who were working on their suffering and who are no longer getting the help they need. I've seen this happen with both adults and children. In fact, I recently asked a pharmacist if he saw the use of medications for psychiatric patients increasing and he said, "Yes." I am not just imagining it. He added that it started to happen just after the clients were no longer able to see therapists as they did before the change in the system. I also talked to a therapist who was told recently to do more groups now because they are more "cost effective!" She was also told that patients are to be moved into and through them as quickly as possible.

C: Would you have the same kind of reaction to the use of what is now being called "manualized" therapy, which is where the treatment plan for a given disorder is laid out in advance and where the clinician follows that plan regardless of their own preference in order to comply with agency or insurance requirements? Manualized care seems to be a growing trend in our field, at least in part, because it is the result of two powerful but somewhat conflicting forces. On the one hand, if research tells us what form of treatment works best for which kind of disorder, which is happening, then in theory, a clinician *should* use it because that is the most efficacious and ethical thing to do. Moreover, treatment is becoming increasingly expensive at a time when the health care dollar is shrinking. Therefore, it can be argued that in the best of all possible worlds, manualized care also means that the patient and the system get the best "bang for their medical buck." Otherwise, a less effective treatment might be selected or treatment might go on for too long, which means others must wait. Ideally, science and economics could work together to create rational mental health care, which is to say cost-effective, good quality care that is widely available.

On the other hand, the same forces can result in negative outcomes if not used properly. For instance, focusing on treatment effectiveness can be defined in ways that mean providing the *minimum* treatment necessary. In this case, the treatment of choice can be defined as the shortest form it can take, which may mean limiting therapy to a small number of sessions even though some evidence indicates that we can expect improvement over longer periods of time (Howard, Kopta, Krause, & Orlinsky, 1986). The treatment of choice may also become understood as being the cheapest form of acceptable treatment, which often involves an excessive use of medications or group therapies, just as you described, or both. Many argue that the financial incentives for insurance companies, government payers, and the pharmaceutical industry, are forcing the field of mental health in this direction more than the other.

J: Well, let's go back to Coco, the horse. Today, I am on this horse called "the modern mental system" and I find myself thinking, "Oh my gosh, I am very fearful of this situation," because I see what can happen with people. In addition to being ineffective, this system actually has greater dangers than those that meet the eye. For example, the lack of good care may play a role in mentally ill people going to prison or suffering bodily harm (because of their erratic behavior), rather than receiving help so they can maintain productive lives. A health care system that overuses medications risks teaching people to be dependent rather than independent, or to avoid facing problems rather than learning how to transcend them. Finally, poor services might have the effect of allowing abusive parenting and partnering to continue or even increase over time. Such an outcome, in turn could affect children in all kinds of negative ways. For instance, they could grow up to become parents or partners who perpetuate the cycle. In addition, emotionally disturbed children who have suffered various kinds of trauma are not receiving the therapy (group and individual) that could help them. Instead, medication seems to be the choice of treatment in many settings. There is no doubt school teachers are working under difficult situations. All of these things and more do not lay the groundwork for a healthy society.

In a way, this situation is why I am glad that I am where I am. In a sense, I am a "catcher in the rye" and that keeps me going. By being willing to ride out the storm instead of letting it eat me up or quitting, I can still feel good about what I am doing because I am trying to serve people, and society, by helping them avoid the dangers. Thank goodness that some people are willing to stay in the saddle, so to speak: The practice of meditation helps me stay in it without going over the edge, which, in my case, would mean becoming depressed, bitter, or despairing, all of which could lead to inadequate care for patients. Fortunately, the Buddha's teachings help me to remember that the personal growth of the health care provider is the crucial factor in our work. A clinician's personality helps determine the direction of treatment and the quality of treatment. For example, even with physicians, who these days are primarily biologically oriented, it is the personality of the doctor that counts. If the physician, and I have seen many of them over a half a century, is a decent human being, he or she is going to be a lot more sensitive to the person for whom they are prescribing medicine. They will take time with them, think about their needs, and couch instructions for selecting, using, and even taking the medication in ways that the patient can hear and appreciate.

C: Well, you certainly are in the thick of things, Joan, with the kind work you do, the kinds of patients you see, and the kinds of settings in which you work. Tell me more about how Zen helps you stay there.

J: I have to be accepting. The principle of acceptance is important here, acceptance of what is happening here and now. Again, I can deny my anger about paperwork, express it by refusing to do it on time, or I can accept what's happening because I cannot reverse it. I can't fight the system any more than it made sense for me to become angry with Coco. Oh, I could fight, but that alone would do no one any good, my patients or myself. I am not going to give in to either burning out or quitting in anger or frustration, because an honest acceptance of reality allows me to stay in the saddle where I might eventually do some good. Accepting that which "is" helps me deal with the rough times because I don't have to waste energy denying or fighting it. Acceptance gives me the ability to see reality for what it is, to know what I am facing, and that allows me to look forward to coming to work where I can at least try to make a difference for someone.

C: Obviously, you have something that works here because we've both seen what happens to therapists who can't find a way to stay in the saddle. How does Zen help you handle the anger once you accept it and that which is causing it?

J: I am doing the same things I've always done. When I am with someone, I am connected with *them,* not the other stuff. I try to do no harm. It is almost like a mantra: Do no harm! I don't deny my feelings, but it does not interfere with me being with somebody. I do not allow the anger to consume me personally either, because I am not stuck with it. The teachings help me to know what feelings I have, learn from them, and move beyond them when necessary. In other words, the anger is often a lesson for me. For instance, sometimes when I feel my anger, it becomes an opportunity to learn about the issue of control, about my desire for it, about how the futility of that desire causes me suffering, and about how to move beyond this attachment to a higher state of freedom in my work and in my life.

C: It seems to me that you may also be communicating this approach to your clients in some ways. For example, your way of responding to anger can stand for them as a model for accepting their own anger or fear or frustration with control and to learn from it, too. We know that modeling is an important part of treatment (Bednar & Peterson, 1995) so it may be that such modeling helps clients to move beyond the kinds of attachments that cause them suffering into a freer life, even though it will still have rough spots.

J: The truth is, Chris, my examining and reflecting on my own anger is no different then talking with someone in therapy. And, yes, I talk about it with clients.

C: Once again, I see some similarities between Zen and a humanistic approach, but with Zen showing a clearer path, which is one of the things that makes Zen appealing to me.

J: It is a lesson. Control has been a real tough one for me, which is why I find the experience with Coco so revealing. This lesson seems to help me accept the changes of my job, too. For example, now I am doing the same thing with my patients. I am now involved in visiting people in their own homes. I think this is a very good idea for some clients and not so good for others. I am learning to be creative and flexible so the time I am with the patient is not compromised too much.

One person, who has PTSD and a Dissociative Disorder, said to me that she was angry at the system because what she was used to had changed and, for a brief time, limited her treatment. She said, "I knew this was going to happen; it always does and there is nothing I can do. I knew that I was not going to be able to continue to see you," and I said to her, "Well, I don't like it either, not one bit. I am not in control, just like you. But I am *here now.* I am here with you now, so let us see what we can do with that." This approach seemed to open up a discussion concerning dealing with things she could not control, which seemed to result in new insights that were helpful for her. Accepting reality for what it is, which is often suffering, enabled us to work together under the new conditions.

The anger has become a lesson for us in control. It is like having to let go of control or of not surviving. I had to give control to Coco, just like I have to give control over to the system. With Coco, it was a matter of my life or at least physical health. I could see other horses stumble in front of me which increased my apprehension, and I didn't want to do anything that would make it worse or to interfere with Coco's ability to get us back safely. I had to let go which was difficult because of this control issue. It was like nothing I have ever done before.

With managed care, I am fearful about what is going on, about what the directions for the future look like. I have seen therapists stumble on their therapeutic horses because they are no longer in control. For example, they lose their sensitivity to patients, become bitter, or even despair of their work. Sometimes, they fall off the edge of managed care, so to speak, and either become ill or quit. Another way is to become too rigid, to become too much a part of the system, which is a kind of reaction formation, I guess. So here as well as elsewhere, although control may be the issue, going through the pain is the process. I cannot avoid my pain. What was helpful from the teachings of Zen was that I do not have to try to hide from that pain, avoid it, or push it away, all of which can cause more suffering and result in a loss of perspective. Going through the pain gives me the edge over it, because I believe that a therapist can only help others face things to the extent that they are willing to face painful things themselves. If I have gone further "into the bush" than my client has, then I can help them go further, too. If I avoid an area that is painful, then I cannot help someone face that kind of thing either. Managed care is but one example of that: It is painful for both therapist and client, and we both of us have to face this form of suffering when necessary because not doing so may do harm and you know how I feel about that.

C: In essence, then, you are doing the same thing with managed care that you are doing in general with Zen. There is nothing different here, which is what you mean by those Zen phrases you sometimes use, such as "It just is, Chris; it is the truth." It seems that not only has this approach helped you to stay in this field longer than most therapists, but that it also helps you grow in the work, even from its difficulties. Is this an example of what you mean by you don't "do" Zen, instead, you "live" it?

J: Absolutely, that is why Zen is in the heart, not in the head. I think I have not burned out because I am *living what is, not what I want.* I don't like what "is," with managed care or any other form of suffering for that matter, but by living it, I am at least not creating illusions, deceptions, and more suffering. I am not doing harm to myself. Patients are already frightened, which is important because in a way they say to us, "I am already frightened; please don't scare me any more." They know that I am not trying to control them or their life, and they respond to that with a reduction in their fear, which is usually good for them, the situation, and for me. Throughout the years I have had no expectations from the standpoint of the work they do, however, I do have expectations of myself not to fail the client. What a client does is entirely up to them; I don't want to burden them with the need to please me, and they can be who they are without reservation.

C: So it is as though the degree to which you can face and ride your own fear helps them face and ride theirs, too.

J: Yes, something happens when those factors are taken into account.

C: Well, Joan, the social scientist in me says that the phrase "something happens" is a bit vague. It is a phrase you use a lot, so please try to open it up a bit.

J: I can understand why you ask for more clarity because it sounds so nebulous. All that I am saying is that something happens when my stuff does not intrude upon the client's stuff and there is a meshing between us. "The Dharma is the most abundant gift of wisdom and like all true gifts, it benefits both the giver and the receiver" (Das, 1997, p. 25). If someone comes in with lots of fear, which underlies most suffering, and if they are not met with fear or with a need to be in control, there is freedom to explore the pain.

C: That sounds rather like a "judo of Zen." But it may be something one has to experience in order to understand fully. I remember that my judo instructor would tell us about the importance of knowing where the opponent's center of gravity is while in a contest. No matter how hard I looked I could never see it. Then, one day I was very relaxed, though I do not know why. At that time, an opponent was moving toward me and I could "see" his center of gravity. It was actually a very specific spot given his body's location at the time and I simply knew where to touch him in order to have the greatest effect. It was really amazing to flip someone completely over with a slight nudge in the "right" direction, but it really happened that way: It was only by letting go of the desire for that kind of perception that I could have it.

J: Right. I am not interested in theory because our work goes beyond the brain. If therapists are not clear on their own issues, then there is a good possibility that they may complicate things. You might call this countertransference or whatever, but the key is that self-knowledge helps make a good connection with the client possible and the lack of self-knowledge, what we call ignorance, may detract the therapist from having a trusting relationship with the client.

C: The world of managed care is also a world of paperwork. When you and I entered this field, paperwork was not an issue: One-page write-ups, a line or two of notes after a session, and a once-every-three-month summary was all that was necessary. Now I find myself telling students in my practicum courses that one of the most frequent causes of being fired at work is poor paperwork habits! We actually spend several sessions on examining and completing the paperwork that they need to fill out at their placement sites. "Paperwork is now the life blood of the organization," I now tell them, "and no paperwork means no money, no money means no therapists, no therapists mean no help, so we are obliged to do this part of our job well, although most therapists can't stand it."

J: I know all that, but it is the control issue at work again, Chris. I have had little use for paperwork and I have been furious about the redundancy. Attached to that anger and other strong feelings is the fear of neglecting people by using up time for paperwork, so once again, we see fear as the problem. For example, I think a complete psychosocial exam is really important, but the manner in which it is asked and used is important, too. For instance, an important question is whether the therapist sees the form as helpful or as a chore? Whether it is seen as getting information they can use or as just an exercise to collect data may make all the difference.

C: Is it possible to say that there is a "Zen of paperwork," too?

J: Perhaps, but only if paperwork is an issue for the therapist. Otherwise there is just paperwork!

ZEN AND ACADEMIC EDUCATION

C: As you know, Joan, I spend most of my professional time in the classroom these days. Some of that work involves lecturing, of course, but some of it includes running clinical internships where I help train future case managers and therapists. As a teacher, I find myself wondering how Zen could apply to clinical education in the traditional college or university setting?

J: Ideally, I would begin at the beginning. I would interview each student interested in this line of work as if I was hiring them for a job. If I didn't feel comfortable with them I doubt if I would accept them in my program, or perhaps accept them on a probationary period, giving them the benefit of the doubt. I have seen far too many clinicians, perhaps 50% of them, physicians and Ph.D.s included, who should not be in our line of work, primarily because of the way they treat clients and how they talk about clients to their colleagues. In fact, I would be hard pressed to refer someone I care about to any therapist I didn't know personally and professionally.

C: Well, on the positive side, this means that at least 50% of us pass the test!

J: In fact, as I think about the professors, nurses, physicians, psychologists, and social workers who taught me at various points in my education or career, I realize that they taught me in various ways what made sense and what didn't make sense. I am very grateful for the bad teachers as well as for the good teachers. There is on-going education in many settings besides the classroom. Basically, I believe that a good teacher of this line of work needs to be someone who has faced themselves and their own problems, just as with clinicians.

> For a teacher the important point is always to be ready to surrender to his disciple. When a teacher realizes he is wrong, he can say, "Oh, you are right and I was wrong." If your teacher has that kind of spirit, you will be encouraged to admit your mistake as well, even when it is not so easy. If you continue this kind of practice, people may say, "You are crazy. Something is wrong with you." But it doesn't matter. (Suzuki, 2002, p. 9)

C: It seems like a kind of catch-22 here. On the one hand, your main criticism of clinicians centers on whether or not they have adequate knowledge about themselves. But on the other hand, the system that trains them to be clinicians may not be giving them the opportunity to do this kind of learning in the first place. In other words, we can either help therapists learn about themselves and how to face their own issues after they are in practice, which is rather hard on clients, or we make sure that the educational system that trains therapists includes preparation in this regard before they actually inflict themselves on others.

J: Yes, I think the problem with how we educate therapists begins with a situation where people, educators, and institutions do not take enough care in selecting and training individuals. Let me tell you what my nine-year-old granddaughter thinks a good teacher is, when I asked her that question recently. She said that a good teacher is, "A teacher who makes school work fun; a teacher who understands what your [learning] problems are in school; a teacher who can help you with your [learning] problems; a teacher who trusts himself or herself about what they know and what they want to teach. They need to know what they know and what is very important for them to teach." I couldn't disagree with her on any point for college teachers as well!

C: Now, as a teacher of this material myself, let me remind you about some of the complexities involved in trying to find and train therapists from my perspective, and then you can respond to that if you like. First, would you agree that a teacher should be an expert on the area being taught?

J: Yes, but on the other hand, not so much an expert that he or she thinks there is no more to learn. Rather, they should always have a "beginner's mind" because being an expert can be a detriment.

C: Well, some research in cognitive psychology indicates that acquiring expertise involves amassing a very, very large amount of information about a subject area. Although the actual size of the number may be disputed, it is clear that the process of becoming an expert takes considerable time, effort, and ability. One way we try to help people acquire this knowledge is to design courses of study and to organize them into various levels called degrees. One accumulates so much of the requisite information in undergraduate school and more in graduate school. Of course, part of this activity means periodic evaluations to make sure that learning occurs. Although testing is relatively good at telling us if the information is being gathered in a reasonable fashion, it does not help us to know if people can use it skillfully. Skill acquisition comes with practice and that is done with gradual exposure to solving real problems with real people in various clinical settings, which is evaluated through the process of clinical supervision. After the formal training is completed, we are still not ready to turn students loose on people, so professional credentialing processes are next, which are usually set up by the state through various licensing boards. Only when students have jumped this third hurdle, which usually takes some time, may they address the population on their own. Now, as you can see, this process is not a simple or ill-designed one. Yet, you tell me it fails at least half the time. What would you have us do differently from a Zen perspective? How could Zen help us do it better?

J: I think the first part of the process makes sense, the undergraduate and graduate requirements. It seems as if as a student goes on to a Ph.D. program, depending upon the student, his or her heart is beginning to bleed and the brain expands, which could result in becoming *less* interested in the humanity part of their work. I wonder if there is the possibility of becoming jaded. Again, the traditional educational format does seem to address the intellectual part of clinical education very well. It does a pretty good job with presenting all the little pieces of knowledge that science develops and may even be somewhat helpful in terms of organizing the information through theories. But the professor is a key factor to me, just as the master is a key factor in teaching Zen. If he or she were too committed toward a particular perspective, then I would say that is a problem because it closes off other points of view. I know that happens a lot today, especially with the biological perspective in medicine. If the instructor is open to a student as a unique individual, like Zen teaches us to be, who is struggling with something in their own life, then, I think traditional education is OK. So what I am saying is that a big part of clinical education depends upon the instructor. If the teacher is open to discussion and is not wedded to one position or approach, is someone who can listen to a person who is struggling and do that with patience, values where the individual happens to be, does no harm to the student, and encourages the student to be open, then the teacher can be an asset. Of course, all of this is built into the teachings of the Dharma.

C: Before you go on, let me add another wrinkle to the complexity of the picture. There are two aspects of the traditional academic world that are of equal importance for clinical and most other purposes: teaching and research. However, although these endeavors are related, they actually require distinctly different mental sets, skills, abilities, and attitudes to do well. Although teaching may seem like it should be the priority, it is usually research that is emphasized, especially among the more prestigious universities. In fact, for various reasons including the history of the academy and funding support, academic institutions are ranked on the basis of their research prowess much more than their ability to teach well. Not surprisingly, researchers are usually given more status, greater resources, and higher income than teachers. Furthermore, even within institutions, individual faculty and students can usually be identified as leaning toward research or teaching with similar results. Clinical programs are no different, so in addition to the challenges associated with teaching knowledge, or what you call "head stuff," we see that there are a mix of factors in regard to what is going to be emphasized in that process.

What we have, then, is a very large educational system that involves hundreds of thousands of people moving through various degree programs, each one of which is characterized by a different mixture of teaching and research emphasis, all of which come from a wide variety of mental health disciplines, while constantly dealing with different types of personalities in both instructors and students, and doing so year after year! I fear that Zen would have very little ability to reform such a large and entrenched system. Perhaps another approach to incorporating Zen into the academic setting might be to focus on individuals, in this case individual teachers. What, Joan, would an ideal teacher or program for clinicians look like from a Zen point of view?

J: The instructor would get to know each student individually, which would involve setting up regular appointments with them right from the beginning and throughout the program. I would ask each one of them why they wanted to do this kind of work, but I would not ask them in the usual way, such as writing an essay on it. I would find a way of conveying to the student that this is an important beginning and that I really am interested in learning the answer to the question. I would try to convey that I want to know something about the person and what draws him or her to this field. Of course, the kind of process I have in mind starts even before admission of students. It would begin with the department heads because it is their responsibility to hire faculty, and they must be very selective in this process, which means that for me, teaching is more important than researching, at least in the clinical program. The teacher is the hub of the wheel; hopefully he will instill into the students that patients have rights and deserve the best they have to offer. The personality of the teacher has a profound affect on what will happen in the future, as well as the personality of the therapist.

Also ideally, the teacher must be a good example to the students, open in terms of genuineness, very similar to the openness of a therapist. Ideally speaking again, the moment the teacher enters the room the students feel welcomed and interested in learning. The teacher is there to help the students grow into their own capabilities. This is a gradual process, but the teacher, like a therapist or master, helps the student to look at him or herself *first and foremost* in the process of becoming a therapist. This kind of teaching environment must be a very safe one, which means that the teachers must not be threatened by students either! For example, how the teacher responds to questions is important; they must *welcome* them because the teacher knows that he or she learns from the student, too. This reciprocity is crucial to the teaching and learning process, just like it is for therapy, where the therapist can learn from the client. Sometimes, like in therapy, the student is the teacher and the teacher must have the strength to be aware of that and even acknowledge it.

C: There is a powerful little book entitled, *The Pedagogy of the Oppressed*, by Freire (1973) that uses a phrase that might describe this kind of teaching relationship, Joan. He says that a good teaching-learning environment is one in which the relationship between teacher and student is reciprocal, dynamic, and interactive. It is that of a "teacher-student and students-teachers" (p. 67), which is to say that teaching and learning is a dialectical process that is created when both parties are partners in learning. This kind of teaching and learning is much different than the more traditional model, where teachers "pour" knowledge in to student "vessels." Does this kind of relationship apply to the kind of learning you are talking about, too?

J: Yes, if the teacher acknowledges that life is suffering and recognizes and talks about that right from the beginning. This makes it possible to talk about the causes of suffering and how to use suffering in order to be free from it. I have found that when I talk with people about The Four Noble Truths and suffering, they often experience a sense of relief because it opens doors that may otherwise remain closed. Remember, from a Zen point of view, our suffering is our blessing for it can be the catalyst of facing our fears and becoming free from sorrow.

C: From a Zen perspective, then, a good clinical instructor would have to begin with helping people understand suffering as the fundamental condition of human life, which is very different from some of the traditional perspectives. This introduction to clinical work would also have to involve teaching about attachment as the cause of suffering, the possibility of being free from suffering through cessation, and the role of learning about one's self in that process, in order to make any of the subsequent lessons sensible. In other words, a primary difference between Zen and other perspectives to teaching clinical material would be in terms of where we start. Instead of beginning with an introduction to the DSM or to the brain, for example, we would begin with The Four Noble Truths and how they apply to ourselves as well as to our work.

J: Right on the button! It would be important to make sure that this process is not an intrusive one because that would be too threatening and might cause more suffering. It is like helping the student to "wake up" to, and to acknowledge, the wisdom of The Four Noble Truths and the Eightfold Path. The process is more like a flower beginning to open up than anything else, a slow, gentle, unfolding that can only be encouraged, not forced, so we are talking some major differences in educational approaches.

C: Of course, Joan, some other perspectives want to see a similar kind of growth, too. For example, the traditional psychodynamic program asks the student to face their own pain by going through their own analysis. In this way, they also come to know the importance of suffering and that the way out is through it. The humanistic approach would also ask students to experience their pain in the here and now as a way of breaking through it. Zen is not the only way to do this, although classical psychoanalysis is the only program of which I am aware that requires the student to be in therapy in order to face themselves. Individual programs often recommend that, but few graduate schools require it and I have met many therapists, especially physicians, who have never been in therapy themselves.

J: I think the Zen approach might be more conducive to long-term growth because it focuses more directly on what we could call the basic human problems of suffering, attachment, learning, and transcendence. From a Zen perspective, whatever happens to us is an opportunity to learn. The psychodynamic perspective might describe this as "more grist for the mill," but it goes beyond that because for Zen this opportunity occurs everywhere in life, in all its ups as well as downs, which means that we have many opportunities to practice and learn! I like the emphasis on "practice, practice, practice," our life is our classroom, our curriculum.

C: Joan, I must confess that even though I have interest in Zen, I would emphasize the DSM, and so forth, because that is part of my obligation as a social scientist and because my students need that for licensure. The best I could probably do as a teacher in the current academic system and remain a social scientist is to dedicate some lectures to The Four Noble Truths and to help people understand suffering better in their internships or supervisory periods. Tell me more about what you would do with them.

J: Well, we already did the first principle, but the second one is important, too. We need to help students understand the ego and what causes suffering if we are to help them understand cessation and how to help people become free of suffering, which, of course, is the Eightfold Path. This is a delicate process. It is one that involves a certain level of mutual respect and trust, just like with a teacher-student relationship in Zen. The approach must make real sense to the professor before he or she engages in it, otherwise there could be confusion for the student.

C: So incorporating Zen into one's teaching is a serious undertaking. Given that prerequisite level of understanding, what would a Zen-based therapy teach about what causes suffering?

J: Well, what I would probably do is to be extremely open and patient with students so that they could hear each other struggle with themselves and with everyday life, too. I would help the students face their struggles instead of filling them with a lot of intellectual information. It would be more like opening up and teaching with the heart instead of the head. Ideally, the teacher would have to be superbly patient and wise. We don't talk much about wisdom and intuitiveness any more, but it is important, especially in our line of work.

C: How would you define wise and how would you make sure your program had wise teachers?

J: Probably pretty simply! I would ask myself if that potential professor is someone I would trust to teach a child of mine. Is the instructor someone who is concerned about the welfare of the student, is knowledgeable and yet open to learn more? Professors don't have to be perfect, but they would not put up barriers between themselves and others, especially students. I have seen far too much of that in academia and in clinical training. Teachers who put up intellectual barriers, status barriers, power barriers, and so forth are worse than not helpful: they may even be destructive.

C: Let me summarize for a moment, Joan, and correct me if I have missed something. Your point here is not that teachers of therapy, regardless of their theoretical perspective, have to embrace Zen, let alone undergo all the rigors of Zen training. Rather, the kind of teaching that is compatible with Zen, regardless of perspective, what we have called the "ideal," involves those who are actively engaged in struggling with their own suffering and who are willing to help students do that, too. This willingness and commitment to self and others, in turn, requires a number of other characteristics, such as the capacity for self-examination, a willingness to be open to experience, and the courage to be honest. Regardless of theoretical orientation or of one's particular mental health discipline, the ultimate teaching and learning goal of the ideal instructor as you describe him or her, is to help students see the importance of suffering and to help them learn how to face suffering in order to learn from it. These two concerns, in turn, involve understanding the causes of suffering and the process of cessation so that eventually students or supervisees could help others do the same, no matter what level of suffering or pain happens to be involved.

J: Yes, and one of the main challenges for teaching, then, is that the teacher must not be afraid to be vulnerable, though not in stupid ways that can only cause more suffering, like being blunt instead of tactful in the use of honesty or by getting involved with students in inappropriate ways.

C: Well, that sure presents a lot of academic issues. Not only do we have to screen instructors for wisdom as well as academic credentials, but we also would put them into situations where student transference and instructor countertransference are more likely, as well as potential litigation if things go wrong. At the very least, the selection processes of new students would have to be greatly revised to reduce these possibilities. How would you go about that?

J: It would be almost like hiring staff.

C: What do you mean by that?

J: This is a tough one, and your scientific mind won't like it, but the word that comes to mind is intuitiveness.

C: What do you mean by "intuitiveness"?

J: I said that it would be tough! Intuitive insight is not just knowledge about the other person because it begins with knowing yourself. There is something inside of me that helps me to determine whether to hire them or not; call it a gut feeling. It is a way of knowing the essence of a person, if you will, or of finding out if they have a certain quality, which is whether or not I, personally, feel comfortable with them. Part of this approach is that I know that I am going to be responsible for them and, therefore, must take hiring very, very seriously. Interviewing a student should be something like interviewing a therapist for a job. It takes a lot of work and time getting to know someone.

A guideline that I use is to keep in mind that I will have to trust them. I need to be able to trust a person because I am going to be responsible for their actions, attitude, and work with patients. This priority makes me look for honesty, for someone who is not performing, who is being themselves with me even during the interview. I must feel that the individual would be someone who, if my son or daughter needed help, I would feel comfortable referring them to for help. I have to feel that the person is sincere, and is worthy of my trust. I listen to my "gut" to see if I feel peaceful with this person. I also look for someone who is "natural," which is to say straightforward and open. I know this is very subjective, but it is the way I do it. I could also say that I know what turns me off and that is important, too.

Maybe it is a two-fold process. I feel uneasy with people who come across with excessive tenseness, disengenuousness, and so forth. Remember that little story about the professor and cup of tea? A professor is said to have wanted to learn about Zen from a master, so the master poured him a cup of tea while listening to him talk about his interest in learning. The master poured and kept pouring and, of course, at some point the cup began to run over. The professor couldn't sit still while that was happening and began to comment about what he was doing; the tea was flowing out of the cup. The master replied something to the effect that the likelihood of being able to teach the professor Zen was very small, about as small as trying to put tea into a cup that was already full! If a student or potential employee doesn't seem like he or she has room to learn or is not open to learning, then I would not hire them and would have doubts about their capacity to be a therapist.

C: OK, then after the student was interviewed, assessed, accepted, and taught The Four Noble Truths, I assume that you would go on to teach about the Eightfold Path, knowing that those lessons would apply to therapy, too, as we saw in earlier chapters, although they may not help the person pass the licensing exam!

J: Absolutely!

C: I think it is only fair to say that many clinical training programs try to do some of these things. For instance, they usually involve an internship where students are expected to do entry-level work, which is supervised, and to discuss their experiences with the supervisor on a regular basis. Most good instructors try to do some of the things you mention, such as making sure the person is open to learning, that they are reasonably conscientious and humane, and so forth. But such things are only one part of an entire program of study. In medicine, for instance, almost all of the educational process concentrates on the body, not behavior. It is only when they get to the resident experience that the training focuses on psychiatric suffering. The same can be said of nursing, although both degree programs "rotate" students through a psychiatric setting for a brief period. In psychology, training in research is just as important as clinical training, even more so at least until the last year when the internship usually takes place. By contrast, social work and counseling programs are more clinically intensive, which may make that a more compatible environment for Zen.

J: Generally, I am really critical of internships because I simply don't think they are thorough enough. I have been around them a lot as a nurse and as a supervisor of mental health services and have seen students come in ill-prepared to work with suffering time after time. Their knowledge of the DSM or medications may be fine, but their understanding of themselves and others is lacking far too often for my comfort.

C: What would you propose as an alternative?

J: I would set it up so that the intern and the instructor would work in concert with the patients and the staff of the setting. I also would want to know what the internship program could offer the student in a very pragmatic way, as well as interviewing the person who would be supervising the student.

C: Many programs try to do something like that, Joan. For example, I teach a practicum where students work in a clinical setting that is of interest to them. They also attend a weekly class meeting with me as a group. The students are required to read a text on clinical practice and discuss it with each other in relation to their experience at the placement sites. They are also required to write journals on what is happening for them at their site each week. Then at the end of the semester, they write a paper integrating their practical experience with the theory they learned earlier in the program. Part of this exercise focuses on what they learned about the strengths and weaknesses of their own helping style, what you might call "self-knowledge."

Many internships try to include some degree of what you are describing, but you seem to be suggesting something that is much more involved. Yet, it is also true that the constraints of reality are such that the kind of program you suggest is likely to be very small, which makes it expensive to run. Also, such a program would be very time consuming, and instructors usually have other classes and research or committee work to do as well. Keeping the realities of the institution in mind here, what would you suggest is actually possible?

J: The basic goal would have to be to develop some connection with the students individually. I think that developing a genuine connection between the student and the teacher is vital. I would also require that there be some method for finding out from the student whether or not they are actually getting what they need from you in order to do this kind of work. I have seen so much of people "performing" for their teachers on tests, or with using the DSM, or with bantering about jargon, that I have to wonder how much of their knowledge is real? I know that you need some way of assessing progress, but my main concern is that things must make sense to the student and have value. I suspect my bias comes from my nursing education and the amount of time and very close supervision we received, we couldn't get away with anything that didn't make clinical sense. When we graduated we had a very strong basis to do our work.

C: Maybe something like an individual learning contract would help, but my question is what can I do in my class to help students learn about Zen and therapy? Should I bring in charts of the Eightfold Path? Should I critique traditional approaches as we have done here and show how Zen can be an alternative? Should I develop individual learning plans?

J: Why not! You could certainly keep The Four Noble Truths in mind because our work deals with suffering and you could focus on The Four Noble Truths. I bet not many of the books currently used in the classroom even talk about them, let alone how they can apply to therapy. Even so, I think you would be best served by focusing on your connection with students—don't ever underestimate its importance. You would benefit by listening to the students, by telling the students to keep an open mind, to avoid succumbing to any preconceived ideas.

C: In summary, there are three things that I could do realistically to help bring Zen to my work as a teacher. The first one is to talk about the principles of Zen, which is to say to introduce students to the role of suffering in our work, how it is caused by attachments, how cessation of suffering is possible, and how that is done via the Eightfold Path. Second, I need to keep in mind just how important being connected with students is in teaching them about therapy. Another thing that is a possibility in almost any program is for an instructor to offer special courses that address various complementary approaches. It is even possible to design classes that could be taught at the undergraduate, graduate, or continuing educational levels. They could be taught as regular academic courses where face-to-face is so important through what I call "mini-courses." It might even be possible to offer them online so that people at institutions that do not offer such courses may have access to them. I have offered similar courses in the past and will in the future. This approach may not be the kind you would envision, but it's very workable in the academy.

J: There is one more thing you can do in the classroom: bring in the teachings of the Dharma pertaining to real life.

C: How am I going to do that?

J: You do it fearlessly! Think about something that pains you that you can share with them and how there is a connection with The Four Noble Truths. You can show them the Eightfold Path in action, with good measure, and when it is appropriate. Remember, the first rule is to do no harm, which should help you with the transference/countertransference problem you mentioned earlier. You have already proven yourself to be a teacher and you don't have to be a master to begin, because in Zen you start *where you are*! As Dogen Zenji has said, "To study ourselves is to forget our selves" (Suzuki, 1970, p. 79). When you forget yourself is precisely when you can really hear other people! To study our self is to learn about us. Learning about ourselves allows us to forget about ourselves. Forgetting about our self allows our mind to be open or clear. An open mind or heart allows us to be able to listen without projecting or interjecting stuff that is not there, and that allows us to be helpful to others. It is the same thing with teaching. Suzuki said,

"You need a teacher so that you can become independent" (Suzuki, 1970, p. 77). It is my sense that a counselor/therapist is similar to a teacher or archeologist. Both are uncovering the spirit of the human being, something that has been buried and is simply waiting to be uncovered to live a peaceful life, a life that everyone wants.

C: My first reaction is to say to you something like, "Gee, Joan, you certainly seem to be asking a lot of teachers for the money that we are not paid!" But then I realize that what you are saying is to simply start where you are and to do the best that you can. In other words, begin wherever you are on the path, continue to walk it until you get to another level, and then try to do the next one as best as you can until you reach the next one and so forth; is that right?

J: Yes. It is a continual process of working on yourself. But remember, it is not a chore; rather, we get in touch with our "soft spot" (Chodron, 1994, p. 48).

C: One problem or "cost" of this approach that I see is that it is not going to lead the teacher down the research path very easily. This may not be such a problem for bachelor or master level programs, but it is for most doctoral programs, not to mention medical school!

J: But there is a beautiful irony here, Chris. When people do this stuff, things like money, status, and the rest don't mean as much as they used to. I guess it is not an easy task for a teacher in this day and age, but it has its own rewards and, as you know, they are quite substantial.

ZEN AND CLINICAL SUPERVISION

C: Joan, as I said earlier, another form of teaching related to our field takes place after graduation because licensing laws in most states for most mental health disciplines require a reasonably substantial period where individuals work in the field under the supervision of a licensed individual before being allowed to practice on their own. In addition, many times even licensed clinicians want to learn more about their work, so they become involved in professional consultation, which is another form of teaching. I know that you have had a tremendous amount of experience as a supervisor in all kinds of settings, such as in inpatient, outpatient, medical hospitals, crisis intervention settings, after-care programs, and so forth, and with all kinds of students, including nurses, counselors, social workers, psychologists, and medical interns as well as residents. Indeed, some of your work as a supervisor was even recognized by the National Institute of Mental Health (Freedman, Kaplan, & Shaddock, 1975, p. 2,318). So let me ask you, how can Zen help supervisors or consultants and the process of supervision or consultation? How do you use the teachings of Zen to select therapists, to train therapists, and so forth?

J: It is most imperative to be truthful with supervisees, which means to be open and honest at all times. For example, if something is going on that is not in the best interest of the patient, I *must* bring that to the forum with the supervisee in a helpful way, even if I only suspect it. After all, dealing with problems is a part of the process of learning, and I would fail the supervisee as a teacher by ignoring such an event no matter how I feel about that particular learner.

C: Are you saying that you are not there for the supervisee, that you are actually there for the client even while with the supervisee?

J: Not exactly, but I can't separate one from the other. Ultimately I am responsible for the client or patient as well as the supervisee. Writing up assessments after an intake might be a good example of what I mean. "The assessment is important," I used to say to supervisees, "because it follows the patient wherever he or she may go—perhaps even for the rest of their lives." Since I am a strong advocate for the patient as well as for an employee, I review all the assessments my supervisees make. Of course, we cannot change the assessment once it is written because that is the law, but I point out things to the authors, especially things that sound harsh or critical or unclear. In fact, I repeatedly mention to the staff, "You write the assessment as if the person is looking over your shoulder or will be reading it for accuracy and sensitivity." The patient is first and foremost; we are this person's advocate.

Of course, the supervisee or employee is just as important as my patients because one affects the other. To me, documentation is always important because of the repercussions it might bring to the client. In fact, when I was a clinical nurse specialist at one job, I used to review all the charts and I would write yellow "sticky" notes to the staff. I would keep a copy, give the original to the staff, and then discuss them at supervisory meetings. Eventually, they had enough of my notes that they said they were going to wallpaper my office with them! But they never seemed to take offense at them, probably because I took pains to make sure that they were always written to be helpful, not punitive, and encouraging, not demeaning.

C: I suspect that Zen helps you get away with that kind of thing without giving offense more often than not, which is quite an achievement, because many clinicians become quite testy when their work is criticized. How do you do that?

J: First, I have no desire, none, to attack people. As I mentioned in chapter 2 when I described various supervisors I've had, I've never wanted staff to feel that I am critical of them. I saw what negative supervisory styles could do and because of that, I want to work with staff as partners: I want them to rely on me as I do on them. I was never interested in anyone being afraid of me, or in being heavy-handed. Such abuses of power offend me. I feel completely responsible for my staff's work, all of it. They know that, so the staff I hire tend to trust me; they know that I am on their side. My staff never saw me bad-mouth their colleagues or put them down, so they know that I wouldn't do that to them, either. I try to create a safe environment for the staff, just like I do for patients and for students.

C: Let me ask for clarification on what you mean by "safe," because that word can be abused, too. For example, I have colleagues in academia who say they want to create a "safe" learning environment so that students can feel free to ask questions, disagree, take risks, and so forth, for learning. But when I examine the grades these instructors assign, it is obvious that safety has come at the expense of scholarship: Typically, they give what I call an "A" for attending, a "B" for being, and a "C," if there ever is one, for caring. Sometimes, I have seen instructors fail to hold people accountable for the quality of their work under the guise of "safe" or "caring," but I would not want those students to become professionals that work on my loved ones, because I don't think they've been trained! To me, such instructors shirk their professional duties.

J: That point is a good one insofar as it concerns students because it is important to weed out those who don't have what it takes before they become professionals, where they can harm people. But supervising employees is different for two reasons: they are not students and they are treating people. Firing people is the hardest thing that I have ever done professionally, and, although it is rare, it reminds me to be extra careful in the hiring process and to be very available to them during their probationary periods. Good people make my job easier, which is why I don't hire people I don't trust or am not confident in: firing them is just too hard on me!

C: What if the supervisor works in an environment where there is a high turnover rate, like in many community mental health settings or with case management positions? Under these conditions, one can become more desperate to fill positions because empty slots have funding implications as well as forcing clients to wait.

J: I try to be very clear with them about what I need and expect and so forth at the beginning. Then, I meet with staff on a regular basis and ask them how things are going. I tell them that I really want to know how things are going, warts and all, and I really mean that. I try to be very tuned into them and what they are doing, in part, because I could not function well myself, either at work or at home, if I didn't have this kind of connection with them. Eventually, we come to look forward to the time we will have together. So, taking this kind of time is as much for myself as it is for patients and staff. Ultimately, if anything gets screwed up, I am responsible, so I try to make sure right from the beginning, that that does not happen.

C: Speaking about "screw-ups," what is your style of handling problems in supervision?

J: I talk with the people involved. It doesn't happen that often, but when there is a screw-up, I talk with them to find out what is going on. It helps that I am very clear in the beginning and try to spend considerable time with staff when they are new so that we can have an honest, trusting relationship. I make myself available 24 hours a day, seven days a week and they know that. I tell them that the only time I would be displeased is if they *didn't* call me and should have. They never call very much, but they know that they could. Although the buck stops with me, it also helps to have fun, especially at staff meetings. Other administrators who walk by my meetings often pop their heads in to ask what was so funny. Later, they tell me that they hear so much laughter at our meetings that they wonder how we get anything accomplished? Yet our meetings are always productive as well as gratifying.

C: Are you saying that having fun is a part of supervision for you?

J: Absolutely, if I am not having fun something is wrong. There are always problems, but that is okay because of the faith I have had in the staff and because of how we worked together as a team. The hiring process is the key for me. If I were hiring someone today, I would do it the same way. I would especially be "hands-on" with them at the beginning until I felt comfortable. When I hire someone, I know that at first I am exposing patients to a person I do not know very well. I take that responsibility very seriously. So I say to new hires that I am available to them all the time and I do not let them work on their own until I feel at ease with what they do. Although time consuming and labor intensive, this practice is well worth the effort, because when they tell me that they feel ready, I usually have a good enough sense of how they are with other human beings, especially those who are suffering, to let them go. In addition, when I know that a new person is on duty alone for the first few times, I make it a point to call and see how they are doing. That's part of the Second and Third Noble Truths. I know that there will still be problems coming up that would cause suffering in one form or another, for staff or for clients, and I have learned that the way to help is to be available.

C: I can see that you make quite a commitment as a supervisor. Being willing to spend so much time with staff stems from your concern with feeling connected, just like the relationship between a Zen master and student. Achieving such a connection cannot be done without time. Although I question the practicality of spending that much time with staff in today's managed care scene, I can certainly see its benefits. It makes them a better therapist, the clients get better help, you feel better at night, and I would suspect that it is better for the system as well. For example, such commitment might reduce staff turnover, which is something that is hard on everyone: the person that leaves, finding someone to replace them, the expenses of training, and most of all, the clients. Perhaps the initial investment is well worth it in the long run.

J: I love supervision because it is like adding a drop of water to a pool. In this part of our work, the supervisor becomes something like a drop of water that is added into the system, first affecting the supervisees and then their clients. The connectedness you develop with your staff or students doesn't stop there because it may ripple through people's lives in ways that you can't foresee. Think of all the people it touches over time!

C: Yes, there is a "ripple effect" in supervising. I like to believe that good teaching works the same way. Zen may facilitate this process because it is always asking people to learn more about themselves and that helps our work. However, the part of Zen that stands out to me here is that your interest in being connected to your staff makes good sense at so many levels, for the development of the clinicians you hire, for the well-being of the clients, for system stability and, ultimately, for yourself. Naturally, I believe that we should also keep our clinical and supervisory eyes on making sure that the treatment of choice is being offered and in the most economically responsible fashion. Yet, I can also imagine an entire staff or mental heath center practicing some of the aspects of Zen you have just mentioned and cannot help but to think it would be a good place in which to work and to which to refer people for help. I don't think such a place can be strongly Zen-like unless it was in a private practice setting, which is in itself an interesting idea, but I could see some benefits from having an increased supervisory awareness concerning the importance of some of these ideas. At the very least, I wouldn't mind having a supervisor like that!

INTEGRATING TRADITIONAL AND NONTRADITIONAL THERAPIES: A CASE FOR ZEN

J: OK, Chris, you have let me express how I find the teachings of the Buddha helpful in my work, but let me ask you something: Why, as a therapist, social scientist, or person, are you even paying attention to Zen in the first place? What do you think you can get out of the teachings that could be helpful?

C: Let me address each part of your question, Joan, which will take a moment, and then you can have the last word to close the dialog as we are nearing its end. There are three reasons I am interested in this project. The first one concerns how practical it seems to me as a clinician. We have already covered the practical possibilities that Zen holds for psychotherapy in chapter 4, so let me simply summarize what is of special interest to me in this regard right now. For me, the first and most clearly complementary practical use of Zen seems to be that it offers a reasonable answer to that basic question I doggedly asked my major professor some twenty years ago: what to do when, as a clinician, I do not know what to do next, especially when I have tried whatever traditional therapeutic strategy I learned in the past, but to no avail. Many of the situations that I have in mind are found while doing crisis intervention work, which both of us have experienced, but include such times as when the therapist is faced with a regular client who is in crisis, too. Another such application of Zen for me is that it could complement my work when a client brings to me something so filled with pain that it is not clear how to respond in a way that could be helpful, or when therapy reaches some kind of impasse, such as a client being stuck in a particular destructive pattern. In other words, Zen is of practical value because it can supplement my work by adding to my existing skills, not replacing them. Since my first response will still be to employ standard, empirically based techniques and strategies, I would be embracing Zen as a complementary rather than as an alternative approach.

In addition to obvious clinical practicality, there is another way that Zen seems practical to me. For lack of a better word, I will call it Zen's "user friendliness." Let me explain. Most therapeutic approaches involve helping the therapist to maintain a certain professional attitude or stance to take toward a client or clinical situation such as supervision. For example, medically oriented practitioners often are encouraged to be "objective" as a part of their scientific and clinical training. Psychodynamic therapists are told about the importance of being "neutral" so that they do not "contaminate" the transference process. Humanistic training stresses the importance of being fully present to the client in order to facilitate an empathic relationship. However, while I can certainly see the value in each approach and have even been trained in some, I have always found getting there to be a mysterious process.

In contrast, Zen actually tells us what we need to do to achieve a helpful state because it provides specific principles that guide thinking and behavior. This aspect of Zen seems enormously practical to me for several reasons. First, Zen identifies the principles of the Eightfold Path: They are not hidden, vague, or hard to find, which means that I can use them more readily. For example, I can memorize them, write them out as a list, create a poster to hang in my office, or find some other way to help me keep their importance in mind and to use them whenever possible. That may seem like a small thing to you, Joan, but to me it is both a help and a gentle way to begin to use Zen. For instance, when I am frustrated with a student, supervisee, or client, it would be helpful to be able to glance at the wall and be reminded about "Right Speech." I am sure it would calm me down a bit if I was reacting to a strong feeling, help me think about what I want to say next and how to say it so that my words are helpful, or to remain silent, if that is appropriate, as silence is often wiser than speaking.

J: Chris, I appreciate the clarity of Zen, too. For me, it is really quite simple. The principles make such good sense; they touch our "soft spot."

C: Yes, and that is second. In addition to being clear, these principles are practical in that they are prescriptive: They remind us that we have choices about how we react to and express things, and that some tend to be more helpful than others. At the very least, then, Zen can be helpful because it offers a place for me to stand, or even retreat if necessary, in the face of uncertainty, frustration, and so forth. Sometimes "doing no harm," as you put it, is either the best thing that one can do or the only thing that one can do without making matters worse.

J: Like with riding Coco the horse.

C: Right. In addition to being consistent with most standard therapeutic principles concerning the importance of listening, empathy, honesty and so forth, the eight principles are useful because they tell or remind us where we should be going in our dealings with self and others. They are also presented in a way that makes taking small steps in that direction acceptable, which is very different from the concept of commandments. In short, the

Eightfold Path can be helpful in reminding the clinician, supervisor, or teacher what high quality human thinking, feeling, and interacting looks like and how to begin to get there in a particular situation. Right Speech, which seems to be my favorite one right now, for example, reminds me about the power of words and at the same time suggests to me that, because of their importance, we should take the time to choose them very carefully in a given situation. I have noticed that we tenured professors often seem to feel free to say anything at any time and that is not always wise. Indeed, the more I think about how such principles as Right Speech and Right Action can apply to helping, training, and teaching, the more impressed by them I become. Their clarity seems quite amazing to me and probably reflects the fact that Zen has had many centuries to discover, articulate, practice, and refine them, unlike all the other approaches we have been discussing.

J: The only real problem that I see with them is remembering to use them more often! Like with so many other things that are good for us, it is a matter of practice, practice, and practice.

C: Just so. The last thing that appeals to me about the practical aspect of Zen is how well it ties into what we know about learning. For one thing, it is important to appreciate the fact that each time one of these principles reduces anxiety or brings about a sense of mastery, it reinforces that behavior. As we know, learning is facilitated under conditions of positive and negative, but especially positive reinforcement, so Zen is consistent with psychology here. For another thing, although I like lists, it is important to remember that the eight principles are organized in the form of a circle, because they are connected to one another. This circularity, in turn, sets up a dynamic process so that one principle leads to another like stepping-stones on a path into the future, which is one reason they constitute an "Eightfold Path." In this sense, Zen possesses the characteristic cognitive psychologists might call a self-fulfilling prophecy, in this case a good one. For example, Right Speech might increase the likelihood of Right Action and vice versa, just as negative speech increases the likelihood of negative perception, experience, or behavior (Burns, 1980). In other words, the more one practices any one principle, the more likely it is that one will be practicing all of them, which facilitates learning. That is an important aspect of Zen because the kind of learning we are talking about involves unlearning very old and very well practiced habits, which makes them hard to change. Behavioral change and personal growth are not easy things to do, so everything that can help is valuable.

J: OK, Chris, Zen interests you because it offers something you can use. How do you respond to it as a social scientist? Do you think it is possible to integrate the teachings and psychotherapy in general?

C: That is the real question here, Joan, isn't it? After all, whether it is really possible to integrate Zen and psychotherapy or not is the basic point of this book. The fact that Zen might have some practical value cannot stand as the only answer to the question, except in a basic way. It might help to think about the fact that the question of how to integrate psychotherapies is becoming increasingly important for traditional approaches, too. In fact, there are over 400 different types of psychotherapy and the number is growing (Arkowitz, 1997, p. 227). Indeed, since at least the 1970s, an entire field called "psychotherapy integration" has arisen in response to this issue (Arkowitz, 1997). Psychotherapy integration is not to be confused with eclecticism where the clinician simply uses techniques from a variety of perspectives. Such an approach lacks the consistency that only an organized theory can provide and would be too haphazard to trust. Arkowitz points out that there are three major approaches to integrating the various theories of therapy that do provide adequate theoretical consistency (Arkowitz, 1997, p. 227), so let me paint a brief sketch of each of them and then we may make a few observations on whether and how Zen could fit into that picture.

The first one, which is called "Theoretical Integration," involves integrating two or more psychotherapies from different perspectives into one model that incorporates all the major principles of both without violating the fundamental tenants of either one so severely that its uniqueness is lost. For example, people have attempted to integrate the principles of the psychoanalytic and behavioral perspectives, largely by translating psychodynamic principles, such as unconscious impulses, into behavioral concepts, such as frustration and motivation (Dollard & Miller, 1950). It is possible to approach integrating Zen and psychotherapy in this fashion. For example, we saw that Mark Epstein integrates many aspects of Zen and the psychodynamic approach, and we explored basic theoretical compatibility between Zen and the humanistic perspective. More recently, I have also noticed people working on the possibility of integrating Zen and the cognitive approach, such as that of Zindel Segal, who has done work on what he calls "mindfulness-based cognitive therapy" (Segal, Williams, & Teasdale, 2001). Of course there are distinct advantages and disadvantages to this approach to integrating Zen and psychotherapies as there are to the others. For instance, although Theoretical Integration suggests that it is possible to create a general or unified theory of helping others psychologically, no one has been able to develop a view that unifies all the perspectives. Even so, it is clear that this approach is one way of integrating the basic principles of Zen with some traditional psychotherapies in a reasonably complementary fashion. ᛒ

J: Perhaps, as Alan Watts said, the Buddha was the first psychotherapist! "Buddha means the Awakened One . . . the man who woke up . . . and the

Buddha was a very, very skillful psychologist, he is in a way the first psychotherapist in history, a man of tremendous understandings of the wiles and deviousness of the mind" (1973). The Buddha went through all his fears, he faced himself, and in doing that he learned all he needed to learn from his self.

C: Another way to integrate different therapies is called the "Common Factors" approach. This approach is based, in part, on the fact that research shows most major psychotherapies are effective, often at the same level, which suggests that it is not their uniqueness that is at work. Instead, it is thought that there must be underlying factors and processes that are characteristic of all good therapies that "really" make therapy work. The earlier versions of this approach to integrating therapies focused on the two things they all have in common, a therapist and a client, which is to say the personal and interpersonal aspects of therapy. Research does seem to show that the qualities of the therapist, such as empathy, genuineness, honesty, and so forth are, indeed, crucial to the process, as are the certain basic aspects of the relationship, including trust, acceptance, shared world view, and the like (Arkowitz, 1997; Torrey, 1972). However, more recent developments focus on another thing that all therapies have in common: change and the process of change. In particular, Prochaska and Norcross (1994) have developed a theory of change as a process that has considerable empirical support based on their work with addictive disorders.

According to this view, therapeutic change occurs in six identifiable and predictable stages: precontemplation, contemplation, preparation, action, maintenance, and termination. Each stage has its own characteristics, issues, and challenges and each of them are addressed more effectively by some therapeutic techniques than others. Consequently, good therapy involves two activities. First comes assessment, which means the ability of the therapist to understand and identify where the client currently is at in the change process. The other one is technique selection, which involves knowing what kinds of therapeutic activities or strategies are most likely to be helpful with a particular individual in a particular part of the change process. This theory also explains why there are such a variety of therapies and techniques available. For example, some theories pertain to some stages better than others, but miss important ones. Similarly, some techniques are more effective for issues tied to certain stages, but are ineffective for others. Add to this picture the fact that each theory or technique fits better with one type of personality than another, and that therapy always deals with at least two of them, and it is not surprising that there are so many approaches available, as well as so many failures in treatment! Change theory is a very elegant and well-supported theory.

It seems to me, Joan, that it might be quite possible to integrate Zen and traditional psychotherapies based on the fact that both approaches have many factors in common in terms of helping people in general. For example, the master-student relationship is very similar in some basic ways to that of therapist and client. In this case, good therapists, supervisors, and teachers share certain personal characteristics, such as the willingness to be honest and the desire to be open to possibilities. Similarly, the qualities of the therapeutic relationship that you emphasize, such as being connected, seem to be consistent with the common factors of care and empathy. In addition, the literature on Zen that you cited often talks about stages of growth and development. For example, Epstein (1995, pp. 15–41) does a remarkable job of describing how Zen involves a process of change in the way he integrates personal and therapeutic growth with the Zen concept of the "Wheel of Life" that describes the various stages one must go through in order to be free of suffering.

J: Once again, I am reminded of the cup metaphor in Zen: A person has to be ready for the next step; it cannot be forced. I can see some correspondence between change theory and Zen here, if we change the word "problem" to "problem and self," because that is where the problem is! The Zen master knows that he or she cannot enlighten the student with the first lesson; the student is going to have to engage in the process of meditation. Learning to meditate effectively cannot be forced. Instead, the individual must live through the process in stages, one at a time. All you can do is what you can do and will do.

C: The third way to integrate psychotherapies is called "Technical Eclecticism." This approach is more empirically oriented than the others because it is actuarial, which means that it is based on what has been shown to work. Here,

> The main criterion used by eclectic therapists when selecting treatments is what has worked best for similar people with similar problems in the past. Theory is not viewed as a particularly important basis for treatment selection. This relative deemphasis on theory distinguishes eclecticism from both theoretical integration and the common factors approach. (Arkowitz, 1997, p. 249)

There are at least three things to appreciate about this way of integrating various therapies. First, it has considerable scientific appeal because it is based on evidence rather than theory, and that means that one can have confidence in it, probably more confidence than in the other approaches. Indeed, it is difficult to argue with the case that we should be using what has been shown to work now that we have progressed to the point where science is beginning to reveal something about what works, with whom, and under what conditions.

Second, de-emphasizing theory for research efficacy does away with many of the complexities of trying to integrate theoretical perspectives, all of which have their own assumptions and priorities that can be difficult to integrate. The research needs of Theoretical Eclecticism are also more straightforward than those of Common Factors, at least those that concern what works "in general," because all that is important is whether a technique can be shown to work or not. In addition, there is considerable harmony between this way of integrating therapy and the medical model or evidence-based therapies mentioned earlier. They are made for each other in that they are all strong on science and compatible with current mental health research, funding, and administrative trends. Unfortunately, however, the possibility of integrating Zen with such an approach is very limited for one very basic reason: Zen is not testable in the way that standard therapies are, meaning that collecting empirical data to support its practices is going to be difficult.

In a word, Zen is probably not compatible with Technical Eclecticism as it now stands, so integrating Zen and therapy this way seems unlikely at least for the foreseeable future. For this approach to integrating psychotherapy, Zen is, and probably will remain, an alternative rather than a complement to our work. All things considered, however, we have seen that a different answer emerges when we ask the question in regard to the other two approaches. In the first case, we see that there is enough compatibility between Zen and several of the traditional perspectives to justify understanding Zen as complementary in this regard. Moreover, the similarity concerning personality, relationships, and the process of change between Zen and the Common Factors approach also seems to be sufficient to achieve a good degree of theoretical compatibility between this nontraditional and those traditional approaches. In sum, although the question of whether Zen can be complementary or must remain an alternative may not be resolved, it does seem fairly clear that it is quite possible to argue for such a position, at least in terms of achieving theoretical integration. Considering all the evidence we have encountered from the beginning, I would argue that Zen, at least the Middle Path, should be regarded as being a complementary approach to traditional psychotherapies and ought to be taught as such. Your thoughts?

J: I am still trying to justify using the word alternative with Zen, because it is what I *live,* not just an idea or theoretical perspective. It is what we live and how we are with people. I've seen it work too much over these 40 some years to dismiss Zen as a mere complement. For example, I think that one thing that has been personally helpful for me, even exhilarating, about Zen is opening up to the knowledge that it is OK to have problems. Problems are going to come. The acceptance of The Four Noble Truths and being aware that you are not stuck because you already know that life is suffering, and looking at the truth of that fundamental fact in order to learn from it, has been *extremely* helpful to the people I talk with in therapy. Where I am coming from is really not just an approach, again, it is the realization that connection is imperative for both parties involved.

C: I can understand your perspective on this matter, Joan, and we will address that issue again. But in some ways the last part of your question, which concerns why I am interested in Zen as a person, is the most difficult one to answer, probably because it involves taking an honest look at myself. There are some things that appeal to me about Zen intellectually and emotionally, or as you would put it, to my "head" and to my "heart."

Intellectually, Zen seems to offer some kind of an answer to a question I have been asking since undergraduate school. In education, we stress something that used to be called "reasoning" and is today usually referred to as "critical thinking." It involves questioning ideas, examining evidence for and against them, and then arriving at some sort of conclusion that is also open to question, which means that critical thinking is a never-ending process that takes one to higher levels of understanding. However, this kind of thinking, and education in general for that matter, comes at a surprising cost: a lack of certainty that is the result of a process of questioning and seeking answers which never stops! Although critical thinking is a good thing in terms of human growth and development, it also seems to make an important problem that we have been dealing with in this book more difficult in a certain way. Critical thinking, the scientific method, and even reasoning itself come to an impasse when addressing the "really big" questions. In this case, it is whether or not there is a spiritual dimension to life and what should be done about that. No one can give a definitive answer, of course, but critical thinking seems to have meant, for me, that it is impossible to simply accept the tenets of any particular religious or philosophical system. As you can imagine, this state of chronic inquiry results in a basic tension that is difficult to resolve.

Zen, however, could present a way of dealing with dualism that allows a person in this situation to live with it more peacefully than is otherwise possible. The question of whether or not the ultimate reality is material or spiritual is akin to one that is often presented to Zen masters about whether there really is a self or not. There is no good way to answer that question. For example, if one says, "Yes," then one must either prove there is a self, which is impossible, or face the possibility of living a lie if it turns out in the end that there is no "real" self. If one says, "No," then everything becomes relative, which ultimately means that nothing is true, or if it turns out that there is a self, then one faces the possibility of living another kind of lie. The Middle Path shows that regardless of the ultimate answer to the question, it is how one lives in the meantime that counts. Since the question of dualism is the same question, perhaps the Middle Path may be a sane response to it as well. At least that position can settle the mind a bit. Emotionally, I suppose that like many others, I experience what might be the central affliction of our times mentioned in chapter 1. I experience some of what David Myers (2000, p. 257) called a modern form of "spiritual hunger," which is a desire for deeper levels of meaning, experience, and connection with others that occurs when one lives in a materialistic culture that is wealthy enough to satisfy physical needs like ours. Perhaps the Middle Path has something to offer in this regard, as well.

J: Then, Chris, I guess that you will have to explore this possibility as critically as the others and who knows where that path will lead!

ZEN AS A COMPLEMENT OR AS AN ALTERNATIVE: A FINAL WORD

C: At this point, Joan, we come full circle and back to the question of the relationship between Zen and traditional therapies. A chief weakness of Zen, of course, is that it is not a scientific theory because it is not based on testable evidence. For example, when you say something like "Zen is truth," I become a bit distressed, because I know we are leaving the point where Zen can be understood as being complementary to a scientific approach and entering the region where it stands as an alternative.

J: Zen is a paradox, Chris: Zen is simple, but it's not simple at all because it talks about truth. For me, the best way to talk about Zen is how it has influenced my life. Zen is not some "idea." My fear is this: I feel responsible for presenting Zen here and do not want people who read this book to think that Zen is simply something else that they can add to their bag of clinical tricks or place on their psychotherapy résumé. The teachings makes sense to me because I can apply it to my *life*. I can apply it to the way I live, to the way that I am with my family, friends, patients, and colleagues, and to help me face my fears. Zen has invited me to look at myself and through looking at myself I have become *relaxed*. I recall my mentor telling me that therapy is a way to help people feel relaxed. At the time I thought that sounded very simplistic—I see what he meant; now. It is a way of life for me, not just an approach to helping.

Above all, Zen has helped me to realize that life is suffering, just as The Four Noble Truths say. When I first heard that, I thought that what the Buddha said sounded very grim and pessimistic. This grim view of the world seemed like everything that I was opposed to, so I did not want any part of it. Then, when I woke up, I realized that life is suffering and I felt a great sense of relief, of not being afraid to look at truth, for the first time in my life. It was like going through a door that I had not wanted to open out of fear and then stepping into a clearer world. After that, it seemed natural to go on to the Second Noble Truth and ask what caused me to suffer? Of course, I discovered that I was bringing it on myself. It took courage to be truthful about my own foibles and how my "stuff" plays a role in my own suffering. From there, I learned what I *can* do so that I don't get caught up in creating unnecessary pain. It has been such a blessing that I can accept the things that I have done without feeling bad. I can even learn from those times!

C: I can see my way to accepting Zen as a complement to my work for the reasons mentioned above, but I wonder what happens when a person takes the next step and embraces Zen as an alternative. At that point, the individual leaves the scientific paradigm altogether, which would cause me considerable anxiety.

J: I think that part of the process is an evolution, the more you practice Zen, the more you find yourself wanting to practice it because you come to terms with yourself. It is facing groundlessness and living a continual sense of transition; for the Zen truth is that we are always in transition.

C: If Zen is like a self-fulfilling prophecy as I described earlier, then does the typical therapist interested in reading this book, learning something about Zen, or incorporating it into his or her work have to worry about losing a scientific foundation or about "converting" to Zen?

J: No! This is the beauty of Zen. It offers an incredible acceptance, an acceptance of many things, such as the fact that I am going to screw up again in life, no matter how hard I work to avoid that, and I do, and that this is as natural as breathing. I will not claim that I am a Buddhist, only that the teachings of the Buddha help me very much. They help me with the people I talk with, too. But let me ask you something, Chris, little by little you seem to be seeing how The Four Noble Truths and the Eightfold Path can help you personally or help you understand something. What do you make of that?

C: Well, I can accept Zen as being complementary, that is consistent with what I have been taught about human behavior and how to change it for the better. I also keep coming back to the way the Middle Path seems to suggest a more gentle approach to living with life's difficult questions and problems than my usual approach at the personal level. For example, Zen may help me to not feel so responsible for everything, which I tend to do far too much, because it may help me accept the fact that I cannot control the future or someone else's behavior. Zen might allow me to better realize that I cannot do *everything*, that I can only do the best I can at the time, both professionally and personally. I also see some potential for Zen to help me to stop doing some things that I don't want to do, some of my "bad habits." For instance, sometimes when I am about to blurt out something or do something that is not particularly admirable, Zen might remind me to ask the question, "Is this Right Speech or Right Action?" and I might have a second chance!

J: Because it is the truth.

C: Maybe, but "why" doesn't seem to matter right now, only the fact that it seems to help a bit. It gives me another tool, and complements the ones I already have without violating them, and that is all I need to know for now. Later on, if I continue along these lines, I might explore it further. But that is not the case right now and it doesn't have to be in order to find value in Zen.

J: That is fine with me!

C: You have the last word here, Joan, and I know you want to tell us more about Zen as an alternative approach rather than a complementary one. What does doing therapy from a Zen perspective look like when it is the primary orientation of the therapist?

J: I think that it involves spirituality, just as we talked about in chapter 1. People are hungry for spirituality, for connecting with something bigger then themselves. As Huston Smith (1991) describes so well in his work, the two greatest influences in the last several hundred years are religion and science. For the first several hundred years, the pendulum swung toward religion. During the Middle Ages, it swung to the extreme points of religion and religion got way out of hand. Now it seems that the pendulum has swung far too much in the other direction, toward the materialism of the scientific side. Today everything is messed up: The meaning of life, the question of fundamental human values, and the need for ethical behavior are all being eroded. Yet, at the same time, people seem to want more of those things, particularly the people we work with who are suffering, but people in general, too. They do seem to hunger for the stability of something deeper in life and sometimes even realize that what they have based their lives upon is like papier-mâché and that it does not make any sense to live this way. Addictions are the clearest form of this problem, but anxiety and depression are manifestations, too. There is an extreme lack of connectedness in our lives, even with our families. The pace of life is too fast, our technology is destroying the planet, and these things are just symptoms. It is like the *Tale of Two Cities*: We are in the best of times and the worst of times. Zen is a genuine alternative to a *merely* materialistic way of life.

C: I see tremendous opportunity and danger, too. Perhaps the Middle Path is a very reasonable one under such circumstances. Indeed, I find that the practical orientation of what is now being loosely called Western Zen can offer some hope to a more scientific mind.

J: Zen has relieved me of a lot a guilt, a lot of fear, of the need to be perfect and it has given me the ability to be much more open, much more forgiving of myself and people. Perhaps learning how to face my own suffering and forgiving myself helps others see that it is possible for them, too. As I move further down the path, I see Zen as a continual waking up to more and more. It is a process, not a destination. Once again, without practice I am at a standstill.

C: If someone turns out to be interested in Zen as an alternative rather than a complement, how would they go about taking that step?

J: First of all, I would warn them: Do not start this path unless you are willing to accept the fact that you will never be the same. You will come to see your "warts" more clearly than you ever have and it will hurt for a while. If you do decide to take the risk, be very compassionate toward yourself. Courage helps, too. But be aware that wherever you are, it is OK. As mentioned in chapter 4, I would look for a good teacher who would be able to teach you clearly about what the *Three Jewels* of Zen mean: Buddha is the guide, the teacher; the Dharma is the way of truth; and the Sangha are the friends that will help you along the way. Fortunately there are many good books, tapes, videos and retreats. There is an advantage going to a meditation or Zen Center because you will be with like-minded people, a community of people who are studying and practicing the teachings of the Buddha.

> Fortunately you have the support of others who are practicing with you. This is not an umbrella to provide shade to protect you but a space where you can have real practice, a space where you can express yourself fully. You can open your eyes to appreciate the practice of others, and you will find that you are able to communicate without words. (Suzuki, 2002, p. 9)

Of course, one must be very cautious in this regard because there is a lot of skullduggery out there, just like with alternative health care in general. I would, for instance, choose authors that have studied the teachings for years, for example, the ones I have mentioned. Meditation Centers, such as the Insight Meditation Society, which is located in Barre, Massachusetts, Spirit Rock Center in Woodacre, California, and the Zen Center of San Diego, are very well respected because of the teachers. I would tell them that I am a novice and am interested in learning more about meditation, the teachings of the Dharma and Zen, whatever the case may be. I would want to have information sent to me regarding the Center and the staff and what would be expected of me.

C: Those suggestions sound realistic, much like the ones a person would do well to ask of a psychotherapist or physician. Now, Joan, in closing this book what would you like to say about what you would *not* want to see happen with a Zen approach?

J: I would not want Zen to become just another technique, like so many others. Nor would I wish to see it be used as just another theory because, "Theories are like patches: However good they are, they will come off" (Sogyal, 1993). It is not just another page in the treatment manual. At the same time, I do want therapists, and people in general, to know how the teachings might be fruitful for them. There are teachings in Zen that lend themselves to easy slogans, catchy phrases, and popularization, so there is some danger that Zen could become another "fad" in therapy, like so many "New Age" therapies. Similarly, I would not like to see Zen become the subject of popular psychology. Those dangers often seem to occur when introducing anything that is new or that is old and made to appear new.

But I am not worried about these dangers in what we have done here, because what we are offering traditionally oriented therapists, supervisors, and educators is more solid. The first and most basic thing to remember is that Zen may be helpful in the clinical, supervisory, or teaching settings. The second is that Zen can also be helpful in terms of offering continuing personal as well as professional development, all the way from reducing the possibility of burnout to offering a new vision of life. Once again, we come back to the issue of Zen as a complement or alternative, and one is free to choose either way.

APPENDIX I

Glossary

Avidya:	Basic ignorance of the mind.
Bodhi:	Perfect wisdom.
Bodhichitta:	One who seeks enlightenment.
Buddha:	An enlightened being; one who is awake; who knows. The first of the Three Jewels.
Buddha-nature:	Our true nature—whether realized or not.
Compassion:	The wish to free all beings from suffering.
Dharma:	The teachings of the Buddha; the ultimate truth; the Buddhist doctrines. The second of the Three Jewels.
Dukkha:	The suffering nature of life. The First of the Noble Truths.
Dogen Zenji:	The founder of Soto Zen in Japan.
Eightfold Path:	The way to end suffering and find liberation. The Fourth Noble Truth.
Four Noble Truths:	The first teachings of the Buddha: the truth of suffering, its origin, its cessation, and the Eightfold Path.

Karma:	Universal law of cause and effect; the actions stemming from thoughts which produce suffering.
Lama:	A Tibetan spiritual teacher, master, or guru.
Maitri:	Loving-kindness, unconditional friendliness, to feel what we feel without judgment.
Mantra:	Sounds or words used in Zen practice.
Marga:	The path that frees beings from suffering, the Eightfold Path.
Middle Path:	Avoiding two extremes.
Nirodha:	Cessation of suffering. The Third Noble Truth.
Roshi:	A Zen master in the Japanese tradition.
Samudaya:	Cause of suffering. The Second Noble Truth.
Sangha:	A spiritual community of friends studying under the same teacher, usually monks and nuns. The third of the Three Jewels.
Sesshin:	A retreat of one or more days, usually a week or more.
Skandhas:	Aggregates of tendencies that form the ego; form, feelings, perceptions, mental formations and consciousness.
Zafu:	A cushion to sit on while meditating; usually round, hand-crafted and filled with buckwheat hulls.
Zazen:	Sitting meditation in the Zen tradition.
Zen:	A way of seeing into your own self-nature.
Zen Centers:	Meditation communities; may include residences.
Zendo:	Practice hall for meditation.

Resources

I. AUDIO CATALOGUES

Audio Literature Inc.
325 Corey Way, Suite 112
South San Francisco, CA 94080-6706
Toll Free (650) 583-9700

Dharma Seed Tape Library
Box 66
Wendell Depot, MA 01380
Toll Free (800) 969-7333

New Dimensions
P.O. Box 569
Ukiah, CA 95482
Toll Free (800) 935-8273

Sounds True
735 Walnut Street
Boulder, CO 80302
Toll Free (800) 333-9185

II. JOURNALS

Buddhadharma: An In-depth, Practice-Oriented Journal for Buddhists of All Traditions

1345 Spruce Street
Boulder, CO 80302-4886
Toll Free (877) 786-1950

Parabola: Myth, Tradition, and the Search for Meaning
P.O. Box 3000
Denville, NJ 07834
Toll Free (877)-593-2521

Shambhala Sun: Buddhism Culture Meditation Life
1345 Spruce Street
Boulder, CO 80302-4886
Toll Free (877) 786-1950

Tricycle: The Buddhist Review
P.O. Box 2077
Marion, OH 43306
Toll Free (800) 873-9871

Utne Reader: The Best of the Alternative Press
P.O. Box 7460
Red Oak, IA 51591-0460
Toll Free (800) 736-Utne

III. BOOKS

Batchelor, S. (1997). *Buddhism without belief.* New York: Riverview Books.

Chodron, P. (1991). *The wisdom of no escape.* Boston: Shambhala Publications.

———— (1994). *Start where you are.* Boston: Shambhala Publications.

———— (1997). *When things fall apart.* Boston: Shambhala Publications.

———— (2001). *The place that scares you.* Boston: Shambhala Publications.

Copra, F. (1988). *Uncommon wisdom.* New York: Simon and Shuster.

de Saint-Exupéry, A. (1943). *The little prince.* Orlando, FL: Harcourt Brace Jovanovich.

Epstein, M. (1995). *Thoughts without a thinker.* New York: Basic Books.

_____(1998). *Going to pieces without falling apart.* New York: Broadway Books.

_____(2001). *Going on being.* New York: Broadway Books.

Farrer-Hall, G. (2000). *The illustrated encyclopedia of Buddhist wisdom.* New York: Theosophical Publishing House.

Hanh, T. N. (1998). *The heart of the Buddha's teaching.* Berkeley: Parallax Printing.

Kaiser, H. (1965). *Effective psychotherapy.* New York: Free Press.

McGaa, E. (1990). *Mother earth spirituality.* San Francisco: Harper.

Surya, D. L. (1997). *Awaken the Buddha within.* New York: Broadway Books.

_____ (1999). *Awakening to the sacred.* New York: Broadway Books.

IV. WEB SITES

A site that offers traditional Zen texts:
http:www.sacred-texts.com/bud/index.htm

An educational site with distance learning capabilities:
http://www.naropa.edu/

Links to sites on Western Zen:
http://www.pcisys.net/~sms.zen/links.htm

A site featuring Pema Chodron's work:
http://www.pemachodrontapes.org/

A site with Thich Nhat Hanh's work:
http://www.plumvillage.org/

A site with Sogyal Rinpoche's work:
http://www.rigpa.org/

An East Coast Zen resource:
http://www.dharma.org/

A West Coast Zen resource:
http://spiritrock.org/

References

Aanstoos, C. (Ed.). (1984). *Exploring the lived world: Readings in phenomenological psychology* (Vol. 23). Atlanta: West Georgia College.

American Psychiatric Association. (1968). *Diagnostic and statistical manual of mental disorders* (2nd ed.). Washington, DC: Author.

American Psychiatric Association. (1980). *Diagnostic and statistical manual of mental disorders* (3rd ed.). Washington, DC: Author.

American Psychiatric Association. (1994). *Diagnostic and statistical manual of mental disorders* (4th ed.). Washington, DC: Author.

Arkowitz, H. (1997). Integrative theories of therapy. In P. Wachtel & S. Messer (Eds.), *Theories of psychotherapy: Origins and evolution* (pp. 227–288).

Baars, B. (1986). *The cognitive revolution in psychology.* New York: Guilford.

Bandura, A. (1997). *Self-efficacy: The exercise of control.* New York: W. H. Freeman & Co.

Barton, A. (1974). *Three worlds of therapy: An existential-phenomenological study of the therapies of Freud, Jung, and Rogers.* Palo Alto, CA: National Press.

Batchelor, S. (1997). *Buddhism without beliefs: A contemporary guide to awakening.* New York: Riverhead Books.

Bayda, E. (2002). *Being Zen.* Boston: Shambhala.

Beck, C. (1989). *Everyday Zen.* New York: HaperCollins.

Bednar, R., & Peterson, S. (1995). *Self-esteem: Paradoxes and innovations in clinical theory and practice* (2nd ed.). Washington, DC: American Psychological Association.

Benson, H. (1975). *The relaxation response.* New York: Avon.

Bloom, P. (2000). *Buddhist acts of compassion.* Berkeley, CA: Conari Press.

Boorstein, S. (1997). *That's funny, you don't look Buddhist.* New York: HarperCollins.

Brazier, D. (1995). *Zen therapy: Transcending the sorrows of the human mind.* New York: John Wiley & Sons.

Bstan-dzin-rgya-mtsho, Dalai Lama XIV. (1995). *The world of Tibetan Buddhism: An overview of its philosophy and practice* (G. T. Jinpa, Trans.). Boston: Wisdom Publications.

Bstan-dzin-rgya-mtsho, Dalai Lama XIV. (1996). *The good heart: A Buddhist perspective on the teachings of Jesus* (G. T. Jinpa, Trans.). Boston: Wisdom Publications.

Bstan-dzin-rgya-mtsho, Dalai Lama XIV, & Cutler, H. C. (1998). *The art of happiness: A handbook for living.* New York: Riverhead Books.

Burns, D. (1980). *Feeling good: The new mood therapy.* New York: Signet.

Burns, D. (1993). *Ten days to self-esteem.* New York: Quill.

Capra, F. (1988). *Uncommon wisdom.* New York: Bantam Books.

Castaneda, C. (1968). *The teachings of Don Juan: A Yaqui way of knowledge.* New York: Ballantine Books.

Chah, A. (2001). *Being dharma: The essence of the Buddha's teachings* (P. Breiter, Trans.). Boston: Shambhala Publications.

Chodron, P. (1991). *The wisdom of no escape: And the path of loving-kindness.* Boston: Shambhala Publications.

Chodron, P. (1994). *Start where you are: A guide to compassionate living.* Boston: Shambhala Publications.

Chodron, P. (1997). *When things fall apart: Heart advice for difficult times.* Boston: Shambhala Publications.

Chodron, P. (2001). *The places that scare you: A guide to fearlessness in difficult times.* Boston: Shambhala Publications.

Chodron, P. (2002). *Comfortable with uncertainty: 108 Teaching* (E. Sell, Ed.). Boston: Shambhala Publications.

Christensen, A., & Rudnick, S. (1999). A glimpse of Zen practice within the realm of countertransference. *The American Journal of Psychoanalysis, 59,* 59–69.

Clark, C. (Ed.). (1999). *Encyclopedia of complementary health practice.* New York: Springer.

Clinician's Research Digest. (1999). Cognitive-behavioral therapy is comparable to antidepressants. *Clinician's Research Digest: Briefings in Behavioral Science, 17,* 11. Washington, DC: Author.

Consumer Reports. (1995, November). Mental health: Does therapy work? *Consumer Reports,* 734–739.

Consumer Reports. (2000, May). The mainstreaming of alternative medicine. *Consumer Reports,* 17–25.

Cornett, C. (1998). *The soul of psychotherapy: Recapturing the spiritual dimension in the therapeutic encounter.* New York: Free Press.

Cortright, B. (1997). *Psychotherapy and spirit: Theory and practice in transpersonal psychotherapy.* Albany: State University of New York.

Crone, C., & Wise, T. (2000). Complementary medicine: Implications toward medical treatment and the patient-physician relationship. In P. Muskin (Ed.), *Complementary and alternative medicine and psychiatry* (pp. 199–240). Washington, D.C.: American Psychiatric Press.

Dalai Lama & Cutler, H. C. (1998). *The art of happiness: A handbook for living.* Riverhead Books: New York.

Das, S. (1997). *Awakening the Buddha within: Eight steps to enlightenment: Tibetan wisdom for the Western world.* New York: Broadway Books.

Dass, R. (1987). *Grist for the mill.* Berkeley, CA: Celestial Arts.

Dass, R. (1979). *Miracle of love.* New York: Viking Penguin.

Dollard, J., & Miller, N. E. (1950). *Personality and psychotherapy.* New York: McGraw-Hill.

Dreyfus, H. L., & Dreyfus, S. E. (1986). *Mind over machine: The power of human intuition and expertise in the era of the computer.* New York: Free Press.

Durand, M., & Barlow, D. (1997). *Abnormal psychology: An introduction.* Pacific Grove, CA: Brooks/Cole.

Ellis, A., & Harper, R. (1977). *A new guide to rational living.* North Hollywood, CA: Wilshire Books.

Emmons, R. (1999). *The psychology of ultimate concerns: Motivation and spirituality in personality.* New York: Guilford.

Epstein, S. (1980). The self-concept: A review and the proposal of an integrated theory of personality. In E. Straub (Ed.), *Personality: Basic aspects and current research* (pp. 83–131). Englewood Cliffs, NJ: Prentice Hall.

Epstein, M. (1995). *Thoughts without a thinker: Psychotherapy from a Buddhist perspective.* New York: Basic Books.

Epstein, M. (1998). *Going to pieces without falling apart: A Buddhist perspective on wholeness.* New York: Broadway Books.

Epstein, M. (2001). *Going on being: Buddhism and the way of change: a positive psychology for the West.* New York: Broadway Books.

Erikson, E. (1985). *The life cycle completed: A review.* New York: W. W. Norton & Co.

Fancher, R. (1995). *Cultures of healing: Correcting the image of American mental health care.* New York: W. H. Freeman & Company.

Farrer-Hall, G. (2000). *The illustrated encyclopedia of Buddhist wisdom.* New York: Theosophical Publishing House.

Freedman, A. M., Kaplan, H. I., & Saddock, B. J. (1975). *Comprehensive textbook of psychiatry—II* (Volume II, 2nd ed.). Baltimore: Williams & Wilkins Co.

Freire, P. (1973). *The pedagogy of the oppressed.* New York: The Seabury Press.

Fisher, S., & Greenberg, R. (1995, September/October). Prescriptions for happiness. *Psychology Today,* 32–37.

Frey, D., & Carlock, C. J. (1989). *Enhancing self-esteem* (2nd ed.). Muncie, IN: Accelerated Development.

Gardner, H. (1985). *The mind's new science: A history of the cognitive revolution.* New York: Basic Books.

Gergen, K. J. (1991). *The saturated self: Dilemmas of identity in contemporary life.* New York: Basic Books.

Giorgi, A. (1971). Phenomenology and experimental psychology: I & II. In A. Giorgi, W. Fischer, & R. Von Eckartsberg (Eds.), *Duquesne studies in phenomenological psychology* (Vol. 1, pp. 6–28). Pittsburgh, PA: Duquesne University Press.

Glassman, B., & Fields, R. (1996). *Instructions to the cook: A Zen master's lessons in living a life that matters.* New York: Bell Tower.

Goble, F. (1971). *The third force.* New York: Pocket Books.

Goldstein, J. (2002). *One dharma: The emerging Western Buddhism.* San Francisco: HarperSanFrancisco.

Hanh, T. N. (1998). *The heart of the Buddha's teaching: Transforming suffering into peace, joy, and liberation: The four noble truths, the noble eightfold path, and other basic Buddhist teachings.* Berkeley, CA: Parallax Press.

Hartzell, J. (1994). Alternatives to psychiatric treatments: Is it safe to be human on a psychiatric unit. Unpublished Manuscript.

Heidegger, M. (1962). *Being and time.* New York: Harper & Row. (Original work published 1927)

Howard, K., Kopta, S., Krause, M., & Orlinsky, D. (1986). The dose-effect relationship in psychotherapy. *American Psychologist, 41*, 159–164.

Hubble, M., Duncan, B., & Miller, S. (1999). *The heart and soul of change: What works in therapy.* Washington, DC: American Psychological Association.

Hunt, M. (1993). *The story of psychology.* New York: Doubleday.

Jackson, M. (1984). *Self-esteem and meaning: A life historical investigation.* Albany: State University of New York.

James, W. (1983). *The principles of psychology.* Cambridge, MA: Harvard University Press. (Original work published 1890)

Kaiser Commission, (2000). The uninsured and their access to health care. *http://www.pbs.org/newhour/health/unisured.*

Kaiser, H. (1965). *Effective psychotherapy* (L. B. Fierman, Ed.). New York: Free Press.

Kimble, G. (1984). Psychology's two cultures. *American Psychologist, 39*(8), 833–839.

Koerner, B. I. (July/August, 2002). Disorders made to order. *Mother Jones, 27*(4), 58–81.

Kopp, S. (1988). *If you meet the Buddha on the road, kill him.* New York: Bantam Books.

Kornfield, J. (1993). *A path with heart: A guide through the perils and promises of spiritual life.* New York: Bantam Books.

Kornfield, J. (Speaker). (1994). *Meditations of the heart.* (Cassette Recording, Tape #A249). Sounds True Audio.

Koudsi, S., & Costa, L. (1998). American vs. the new Europe: By the numbers. *Fortune, 138*(12), 149.

Lasch, C. (1978). *The culture of narcissism: American life in an age of diminishing expectations.* New York: Norton.

Leiper, S. (May, 1999). Wavy Gravy: A humorous humanist. *Connections*, No. 7. Institute of Noetic Sciences: Sausalito, CA (ISSN: 1096–7303).

Levin, J. D. (1993). *Slings and arrows: Narcissistic injury and its treatment.* Northvale, NJ: Aronson.

Linehan, M. (1993). *Skills training manual for treating borderline personality disorder.* New York: Guilford.

London, P. (1986). *The modes and morals of psychotherapy.* New York: Hemisphere.

Mascaro, J. (1962). *The Bhagavad-Gita.* New York: Viking Penguin.

Maslow, A. (1968). *Toward a psychology of being* (2nd ed.). New York: Van Nostrand Reinhold.

Maslow, A. (1971). *The farthest reaches of human behavior.* New York: Viking.

Masters, K., & Bergin, A. (1992). Religious orientation and mental health. In J. Schumaker (Ed.), *Religion and mental health* (pp. 221–232). New York: Oxford.

McGaa, E. (1990). *Mother Earth spirituality: Native American paths to healing ourselves and our world.* New York: Harper & Row.

Miller, R. (Ed.). (1992). *The restoration of dialogue: Readings in the philosophy of clinical psychology.* Washington, DC: American Psychological Association.

Miller, W. (Ed.). (1999). *Integrating spirituality into treatment: Resources for practitioners.* Washington DC: American Psychological Association.

Minsky, M. (1986). *Society of mind.* New York: Simon & Schuster.

Misiak, H., & Sexton, V. (1973). *Phenomenological, existential, and humanistic psychologies: An historical review.* New York: Grune & Stratton.

Moore, P., Adler, & Robertson, N. (2000, October). Medical malpractice: The effect of doctor-patient relations on medical patient perceptions of malpractice intentions. *Western Journal of Medicine, 173*(4), 244–250.

Moyers, B. (1993). *Healing the mind volume 1: Mystery of chi.* [Film] Available from Ambrose Videos, David Gruber Productions and Public Affairs Television, 290 Boulevard of the Americas, Suite 2245, New York, New York, 10104.

Mruk, C. (1999). *Self-esteem: Research, theory, and practice* (2nd ed.). New York: Springer Publishing.

Mruk, C. (1994). Phenomenological psychology and integrated description: Keeping the science in the human science approach. *Methods: A Journal for Human Science* (annual edition), 6–20.

Muskin, P. (Ed.). (2000). *Complementary and alternative medicine and psychiatry.* Review of Psychiatry 19. Washington, DC: American Psychiatric Press.

Myers, M. (2000). *The American paradox: Spiritual hunger in an age of plenty.* New Haven, CT: Yale University Press.

Nathan, P., & Gorman, J. (Eds.). (1998). *A guide to treatments that work.* New York: Oxford University Press.

Pargament, K. (1997). *The psychology of religion and coping: Theory, research, and practice.* New York: Guilford.

Peeke, P., & Frishett, S. (2002). The role of complementary and alternative therapies in women's mental health. In K. Zerbe (Ed.), *Women's mental health. Primary Care: Clinics in Office Practice, 29*(1), 183–197.

Prochaska, J. O., & Norcross, J. C. (1994). *Systems of psychotherapy: A transtheoretical analysis* (3rd ed.). Pacific Grove, CA: Brooks/Cole.

Ramis, H. (1993). *Groundhog Day.* [Film] Available from Columbia Tristar, Trevor Albert, 3400 Riverside Burbank, CA 91505.

Rathus, S. (1999). *Psychology* (7th ed.). San Francisco: Holt, Rinehart & Winston.

Richards, P. S., & Bergin, A. E. (1997). *A spiritual strategy for counseling and psychotherapy.* Washington, DC: American Psychological Association.

Reid, E. (1959). *The great physician.* Oxford: Oxford University Press

Rogers, C. (1951). *Client-centered therapy: Its current practice, implications, and theory.* Boston: Houghton Mifflin.

Rogers, C. (1977). *Carl Rogers on Carl Rogers.* New York: Delacorte Press.

Rosenbaum, R. (1998). *Zen and the heart of psychotherapy.* New York: Brunner/Mazel.

Rubin, J. (1999). Close encounters of a new kind: Toward an integration of psychoanalysis and Buddhism. *The American Journal of Psychoanalysis, 59,* 5–24.

Saint-Exupéry, A. de. (1943). *The little prince* (K. Woods, Trans.). New York: Harcourt Brace & World.

Schumaker, J. (Ed.). (1992). *Religion and mental health.* New York: Oxford.

Scotten, B. (1996). Introduction and definition of transpersonal psychiatry. In B. Scotten, A. Chinen, & J. Battista (Eds.), *Textbook of transpersonal psychiatry and psychology* (pp. 39–51). New York: Basic Books.

Segal, Z., Williams, J. M., & Teasdale, J. (2001). *Mindfulness-based cognitive therapy for depression.* New York: Guilford.

Seligman, M. (1995). The effectiveness of psychotherapy: The Consumer Reports study. *American Psychologist, 50*(12), 965–974.

Shafranske, E. P. (2000). Religious involvement and professional practices of psychiatrists and other mental health professionals. *Psychiatric Annals, 30*(8), 25–32.

Shafrankse, E. P., & Malony, H. N. (1996). Religion and the clinical practice of psychology: A case for inclusion. In E. P. Shafranske (Ed.), *Religion and the clinical practice of psychology* (pp. 561–586). Washington, DC: American Psychological Association.

Silberner, J. (2002, May 3). Talk of the Nation/Science Friday. Washington, DC: *National Public Radio.*

Sills, M. (2002). Licking honey from the razor's edge. In G. Watson, S. Batchelor, & J. Claxton (Eds.), *The psychology of awakening.* York Beach, ME: Samuel Weiser.

Smith, H. (1991). *The illustrated world religions: A guide to our wisdom traditions.* San Francisco: HarperSanFrancisco.

Smith, H. (Speaker). (1995). *Religions of the World: Buddhism.* (Cassette Recording, Tape #3). Sounds True Audio.

Sogyal, R. (1993). *The Tibetan book of living and dying.* New York: HarperCollins Publishers.

Soldz, S., & McCullough, L. (2000). *Reconciling empirical knowledge and clinical experience: The art and science of psychotherapy.* Washington, DC: American Psychological Association.

Spilka, B., & McIntosh, D. (Eds.). (1997). *The psychology of religion: Theoretical approaches.* Boulder, CO: Westview.

Suzuki, S. (1970). *Zen mind, beginner's mind* (T. Dixon, Ed.). New York: Weatherhill.

Suzuki, S. (2002). *Not always so.* New York: HarperCollins.

The song of God: Bhagavad-Gita (Swami Prabhavananda & C. Isherwood, Trans.). (1972). New York: New American Library.

Toms, M. (1984). New Dimensions. San Francisco: (Cassette Tape, #1735) *National Public Radio.*

Toms, M. (2001a). New Dimensions. San Francisco: (Cassette Tape, #2861). *National Public Radio.*

Toms, M. (2001b). New Dimensions. San Francisco: (Cassette Tape, #2783) *National Public Radio.*

Torrey, E. F. (1972). *Witchdoctors and psychiatrists: The common roots of psychotherapy and its future.* New York: Harper & Row.

Trungpa, C. (1973). *Cutting through spiritual materialism* (John Baker & Marvin Casper, Eds.). Boston: Shambhala Publications.

Trungpa, C. (1984). *Shambhala: The sacred path of the warrior* (Carolyn Rose Gimian, Ed.). Boston: Shambhala Publications.

Trungpa, C. (1996). *Meditation in action.* Boston: Shambhala Publications.

U.S. Department of Commerce, Economic & Statistics Administration. (1998). Higher education means more money, census bureau says. *Census Bureau Press Release.* http://www.census.gov/press-release/cb98-221.html.

Valenstein, E. (1998). *Blaming the brain: The truth about drugs and mental health.* New York: Free Press.

Vash, C. L. (1994). *Personality and adversity: Psychospiritual aspects of rehabilitation.* New York: Springer Publishing.

Wachtel, P., & Messer, S. (Eds.). (1997). *Theories of psychotherapy: Origins and evolution.* Washington, DC: American Psychological Association.

Wagner, D. (1998, August 17). Friend or enemy? *Insight on the News, 14*(30), 8–10.

Watts, A. (1961). *Psychotherapy east and west.* New York: Pantheon Books.

Watts, A. (Speaker). (1973). *Philosophy of Asia series: Introduction to Buddhism.* (Cassette Recording, Tape #4.) Electronic University.

Watts, A. (1989). *The way of Zen.* New York: Vintage Books.

Wilber, K. (1996). Foreword. In B. Scotten, A. Chinen, & J. Battista (Eds.), *Textbook of transpersonal psychiatry and psychology* (pp. xvii–xx). New York: Basic Books.

Williams, J. (2000, July 29). Talk of the Nation. Washington, DC: *National Public Radio.*

Wilson, O. (1998). *Consilience: The unity of knowledge.* New York: Knoff.

Wolitzky, D., & Eagle, M. (1997). Psychoanalytic theories of psychotherapy. In P. Wachtel & S. Messer (Eds.), *Theories of psychotherapy: Origins and evolution* (pp. 39–96). Washington, DC: American Psychological Association.

Wong, P., & Fry, P. (1998). *The human quest for meaning: A handbook of psychological research an clinical applications.* Mahwah, NJ: Lawrence Erlbaum Press.

Index